His Holiness the Dalai Lama, Maria Shaneman & Jhampa Shaneman

Foreword from His Holiness the Dalai Lama

The ultimate purpose of Buddhism is to serve and benefit humanity; therefore I believe that Buddhist ideas have a positive contribution to make to human society whether in the East or the West. On the one hand, this is because Buddhist thought gives a significant role to logic, which corresponds closely with a modern scientific outlook. On the other hand, the goal of Buddhist practice, inner peace, has a universal relevance. If we have inner peace we can face difficulties with calm and reason, while our inner happiness is unaffected. The teachings of love, kindness, and tolerance, the conduct of nonviolence, and especially the Buddhist theory that all things are relative are a source of that inner peace.

People who use astrology on a regular basis may derive beneficial inspiration from the Buddhist practices of mindfulness, compassion, and wisdom as they make their decisions. Indeed, I believe compassion and wisdom are not merely useful, but necessary in all aspects of our day-to-day life.

June 21, 2002

About the Authors

Jhampa Shaneman (British Columbia, Canada) has been an astrological consultant for twenty years and a Buddhist for over thirty. He is one of the first Western practitioners to be given permission by His Holiness the Dalai Lama to teach all levels of Mahayana and Vajrayana Buddhism. In 1980, Jhampa entered the traditional Great Retreat and spent the next three-and-a-half years on the mountain above Dharamsala, India.

Jan V. Angel (Colorado) is a professional astrologer with an extensive focus on Eastern and Western transformative psychology.

To Write to the Authors

If you wish to contact the authors or would like more information about this book, please write to the authors in care of Llewellyn Worldwide and we will forward your request. Both the authors and publisher appreciate hearing from you and learning of your enjoyment of this book and how it has helped you. Llewellyn Worldwide cannot guarantee that every letter written to the authors can be answered, but all will be forwarded. Please write to:

Jhampa Shaneman and Jan V. Angel
% Llewellyn Worldwide
P.O. Box 64383, Dept. 0-7387-0315-X
St. Paul, MN 55164-0383, U.S.A.

Please enclose a self-addressed stamped envelope for reply, or $1.00 to cover costs. If outside U.S.A., enclose international postal reply coupon.

Many of Llewellyn's authors have websites with additional information and resources.
For more information, please visit our website at
http://www.llewellyn.com

CHART INTERPRETATION
FROM A BUDDHIST PERSPECTIVE

BUDDHIST
ASTROLOGY

FOREWORD BY HIS HOLINESS THE DALAI LAMA

JHAMPA SHANEMAN & JAN V. ANGEL

2003
Llewellyn Publications
St. Paul, Minnesota 55164-0383, U.S.A.

Buddhist Astrology: Chart Interpretation from a Buddhist Perspective © 2003 by Jhampa Shaneman and Jan V. Angel. All rights reserved. No part of this book may be used or reproduced in any manner whatsoever, including Internet usage, without written permission from Llewellyn Publications except in the case of brief quotations embodied in critical articles and reviews.

First Edition
First Printing, 2003

Book design by Donna Burch
Cover art © 2002 by Photodisc
Cover design by Kevin R. Brown
Editing by Andrea Neff

Library of Congress Cataloging-in-Publication Data

Shaneman, Jhampa, 1950–
    Buddhist astrology : chart interpretation from a Buddhist perspective /
Jhampa Shaneman & Jan V. Angel.— 1st ed.
        p.   cm.
    Includes bibliographical references and index.
    ISBN 0-7387-0315-X
    1. Buddhist astrology. 2. Astrology, Tibetan. I. Angel, Jan V., 1951– II. Title.

    BF1714.B7S53 2003
    133.5'9443—dc21   2002044433

Llewellyn Worldwide does not participate in, endorse, or have any authority or responsibility concerning private business transactions between our authors and the public.
    All mail addressed to the author is forwarded but the publisher cannot, unless specifically instructed by the author, give out an address or phone number.
    Any Internet references contained in this work are current at publication time, but the publisher cannot guarantee that a specific location will continue to be maintained. Please refer to the publisher's website for links to authors' websites and other sources.

Llewellyn Publications
A Division of Llewellyn Worldwide, Ltd.
P.O. Box 64383, Dept. Dept. 0-7387-0315-X
St. Paul, MN 55164-0383, U.S.A.
www.llewellyn.com

 Printed in the United States of America on recycled paper

Dedication

This book is dedicated with supreme admiration and esteem to the glorious spiritual mentors who help us realize how to live in harmony with each other in constructive and beneficial ways. Heartfelt love is offered to all mother sentient beings that give us these bodies we currently inhabit and also the opportunities for sharing and growth. Our deep appreciation goes to this full and complete universe we are currently, for this short time, conscious of, interdependent with, and learning lessons from.

In Gratitude

We are deeply grateful to His Holiness the Dalai Lama for his kind contribution of the foreword to this book. His words express with crystal clarity the genuine heartfelt intent of the effort. We offer gratitude to gifted and respected astrologer Steven Forrest for his vision and encouragement in the earliest stages and his generosity in providing an exquisite introduction. We are grateful to Stephanie Clement at Llewellyn for her foresight, receptivity, and creative input. We appreciate the wise expertise of our kind editor at Llewellyn, Andrea Neff. Thank you to all at Llewellyn who participated in ways large, small, and unseen. Our sincere appreciation goes to Dr. Nicholas Ribush, founder of the Lama Yeshe Wisdom Archive, and Jeffrey Cox at Snow Lion Publications for their valued dialogue and continued encouragement.

Acknowledgments

I offer my personal warmth and affection to my family, Maria, Aimee, and Tenzin, who were patient with the process. My appreciation goes to Jan Angel, my angel of inspiration; to my first astrology teacher, Michael Layden, who opened the door to astrology; to Lura McCallum, for her assistance as I wrote; and finally to all the people who assisted me as the book was being produced. Whatever we do is an interdependent production, no matter what the goal may be. Thanks to all of you.

—Jhampa Shaneman

I offer my heartfelt appreciation to my husband, Eric; my children, Theresa, Erin, Maureen, and Erica; and my sister, Barbara. Thank you to supportive friends Pat Koerner, Barbara Goodfriend, Evelyn Dykman, Diana Ford, James Shaffer, Christine and Randall Klein, Nancy MacDowell, Jacqueline Shuler, Martha Urioste, Hiroko Kaska, Mary Jo Osborne, Florence Wells, Dr. Cherie Cook, Marjie Carlstedt, and April Boyer. I offer gratitude to my first astrological mentor, the brilliant Mr. Noel Tyl, who patiently helped me set a balanced foundation. Thank you to astrologer Steven Forrest, whose books and lectures are a continual inspiration. Finally, thank you to Jhampa, who made this all possible. I deeply appreciate you and especially your day-to-day wisdom that joyfully permeates all our efforts. You have helped me gain a deeper appreciation of the beauty of the Buddhist path in a practical way.

—Jan V. Angel

Contents

Introduction
  Steven Forrest . . . *ix*

Preface
  Jhampa Shaneman . . . *xv*

Preface
  Jan V. Angel . . . *xix*

Chapter One
  Buddhist Astrology . . . 1

Chapter Two
  Buddha's Natal Chart . . . 11

Chapter Three
  The Wisdom of Siddhartha . . . 49

Chapter Four
  The Deeper Wisdom . . . 73

Chapter Five
  Love and Compassion . . . 91

Chapter Six
  The Houses . . . 105

Chapter Seven
  The Planets . . . 117

Chapter Eight
  The Moon and the Sun in the Houses . . . 129

Chapter Nine
  The Inner Planets in the Houses . . . 145

Chapter Ten
The Outer Planets in the Houses . . . 181

Chapter Eleven
Aspects of the Moon and Sun . . . 205

Chapter Twelve
Aspects of the Inner Planets . . . 231

Chapter Thirteen
Aspects of the Outer Planets . . . 273

Chapter Fourteen
Buddhist Meditations and Personal Astrology . . . 279

Chapter Fifteen
Meditation . . . 303

Chapter Sixteen
Biographical Sketch of Jhampa . . . 309

Glossary of Buddhist Terms . . . 339

Bibliography . . . 353

Index . . . 357

Charts

1. Siddhartha's Natal Chart . . . 15
2. Siddhartha Renounces Palace . . . 52
3. Siddhartha Achieves Enlightenment . . . 80

Introduction
Steven Forrest

Sky and mind mirror each other: that perception is the elemental heart of astrology. As there is infinite depth in the sky, there is infinite depth in the mind. As there is longing in the heart of the mind, there is also longing in the sky.

How strange that last sentence sounds! *Longing* in the sky? And yet the logic of astrology dictates that it must be true. As we long for the sky, the sky longs for us. They mirror each other.

And sky is mind.

The great Mind of the sky calls the little human mind, longs for the little human mind to join it.

Is this Buddhism? Sure. And Christianity and Islam and Shamanism and Druidism and Judaism and Hinduism. Strip religions of their mythology and cultural contexts, and they boil down to the same feeling in the human heart: our longing to go beyond the boundaries of separateness. And, as we proved in the first 107 words of this introduction, that perception exists inescapably in the core logic of astrology too.

How odd it is that this mystical, spiritual hunger is so absent from most contemporary astrological writing. In our zeal to describe the psychology of the personality, we astrologers have mostly forgotten to wrestle with the more fundamental questions: *Why* do we have these personalities? Do these vehicles have a destination? Are we *going anywhere*?

Carl Jung famously remarked that the most important event in contemporary history was the arrival of Buddhism in the West. I think he may very well be correct. I am personally quite certain that Buddhism's arrival here is at least the most important event in contemporary astrological history. Buddhism is theologically and metaphysically compelling, but it is also very practical. "Step-by-step" instructions for the evolution of consciousness abound, and within its tenets every down-and-dirty psychological state is embraced realistically, integrated, and brought to light. It is precisely the spirit-medicine modern astrology needs.

Jhampa Shaneman's *Buddhist Astrology* bridges familiar astrological thinking with dharma. It will help us put God and soul back into Western astrological practice. I take naughty delight in using those two words: God and soul. Among strict Buddhist theologians that language isn't, shall we say, *kosher*. God, as we understand the term in the West, is not a part of the Buddhist view. The individual soul is seen ultimately as an illusion.

So why my naughty delight? It's because as Buddhism comes to the West, both will be changed. Neither one needs to bow down to the other. Western Buddhism may wind up embracing rich, metaphorical words such as *God* and *soul* and weaving them right into Gautama's eightfold path. Let the tectonic plates grind! Let Buddhism meet physics and Western paganism. Let it meet Christians who glow in the dark with the power of their path. Let it meet naguals and medicine people. Let it meet feminism. The synthesis and the interdependency is where the creative magic will happen. And those antiquarians who fear the change, on either side, will huff and puff predictably and entertainingly.

Jhampa Shaneman is a Canadian who went to India as a young man. He spent fourteen years there, and had the strenuous privilege of studying Tibetan Buddhism under the direct guidance of teachers who could trace their lineage right back to Buddha himself. One of his preceptors, Kyabje Ling Rinpoche, was actually senior tutor to the Dalai Lama. One great joy awaiting you on these pages is his telling of that autobiographical tale. I speak of it here only to indicate that Jhampa is uniquely positioned to link East and West. He is one of the bridge-builders, linking the tectonic plates.

I suspect he also sometimes feels as if he is being ground to pieces where those tectonic plates are colliding.

To most Western astrologers, Tibetan astrology would be as indecipherable as the Tibetan language itself. For one thing, it's got a lot more in common with constellation-based Vedic astrology than with season-based Western astrology. For another, it's full of Chinese elements and Tibetan folklore. In astrology, as elsewhere, the smaller the mind, the more partisan it tends to be. I'm saddened by the arguments and tensions that sometimes exist among the practitioners of various astrological traditions. Certainly Vedic and Tibetan astrologers can help people. Certainly people practicing any of the various Western systems do that as well.

Just as a dream might have more than one correct interpretation, so does the infinite sky.

Yet Jhampa, in these pages, uses Western astrological techniques, and applies them in quest of Buddhist perspectives and insights. I'm sure that will raise some eyebrows among practitioners of Eastern forms of astrology. I love it: He's bravely standing in the middle of that shaky bridge, joining worlds. He's speaking Buddhist truth in Western language. And, like a good Buddhist, he's placing Mind itself at the center, not some cerebral argument over technique. Buddhism has been absorbed into many different cultures. It can be absorbed into many different forms of astrology, too.

When people ask me about my own religion, I generally give a wiseacre answer. I'm a "Crypto-Buddhist Druid for Christ." I've read Buddhism for a long time, and I've been blessed with several opportunities to sit with Buddhist teachers. I can honestly say that no other single religion has so formed my basic view of astrology. Still, in its heart, my own astrological writing has been something of a *jihad* for the reintegration of free will into the moribund astrological traditions of inescapable prediction and the "delineation" of personality. That's been my astrological "religion." I see my clients making choices. I see them proving rigid astrologers wrong every day. And, in common with anyone who looks at astrology with an open mind, I also often see those rigid predictions and delineations working quite accurately. Why does that kind of deterministic astrology work sometimes and fail other times? I have written extensively about my own notions in that regard, and I was delighted to see that those notions were echoed in Buddhism. In Jhampa's words, "Mindful individuals are not as predictable. Buddhism explains that free will is proportionate to the amount of awareness and wisdom an individual exercises at any particular moment."

So here's the recipe Jhampa has brought home from his years in the East:

Free will.

The purposefulness of life in this mysterious universe.

An astrology that is centered on the evolution of consciousness.

A view of the universe that is centered on Mind.

It's good to know that men and women in the Himalayan Outback came to those same kinds of conclusions long ago. It's good to know that they integrated those insights into a powerful, practical system for working on the endless task of becoming fully human. And it's good to know that Jhampa Shaneman, in these pages, is a living, breathing bridge between their world and our own.

Come stand in the middle of that quaking bridge with him, and enjoy the view.

Steven Forrest
Chapel Hill, North Carolina
The Feast of Lamas, 2001

Steven Forrest is a popular lecturer and the author of eight astrological bestsellers, including The Inner Sky, The Book of Pluto, *and* Skymates.

Preface
Jhampa Shaneman

I have taken a great deal of pleasure in writing *Buddhist Astrology* with Jan Angel. The book resided in my mind for years until Jan's interest and dedication helped it take birth. She was an inspiration and a soft feminine voice reminding me not to pontificate. The process took several years to reach the final product you now read.

I have a feeling that professional astrologers will say the that book is an interesting start but lacks astrological depth. What happened to the Zodiac and Ascendant? These are good questions to which I would like to offer a short response.

As a Buddhist, I look for the karmic connection between phenomena. His Holiness the Dalai Lama is my mentor when using critical thought. For example, traditional Buddhists refer to the world as being flat. His Holiness said that that worked when people did not know any better. He currently states that there is no loss of faith in embracing a round-world concept. This is an echo of the Buddha's inspiration to investigate any truth and prove that it works for you. The same applies to astrological thought. At one point, it was believed that the earth was the center of the solar system. The revelations of Copernicus and Galileo, that the sun is in fact the center of the solar system, did not destroy astrology; astrology shifted with these insights.

I find karmic connections exist when looking at the planets in the natal chart. The Zodiac is a different matter. Ptolemy fixed the constellations 2,000 years ago and set the stage for Western astrology. This was fine for a few hundred years, but as time passed the discrepancy between the physical constellations and the Zodiac grew and grew. Now we have more than 26 degrees between these two phenomena. The use of his Zodiac becomes an object of dogma for Western astrologers instead of an investigation into the dynamics of the universe and our solar system.[1]

My objective is not to be controversial, but I need to be true to my own beliefs. I do not think that a Buddhist perspective on Western astrology needs to be exclusive of the current Zodiac. The philosophical points work in any environment. I am happy to introduce the philosophy and let others run with it.

I have done astrological consultations for twenty years and only focused on the planets, houses, and aspects. People are appreciative of the insight they gain. I do use the Ascendant and Midheaven with transits to the natal chart. It would be inconceivable to not do so. My own life has provided ample examples of the importance of these points. I simply don't comment on the degree of the Ascendant when reviewing the natal chart. This works for me. The only criticism I see is that it presents a limited vision of astrological influence. I am willing to accept that criticism. Everyone is welcome to an opinion. That is the ground for fertile discussion. I think that working with the planets, houses, and aspects is sufficient.

I look forward to the future of astrology. Historically, astrologers were valued members of society. That view is returning finally. There is ample room for us all to maneuver if we are open-minded. I hope you enjoy the book. It is the product of many hours of thought and reflection. I think it adds to the total picture of what astrology has to offer.

1. In the article "The Great Zodiac Debate" in the April/May 2002 issue of *The Mountain Astrologer*, Bruce Scofield describes Kepler's solution to this problem:

> "The great astrologer Johannes Kepler had a solution to this problem (of the zodiac question): He basically abandoned the zodiac and built his astrological system around the aspects between the planets. He believed that the zodiac itself was merely a human geometry exercise that served primarily to aid the memory of astrologers as they computed aspects in their heads.
>
> "To the argument that the zodiac reflects the cycle of the season, he responded: 'There is no experiment that proves that the twelve signs are divided up into various qualities—especially in view of the fact that, in the other (i.e., Southern Hemisphere) temperate zone those signs that make us warm would have to be considered cold and vice versa.'"

Kepler quote: Johannes Kepler, *Kepler's Astrology Excerpts*, trans. Ken Negus, Princeton, N.J.: Eucopia, 1987, p. 11.

Preface
Jan V. Angel

Seeking the Essence of the Horoscope

Astrology is experiencing a widespread renaissance. Astrologers of recent decades have presented increasing evidence that the horoscope is a dynamic, transformative tool. Psychology and spirituality are now focal points in Western chart interpretation.

Amid these genuinely exciting times for astrology, I privately yearn for a technique to peel through the layers of the chart to uncover the distilled "essence." I envision future insightful astrologers offering small scrolls containing only one or two meaningful lines to contemplate relative to the particular chart dynamics. My desire to discover the essence of the chart led me to contact Buddhist teacher Jhampa Shaneman about his work with Buddhism and astrology.

Essences in Healing

Homeopathic medicine activates the body's natural healing system from a distilled "essence" of a denser substance. Flower essences also originate from a distillation of a flower. Both methods are widely used to promote health and well-being.

It is my belief that astrology can work similarly in these subtle forms as a catalyst for spiritual progress. To be a good astrologer is a delicate work. We desire to present just the right "essence" of the horoscope to benefit our clients.

Too much information about a chart is fascinating but often difficult to assimilate. A cookbook interpretation or impersonal chart description leaves us feeling far from satisfied. The astrologer who wisely presents a significant and timely "essence" may offer the finest gift.

Why Buddhism and Astrology?

I wanted to find out if Buddhism and Western astrology could find a meeting ground. Jhampa, a Buddhist teacher and Western astrologer, effectively combines the two systems in his counseling practice. His spiritual journey is not separate from his work. He intermingles his Buddhist training effectively with his interpretive process.

I first met Jhampa in 1998. We soon discovered that we had had a similar adventure in the early 1970s. When we were each nearly twenty years old, we traveled to Asia. Jhampa left from Canada and I from California. Many Westerners during those years arrived in Nepal and India to experience ashrams, gurus, and spiritual teachers. This culture of the Western youth in Asia was an exciting extension of the sixties, a time when many youth were seeking to find deeper meaning from the superficialities of modern life. Ram Dass and others brought back stories of experiences with spiritual teachers and teachings.

Jhampa's path quickly led him to become one of the first Western Buddhist monks under a bright and joyful teacher named Lama Yeshe. You can read the fascinating story of Jhampa's journey and subsequent Buddhist immersion in the last chapter of this book.

I studied yoga and meditation in northern India for a number of years, but Buddhism did not enter my life until I returned to the United States. It was in the mid-1970s when I, too, met Lama Yeshe in southern California.

Jhampa and I shared the same initial impressions upon meeting this lama who introduced us to Buddhism on different continents. It was the first time either of us had encountered anyone teaching spirituality who embodied such humor and joy. Lama Yeshe seemed to radiate a brilliant happiness and inner peace as he exquisitely shared the Buddhist teachings with Westerners.

A Single Second in Consciousness

Lama Yeshe pointed out that in a world of nonstop change, most of the complex problems we face are rooted in our denial of the fact that change is a natural experience in life. Impermanence collides with our desire for circumstances to remain the same.

Astrology expressed within a Buddhist context is exceedingly valuable. The essence of the chart becomes active and experiential, and less analytical. We study astrology to discover continuity or meaning and to look to the future. Our future, in Buddhist terms, and according to many spiritual traditions, is determined by the quality with which we embrace the present moment.

What happens if Buddhist concepts like impermanence, interdependence, and the law of cause and effect are integrated into chart interpretation? These ideas reduce the fixity of chart definitions. The variables of outcome begin to widen based on our wisdom, compassion, and awareness.

The effect of free choice is far-reaching if "all" is truly interdependent. Buddhists discuss losing solid ground, a sign of progress. Astrology, as a study, is in the process of losing solid ground as it gives up the older, more authoritative definitions of signs and symbols.

Buddhist Practices and Chart Dynamics

Jhampa offers Buddhist practices that are helpful to individual chart themes. Some are described in this book, but there are many more. A good example is the practice of *bodhicitta*. Buddhists learn to generate bodhicitta, or loving-kindness, through meditation and visualization. Jhampa describes the Giving and Taking Meditation to develop bodhicitta and altruism in chapter 5.

Perhaps the essence of a chart is not to be found in new interpretation, but through techniques such as these. My belief and experience is that meditations and visualizations can work deeply into our awareness. These can elevate and enrich our experience of chart themes and patterns we know all too well.

Lama Yeshe made a lifelong impression on me during the year in which I studied with him. He focused teachings on the changing stream of consciousness. He emphasized that we are free to progress out of old habits, patterns, and conditioning; it just takes time for us to understand ourselves. We can actively approach old lessons with new awareness. He often admonished disciples to "check up" to find out what was going on within instead of responding to what was happening (often repeatedly) in their external experience.

Today Jhampa exquisitely teaches Buddhism to Westerners. I discovered in Jhampa's teaching style the joy and fun so alive in Lama Yeshe. Jhampa spiritually "grew up" with this lama, who naturally expressed simplicity and freedom of consciousness. Jhampa makes it look so easy as he brings these two systems together. It is liberating to consider the chart from this perspective. He encourages his clients to develop greater wisdom and compassion toward themselves and others when he conveys chart dynamics.

The world is far more receptive to the ideas of karma, interdependence, and impermanence than ever before. These ignite the awareness that our freedom to be compassionate toward ourselves and others arises from moment to moment. What if we consciously choose the compassionate way to face the depths of a Pluto transit or approach the summit of a major Saturn cycle? Does such a response set up an array of rippling effects? If you are a student of astrology, the Buddhist ideas shared in this book offer a refreshing approach to the horoscope.

My participation in this book is from the viewpoint of a contemporary Western astrologer. I now apply these three components, or the three *Wisdoms*, in my own astrological work. I find increasingly that the consideration of these points contributes to an enhanced quality of vital communication with clients of many different orientations.

It is my belief that Buddhism and other mystical-spiritual paths can continue to blend with Western astrology. Prominent and perceptive Western astrologers, like Steven Forrest and Jhampa, recognize that astrology is a tool to unveil deeper and deeper meaning for the individual. These astrologers view the chart as a whole that precisely reflects past actions—the law of cause and effect, or karma. The question arises, "What can we learn from our chart?" Many astrological systems now embrace the horoscope as a truly illuminating tool.

I am extremely grateful to Jhampa for inviting me to join him in this project and for his patience and care as he answered many questions. I am grateful for Lama Yeshe's impact on both our lives. You might discover Lama's ever joyful and kind presence shining brightly through these pages.

One
Buddhist Astrology

Buddhists say that Siddhartha was the product of eons of positive intention and action. Whenever Buddhists pray before a statue of the Buddha, they pray for inspiration. This is the positive inspiration to deal effectively with each day. Inspiration moves one to make life meaningful with positive action. Buddha attained enlightenment to show and inspire others on their path to enlightenment. The inspiration to be an enlightened individual has astrological implications.

Siddhartha's past-life birth stories, in Buddhist scripture, are a good example of the process of dealing with many different levels of influence. As a *bodhisattva*—someone who works toward enlightenment for the benefit of all sentient beings—Siddhartha cultivated positive qualities and wisdom over millions of rebirths. Those positive qualities helped him deal with life and all its various dimensions. The stories are read to Buddhist children to inspire them to be virtuous. They culminate in Siddhartha's final rebirth when he attains enlightenment. The glory of that last lifetime is due to the accumulation of vast wisdom and virtuous action.

A Buddhist review of Siddhartha shows that he is a multidi-
mensional character, an archetype. There are so many ways to
view the man and his life, and they are all interdependent. Siddhartha's life as a crown prince, his astrology, and his lineage
of rebirths all interconnect. This is the wisdom of the Buddha,
which is the wisdom of enlightenment. It sheds a wonderful
new light on the practice of astrology.

Shortly after the birth of Siddhartha, the man destined to
become Lord Buddha, an aged and wise Vedic astrologer visited
his mother and father. It was traditional in India for astrologers
to make predictions when a child was born. Siddhartha's father
was the king of a small country on the border of Nepal and
India. His first child was a boy, and that was auspicious. He
hoped his son, the crown prince, would be blessed by the planets. The old astrologer viewed both the boy and the calculations
of his planets and then started to shed many tears. Siddhartha's
father was shocked. Was his son doomed to a horrible rebirth?

When the old man composed himself, he explained the
tears by saying, "I cry because I will not see the great person
this child is destined to become. Siddhartha can be the lord of
all India or he can become an enlightened being, a Buddha in
this very life." The father was overjoyed that his son would be
the next ruler of India. The thought of his son becoming a
Buddha was meaningless to him. Of course his son would become a great king; what cause was there for other options?

The astrologer did see the options available to Siddhartha.
Buddhism holds the ideal that life is not inherently fixed or
fated. All phenomena, animate and inanimate, are interdependent. The intention of this book is to present a Buddhist view
of astrology.

No phenomena, sentient or inanimate, are separate from the
causes and circumstances that create them. Siddhartha is an excellent example of this. He was the product of a wide spectrum
of causes and circumstances. Siddhartha's parents were the first

and primary cause. Their DNA, from the very start, established a set of physical characteristics that he inherited. Siddhartha's rebirth was auspicious in this way. His father was handsome, healthy, wise, and virtuous. His mother was attractive, healthy, intelligent, and virtuous as well. They were both from the warrior ruling caste of India.

Siddhartha's mother, in particular, was spiritually aware of Siddhartha's qualities. She had dreams indicating that her son's rebirth lineage was special. She dreamt on the night of his conception that a six-tusked elephant entered her womb. This symbolized Siddhartha's power and qualities. Historical accounts say that she was joyful during the pregnancy. Mahayana Buddhists say that she was the incarnation of a goddess who promised to be the mother for Siddhartha. She currently resides in Tushita Pure Land and waits for the next Buddha Maitreya. She is prophesied to be the mother for every Buddha to come. All these births will cause her no discomfort, due to the pure qualities of these beings.

Siddhartha's external life situation is another area of interdependence. This includes his physical environment, his socioeconomic situation, and his education. The physical environment was a palace in ancient India. His socioeconomic situation was one of immense wealth and prestige. Siddhartha's education was the best available at the time.

Siddhartha was also trained in a traditional manner as a member of the warrior caste. His training included literature, logic, philosophy, and arms. Historians say that he excelled in all these activities. He even won the hand of his wife-to-be on the basis of his athletic and academic skills. Siddhartha's father was careful not to stimulate Siddhartha with religious speculation. The general ideas of past and future lives, the ethics of a monarch, and generosity to the poor were taught to him. The historical references say that his father spared nothing in the worldly sense for Siddhartha's education.

The influences to stimulate, support, and create Siddhartha were innumerable. These ranged from coarse and manifest aspects to subtle and invisible aspects of influence. Coarse aspects were the physical environment and social setting. Subtle aspects were less obvious to observe. Astrology is considered a subtle influence. It is considered an environmental influence of secondary importance.

To show how astrology may have played a role in Siddhartha's life, I have cast a natal chart for him. The actual birth chart of Siddhartha can only be speculated. There are various years given for his birth, so I have picked the year that best represents historical reports.

We can surmise from the comments of historians that Siddhartha's natal chart was impressive. He was born in the springtime. Most Buddhist traditions place it in May or June. We know he was born during the daylight hours as his mother was traveling to Nepal. She was walking about in the forest to get exercise when her water broke. Shortly after, she grasped the branch of a tree and gave birth to him. This was at noontime. His destiny was to become great, so the Sun was close to the Midheaven and it was a Full Moon day. That indicates a Taurus Sun with a Leo rising sign, definitely a strong set of supporting influences for a man destined to become either an emperor or a Buddha.

Astrology in General

Astrology is an environmental influence. It is a map of the physical world around the planet Earth at the moment of birth. This map includes the exact placement of the Sun, Moon, and all the other astronomical objects related to the Earth.

The placement of these objects naturally causes global influence. We can easily see this reflected in the world around us. The Moon is an excellent example of interdependence. Farmers plant crops with awareness of lunar cycles. If a farmer plants a crop to coincide with the correct phase of the Moon, the germinated seeds sprout faster. The waxing effect of the Moon assists the quick growth of the sprouts. When you consider the size of a seed and its sprout, the subtle effects of the Moon become obvious. The Moon affects the world on a grand scale as well. The Moon's immense gravitational pull shifts the waters of the ocean in a rhythmic tidal movement. The Moon and its effects are constantly present in everyday life. The world is interdependent with the solar system on many levels.

The Moon and human body have strong indications of interplay. The body is made up of 75 percent fluids, and the Moon's twenty-eight-day cycle can affect the emotions and temperament. The Full Moon phase occasionally stimulates people adversely. Historically the label *lunatic* refers to someone who is sensitive to phases of the Moon. The feminine menstrual cycle demonstrates synchronicity with the lunar cycle. Many cultural groups refer to the menstrual cycle of a woman as *Moon Time*. All living beings are part of the great interplay of environmental factors, even though they are mobile upon the planet. Mobility does not exclude them from the total scope of influences, including astrology.

Buddha commented on the physical and emotional interplay of influences. He said, "Individuals with mindful awareness are free of harmful influences." What the Buddha meant is that people who lack self-awareness and wisdom respond unconsciously to stimulation within their physical and emotional environments. They become stimulated by delusion, habit patterns, and instinct. They may be predictable or fated because of the lack of awareness. This encompasses all aspects of influence, including astrology.

Individuals with mindful self-awareness draw on the wisdom of past experience and education, which provides them with a variety of choices. Having a selection of options demonstrates a greater expression of free will. Mindful individuals are not as predictable. Buddhism explains that free will is proportionate to the amount of awareness and wisdom an individual exercises at any given moment.

Buddhism divides experience into internal and external events. Inner events refer to feelings, emotions, thoughts, and attitude. External events refer to the outer world of people, possessions, and the body. Aware individuals have more options in both of these areas. When inner feelings and thoughts arise, they are mindful of what response best suits those emotions. To deal with external events, they are mindful of actions of body and speech. Their intent is to respond in a virtuous, positive, and constructive manner.

Realized Buddhist practitioners have little concern for astrological influences. They apply mindful wisdom to whatever stimulations are felt internally or externally. They do not even have to know it is an astrological influence. Their wisdom and awareness give perfect advice. Their decisions and actions benefit everyone. This is an excellent example of enlightened activity.

It is possible to go a step further with awareness and wisdom. Everything is interdependently connected. The practitioners of the Kalachakra Tantra, in Tibetan Buddhism, utilize this awareness. These practitioners know what is happening astrologically without even seeing the heavens above. The advanced Tantric stages of the Kalachakra system are done in closed, dark cells. They know the phase of the Moon and positions of the planets even though they are in a cell. Their wisdom and awareness senses the changes in the body to reveal the exact position of the Moon or Sun. The movement of energy in their nerve channels tells them what is happening in the external world.

People generally live in a realm somewhere between being conscious and unconscious. Their inconsistent awareness may lack wisdom as things unfold. They respond to situations spontaneously, without foresight or consideration. It is an advantage to be aware of the influences. This is how most Ti-

betans look at life. They use astrology to select the most fortu-
itous time to accomplish their goals.

It is interesting to view how Tibetans use astrology and
other forms of divination on a daily basis. There are two principal forms of astrology studied in Tibet. The astrology from
India is called *Kar tse*, and the astrology from China is called
Nag tse. The *kar* refers to the color white and the country of
India where people wore white clothes. The *nag* refers to the
color black and to China where black was principally worn.
The word *tse* means measurement or measuring the movement
of various cycles. The Tibetans use both Indian and Chinese astrology to anticipate auspicious and inauspicious times.

The Indian system used by the Tibetans is not exactly the
same as the Vedic astrology presently used in India. The main Tibetan source is the *Kalachakra Tantra,* or *Wheel of Time Tantra.* This
Tantra tells the position of the first six planets, Ketu, Rahu, and
other astrological phenomena considered important. There is a
second system in Tibetan Tantra called the *Raising Vowels* astrological system. This system is held as secret and deals with
prophecy.

The Chinese system of astrology has nothing to do with astrological bodies. It is based on a twelve-year minicycle in conjunction with the five elements of earth, fire, water, air, and
metal. The total cycle takes sixty years to complete, created by
multiplying the twelve animals and five elements. Divinations
are based on the compatibility of the animals and elements
with one another.

There is a third form of astrology developed solely by the Tibetans. It is based on the seasons and crops. It is used in agricul-
ture and not for the prophesy of human events. Tibetan clients
receive the results of the Indian and Chinese astrological inter-
pretations at the same time. Both systems are used as a form of
divination, and they can contradict each other. It is common
for an astrologer to tell a client that it is auspicious from the

Chinese side but inauspicious from the Indian side. This makes the situation appear confused.

The Tibetans tend to be practically minded and weigh the options as they appear. If both the Chinese and Indian systems bode well for a trip or project, then it is viewed as a definite sign of success. If the two systems differ in opinion, then the project is debatable. If they both say it is inauspicious, then the Tibetan seriously reconsiders the activity.

A third and even more important process of divination outside of astrology is available to Tibetans. It can be used to complement the previous two systems, or clarify disagreements. This is the use of a *mo*, or divination performed by a monk, nun, or holy person. Those who do the mo are normally well-known in the area for the accuracy of their divinations. The lama or layperson will use either dice or a rosary to predict the event.

If all three divinations are supportive, the project is almost sure to succeed. If the two astrological systems contradict each other, the mo is used as the deciding factor. If all three divinations give a bad indication, it is definitely not an auspicious time for action.

The dedicated Tibetan has yet another option if a desire is strong and requires action. If all aspects of divination indicate little hope for success, the client has this solution. It is the use of prayer, meditation, and ritual to turn the project in a positive direction. The prayers and meditation normally involve Green Tara, the female Buddha of activities. She is invoked to help correct bad indications and bring forth the best possible solution. Her name means "the savior." Buddhists believe that Green Tara is a benevolent and powerful deity who removes fear and interferences.

Tibetans also use more forceful intervention to assure success. They may turn to a Wrathful Buddha or a Dharma Protector for help. These rituals are often done to rectify health problems and avoid foreseeable disasters. This is because there are no options if the client remains inactive. There is something that can be done even if the problem seems overwhelming. No Tibetan ever looks at a situation as being completely lost. They weigh how much spiritual intervention is required to swing the balance in their favor. To accomplish this requires earnest faith, prayer, mantra recitation, and reliance on the deities.

The underlying structure for all Tibetans is the belief in Buddhism, which gives the wisdom to deal effectively with whatever transpires. If all forms of intervention were attempted and still the event was a disaster, it then indicates extensive bad karma. The Tibetans would listen to the counsel of their Buddhist teacher and accept the failure. This is regarded as a life lesson. They take inspiration and apply it toward future projects. This will often translate into the accumulation of positive activity to enhance their karmic potential.

Karmic potential is the product of motivation and action. If desires and wishes are difficult to realize, then there is a need to accumulate more positive actions. This is accomplished through kindhearted and positive motivations. Persistent positive action both purifies previous negative actions and accumulates new positive potential. Buddhists believe that the success of any action depends on the accumulated positive activity of the past.

Two
Buddha's Natal Chart

In this chapter we will analyze the birth chart of Siddhartha, the crown prince of the Shakya clan, born 2,500 years ago. This analysis reviews Buddhist astrology in conjunction with Siddhartha's life and natal chart. This report uses a Buddhist's view of the factual aspects of astrology that are in harmony with karma and interdependence. The chart is interpreted without reference to the zodiac. This is because the Western zodiac is no longer harmonized with the actual constellations. This means, from a Buddhist standpoint, that the Western zodiac is not causally connected with any actual phenomena. This approach may initially appear simplistic. I find consistently, in my own astrological practice, that the chart theme normally ascribed to the zodiac is also recognizable using the planets, house systems, and aspects. All other general components of Western astrology are used in this book, such as the Placidus house system and standard orbs and aspects.

Astrology for a Buddhist practitioner falls into the category of being an external influence. This is similar to investigating a healthy diet. The study of good dietary needs increases knowledge regarding the finer details of health and well-being. Buddhist astrology reviews the body and mind. The study stimulates understanding of the dynamic influences between action and consciousness. Astrology is one of those dynamic influences. One can gain a certain level of freedom from unconsciously stimulated actions if a better understanding of oneself and the world is developed.

Siddhartha's conception and birth were auspicious from the point of view of his karmic potential. Buddhists state that he amassed a huge collection of positive actions in numerous past lives as a bodhisattva. The karmic power of those actions played a strong role in the final life of Siddhartha. This life had a great impact on humanity.

The original astrologer who cast his birth chart predicted an attainment of great power. The astrologer based his prediction on the birth data and observation. Siddhartha was a crown prince of a small kingdom. The priest could not predict, even with all this data, the exact direction Siddhartha would choose for his life, just the possibilities. He saw indications that Siddhartha was to become either a great ruler or a saint.

What is interesting about this prediction is the effect it had on Siddhartha's father. The king had an agenda for his son. The astrologer said that Siddhartha had the potential to become an enlightened being, a spiritual leader, if he chose a spiritual life. The king thought he was wise when he organized life in the palace to provide only luxury and comfort for his son. What Siddhartha's father did not see was that he had set the stage for comparison. Palace life allowed Siddhartha to perceive the strong contrast between his life and the lives of his subjects. Remember, Siddhartha fled from the palace when he was twenty-eight to seek the meaning of life. He led such a protected life until that time that he could not understand the suffering and pain he saw among the populace. His father inadvertently set the circumstances for Siddhartha's shock at the difference between his palace reality and the common world.

This review of Siddhartha's life looks at the astrological interplay of the many factors that stimulated him over the years. Buddhists see that his positive karmic potential from past lives gave him the qualities of health, power, influence, and intelligence. This manifested with his mastery of worldly skills. Historically, those qualities were demonstrated in the contest he won for the hand of his future wife. History mentions that he outperformed all the rival princes in northern India. He was recognized as the best husband for Yodishvara, the daughter of an important king. The contests were the arts, poetry, literature, strategy, and combat skills.

Siddhartha's marriage lasted for approximately two years. This culminated in his great quest for spiritual meaning. When he left the palace, Siddhartha's spiritual journey involved meeting two famous meditation masters of the time. Buddhists say that his past-life karmic potential met positive circumstances. The circumstances ripened his accumulated spiritual capacity. He quickly mastered deep states of meditative concentration. He meditated so well that one of the teachers offered Siddhartha his meditation center and spiritual lineage. Siddhartha refused this offer because he was not satisfied. He could escape from distracted mental states through meditation, but he did not yet understand reality and the meaning of life.

Siddhartha spent the next six years in strict meditation. Determined to discover the meaning of life, he performed extreme acts of asceticism. He starved himself, eating only one grain of rice a day for several years. He mastered even deeper states of meditation and self-control due to his determination. He abandoned self-mortification as a technique for spiritual realization at age thirty-five. He started to eat food again and sought a middle-path approach to attaining enlightenment. He attained enlightenment on the Full Moon night of May 15, 539 B.C.

Siddhartha taught the Buddhist path after enlightenment until his eighty-first year. This included three major presentations of spiritual practice. The first *Turning of the Wheel of Dharma*, as Buddha's teachings are called, was in Sarnath, at a deer park. The second Turning of the Wheel of Dharma was the bodhisattva vehicle at Rajgir, Bihar State. The last Turning of the Wheel of Dharma was a collection of various teachings given over several years. He entered *Parinirvana*, the Buddhist term for a Buddha's death, on the Full Moon in May of 494 B.C. We will cover these events considering his astrological birth chart and the transits over the years.

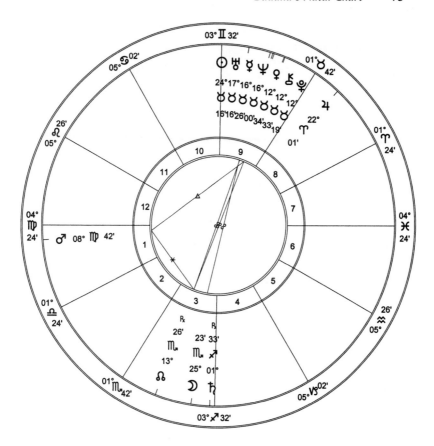

Chart 1
Siddhartha's Natal Chart
May 23, 575 B.C. / 12:30 P.M. LMT
Patna, India 25N36 085E07 / Geocentric Tropical Zodiac
Placidus Houses, True Node

"The birthchart is a remarkable tool. But to use that tool you must learn a lost art. You must become a symbol reader."

—Steven Forrest in *The Inner Sky*

Moon in the Third House

The third house relates to the astrological influences stimulating how one learns. There are three areas to consider in the third house. These are the early years of education, the mature years when that knowledge is used, and finally sharing knowledge with others. This house indicates how one learns, not the level of intelligence. When an individual is young, planets in the third house also represent the subjects he or she may easily gravitate toward and what types of teachers offer the best influence.

This information is especially useful when choosing a spiritual teacher. All spiritual teachers are valuable, but individual preferences help one learn more quickly. Students often become similar to their teachers. The influence the teacher has may depend on which planet is in the third house. If more than one planet is there, one has multiple dynamics for study. No planets in this house may mean that other considerations will motivate the individual.

The Moon is similar to the Sun in that it has a great influence on the individual. The Moon represents soft emotions such as empathy, compassion, and receptivity. It further represents emotional sensitivity to the immediate environment and finally relationships with women. The Moon indicates some of the dynamics relating to the mother, sisters, female relatives, and women in general. It is not limited by gender. The Moon's influence can attract men who demonstrate a compassionate nature. The Moon represents and attracts soft emotions.

The Moon empowers meditation practices focused on compassion. If it is well aspected in the chart, the person can express both sensitivity and compassion. An individual with a Moon with stressful aspects may express compassion with a higher sensitivity. This stress is beneficial to the development of empathy and an open heart. Compassion often does not have a solid foundation without some experience and acceptance of suffering. Empathy allows compassion to be sincere and authentic.

A spiritual practitioner needs both loving compassion and wisdom to be an effective spiritual entity. These are seen as the two legs that carry one to enlightenment. Wisdom often comes from the experiences related to suffering. Suffering is a great motivator. Suffering creates a challenge, and wisdom decides how to solve the problem. Love and compassion arise from recognizing the equality of the self and others. Everyone equally desires happiness and wishes for no suffering; clarity with this point establishes empathy, compassion, and altruism.

The Moon in the third house gave Siddhartha an affinity to compassionate instructors. Siddhartha also was inclined toward subjects focused on emotional relatedness. The humanities, social welfare, and psychology would be natural choices for him. This compassionate interest in the emotions of others was a good support for his spiritual journey. To be able to understand others, he had to understand his own emotions.

The third house seeks knowledge, in this case emotional knowledge because of the Moon's placement. Siddhartha's enlightenment was a profound investigation into the nature of existence for all living beings. It was not an intellectual journey, but a journey of emotional inquiry. Enlightenment revealed for him the suffering nature of delusion. He separated deluded thoughts and feelings from clear-minded awareness and skillful compassion. He described a path to liberation and freedom. *Nirvana*, in Buddhist terms, is called everlasting happiness, or enlightenment that embodies supreme fulfillment.

Saturn in the Third House

Saturn in the third house stimulated a conservative and reflective nature in Siddhartha. It influenced him with a practical, pragmatic, and reasonable approach to life.

Saturn's astrological influence ripens people slowly. They might move gradually in new directions of interest. Saturn suggests a sense of hesitation. It may generate a tendency toward insecurity and fear until the individual feels confident about a new situation. It stimulates people to make safe, conservative decisions.

Individuals with planets that are negatively stimulated by Saturn tend to develop a stubborn attitude. They can be resistant to change because of fear and insecurity. A negative aspect with Saturn can be like an anchor to the other planets, dragging them back with fear and insecurity. The feelings of security and insecurity are the main issues for Saturn.

Saturn's influence can be introverted or extroverted depending on the personal attitude. The attitude an individual has toward life has several sources. These can include family structure, upbringing, and social position. For individuals with weak willpower and low self-esteem, there is a tendency to be introverted. Saturn may stimulate them to hesitate and be fearful. An introverted attitude may limit their self-expression. It is the attitude that cripples, and Saturn exacerbates the effect of negative feelings and insecurity.

Insecure individuals with an extroverted personality may express aggression. These individuals experience insecurity, but due to their extroverted personality they hide it under a strong show of assertiveness. If there is minimal self-awareness, they can be stubborn and resentful toward others.

In cases of introversion or extroversion, the issue is the same. Fear and insecurity motivate the person. If there is little self-awareness, these people will repeatedly select goals that protect them from fear. They wish to have a safe and secure life. As they become more self-aware, there is the opportunity to grow beyond a fearful response to life. Wisdom can change situations dramatically. By investigating negative feelings, one can gain profound insight. Saturn's strengths can be enhanced with the cultivation of a positive, reflective attitude.

Saturn's spiritual side greatly assists deep, thoughtful growth. It supports the development of profound wisdom because it bestows insight. Saturn is reflective, calm, and constructive when coupled with a meditative attitude. If altruism is combined with this mixture, the individual can become a source of support for others.

Saturn in the third house assisted Siddhartha to be diligent in his studies. His early years of study may have been difficult. Saturn's influence in any part of the horoscope can indicate slow development. Siddhartha needed time to become familiar with the subject matter. He may have gradually established good study habits through the years. This placement can bestow deep wisdom.

Saturn can be a stickler for details. The practical aspect of Saturn stimulates the self-absorbed pursuit of perfection. Saturn could be overly intellectual in the third house. There is a need for a balanced, positive attitude to avoid overintellectualization. Historically, Siddhartha's later years demonstrate that he developed a balance between knowledge and compassion.

Saturn in the third house supported the authority Siddhartha carried throughout his life. This was the influence of Saturn's steady and organized manner of presentation. Considering that Siddhartha became the Buddha and was known for being serene and peaceful, it appears that his attitude and Saturn's influence were mutually supportive of positive expression.

Aspects to the Moon

Moon Opposite Sun—1°13' Separating Orb

The sense of self and sensitivity are in opposition. It is the Full Moon day. An astrological opposition is similar to a pendulum swinging back and forth. One can look at the two planets to get a sense of the dynamics that may influence the individual. On one side there is sensitivity, and on the other the sense of self. This placement indicates a strong sensitivity and compassion toward others. It may attract many women into one's life. In astrology, the Moon and women are strongly related. This aspect also attracts compassionate people. There may be a problem learning to establish boundaries between oneself and others. There is a need to be aware of one's own needs and yet to be sensitive toward others.

Siddhartha's Sun-Moon opposition motivated him with a compassionate determination to seek enlightenment. His compassion was strong and expressive. Because the Moon was in the third house, he sought to know more about emotions and feelings. Once he became enlightened, he expressed his teachings in a compassionate, knowledgeable manner.

Moon Conjunct Saturn—6°03' Applying Orb

Sensitivity and a conservative nature combine. There can be realism and practicality within emotional expression. These individuals may appear cool in situations to the point of showing no emotional expression. The simple explanation for this may be that their compassion responds slowly. They want to see what is happening with the situation before they respond. Saturn reflects on situations in a slow and calculated manner. This conjunction could mean a slow development of the emotional life. Deep down the person is thinking about things. The negative side of this aspect is to be cold and detached, and distant from feelings.

Siddhartha was a reflective young man. At birth he lost his mother, causing a limitation on his emotional expression. Although a cousin replaced his mother, the love of his original mother was not there. This external situation may have stimulated an emotional hesitancy in Siddhartha. Add to this Saturn's conjunction to the Moon and greater stimulation arises for a hesitant emotional response. He might have reflected on his mother and felt a great wonder and loss about her.

When Siddhartha married and fathered his son, Rahula, he was twenty-seven years old, a mature age at a time when the average life span for people was about forty-five years. Even as a member of a royal family, the life span was not that long. It appears that he was hesitant to move into the responsibilities of marriage and family life.

Siddhartha may have taken his emotional responsibilities seriously after the marriage. This is a common influence for Saturn. Saturn appears to assume a responsible position to life's circumstances. Siddhartha's Moon was conjunct Saturn. He strongly reflected on what it meant to be a husband and father. His emotional life moved slowly and he took everything seriously. Saturn's energy needs to be practical. Saturn's placement in the third house needs to understand the responsibilities of family life.

It is interesting to consider that he left his wife shortly after the birth of their son. Siddhartha grew up with no mother and may have personally felt abandoned. Here he faced the responsibility of caring for two people. He was reflective about what that meant to him. His Saturn-Moon conjunction made him serious about the emotional implications. His responsibilities were great because he was also the crown prince. He would soon be the ruler of a kingdom and have the responsibility of the whole Shakya clan upon his shoulders. He may have felt quite insecure with all this responsibility. Could he really help all these people? The negative influence of Saturn might have stimulated feelings of fear and insecurity. The responsible side of Saturn could have made him feel like he was carrying a great burden. The internal conflicts that Siddhartha faced relate clearly to his natal chart.

Siddhartha left the palace after taking four journeys into his kingdom. He saw an ill person, an old person, a death procession, and finally a meditating monk. When Siddhartha reflected on how his wife, their child, and the subjects of his kingdom were all subject to illness, old age, and death, he was strongly moved. The final vision of the monk stimulated a strong desire in him to meditate. Monks look for serious answers to life's questions. They drop all distractions and meditate on the meaning of life. Siddhartha did not need to become a monk, but he was serious and responsible. A monk's lifestyle may have appeared to be the best solution for someone so serious about life.

Siddhartha's Saturn-Moon conjunction combined with a Sun-Moon opposition to accentuate his compassion. One of the influences of a Sun-Moon opposition is a difficulty setting boundaries between oneself and others. Siddhartha's compassion was in direct opposition to his sense of self. This compassionate influence may have torn him apart. How could he not seek a solution to this dilemma in his life? He was destined to become the king and serve his people. His sense of responsibility and compassion required total dedication, like the commitment a monk has for meditation.

Siddhartha practiced meditation strictly during the six years between his twenty-ninth and thirty-fifth birthdays. It required incredible emotional control to starve himself and yet maintain spiritual determination. He abandoned all comforts and sat on the ground under a tree to focus his mind. He already had a deep meditative capacity. He could attain a high state of meditation with no distraction, which required deep emotional discipline. His Saturn-Moon conjunction bestowed part of this resolve, and his first-house Mars supplied added determination and willpower.

Siddhartha manifested a powerful aspect of detachment after enlightenment. He was a celibate monk. How much more detached can one be? He never returned to worldly life. His main message was that attachment and aversion cause unnecessary suffering and are based on delusions. Because of his analytical nature with the Saturn-Moon conjunction, he was able to go deeply into emotional issues. His enlightenment demonstrated the path he taught. Buddha's message is an investigation into the nature of the self.

Siddhartha taught the path to enlightenment for the remaining forty-six years of his life. This started with a sense of

responsibility and compassion that surfaced after his initial realization of enlightenment. He first taught the five other mendicants who practiced with him for five of the six years. Siddhartha walked and taught all over northern India until his
Parinirvana at age eighty-one.

Sun in the Ninth House

The ninth house deals with a deep investigation into the world
around us. A good word for this investigation is *context*. One
strives for context in order to view and understand what is happening. The search for context leads people to philosophy and
finally spiritual and religious expression. The ninth house is
the area of vast and profound thought. Whenever planets are
placed here, the individual becomes philosophical to satisfy the
need for a logical life. This search may be expressed on many
levels, such as pursuing a university degree, asking endless
questions, or reviewing many religions. Buddhism does well
with ninth-house planets. Buddhism emphasizes logic and investigative insight. With planets in this house, people seek to
clarify what is important. Organizing personal context clarifies
how to deal with life and the world outside. Religions and
philosophies all strive to accomplish this. They offer a context
in which to understand the world.

The Sun is the largest body in the solar system and exerts
the greatest influence on the individual. It represents the central sense of self. It indicates the greatest areas of interest. The
Buddhist point of view states that our sense of self is an interdependent phenomenon. Reflection on the self considers many
factors: the birth family, the education, the socioeconomic
structure, and finally the cultural and ethnic environment. All
of these things together, plus other subtle factors such as astrology, create the holistic total of self.

The Sun's placement and aspects in the chart identify the
astrological factors of influence to the self. The self only gains

expression through all the factors combined. It has no capacity to create an independent existence. Thus the vision of interdependence plays a central role in the Buddhist review of astrology. Individuals can reflect on the Sun's placement in the natal chart to understand themselves astrologically.

If wisdom and awareness are strong, an individual will express the positive attributes of the Sun's placement. The job of spiritual seekers is to take whatever circumstance they find themselves in and "turn it to the path." This is the central practice of attitude transformation in Mahayana Buddhism. All situations and influences can be used as grist for the spiritual mill. This expresses the Mahayana attitude that all experiences are transformable into components of spiritual realization. The sense of self is a multifaceted play of dynamic factors. A positive attitude is one of the more important factors.

Siddhartha was a natural philosopher with his Sun in the ninth house. He wanted to understand a greater vision of life. He sought answers to his questions. Whether Siddhartha was in the palace or outside with the masses, he reviewed his experiences, seeking to understand them. He wanted context. This is a natural question for a philosopher. Siddhartha's ninth-house Sun benefited greatly by the opposition to the Saturn-Moon conjunction in the third house. This opposition made him emotionally serious in his search for solid, practical answers to his questions.

When we consider the other circumstances of Siddhartha's life, we can surmise why he acted as he did. He was a crown prince, well educated, and living a life of luxury. He was destined to take a position of responsibility. He accepted the limited reality his father had portrayed for him. He believed that everyone lived as comfortably as he did. His father was careful to control Siddhartha, keeping him isolated in the palace. As time passed, Siddhartha formatted his experiences according to that environment. His ninth-house Sun would influence him to create a context.

Siddhartha became an adult and looked for greater context to life. He had a beautiful wife, servants, wealth, and prestige. When he went out of the palace to see the kingdom, he may have expected the kingdom to be equally perfect. He was the king's son and these were his subjects. Everyone should be happy, or at least have the potential to be happy. The kingdom his father had was a good place. This was the idealistic context he may have held because of the protective environment his father had built around him.

Individuals with a ninth-house Sun constantly ask questions and seek answers. When Siddhartha came up against old age, illness, and death, he was deeply shocked by the implications. He asked for his charioteer's opinion as he confronted each individual experience. The charioteer responded politely that this was the lot of everyone. All beings will experience aging, illness, and finally death. Siddhartha ventured out of the palace three separate times and saw one of these realities of life each time. These experiences fueled his desire to seek answers about what he had seen. He wanted to expand his context based on these new experiences. He was trying to format new information into a meaningful context.

The final experience was to see a monk meditating. This must have been a powerful stimulation for an individual with a ninth-house Sun. Here was an individual who seriously questioned reality. Siddhartha's father was successful at keeping his son in the dark about spiritual matters. Siddhartha didn't even recognize the meditator as a spiritual mendicant. He had to ask the charioteer about the robed fellow. The charioteer explained that the man sought the meaning of life through meditation. This must have deeply inspired Siddhartha's interest in spiritual questions.

Siddhartha approached his father after the last chariot ride and stated his desire to pursue spiritual answers. He wanted to go out into the world and discover deeper meaning. His father refused the request. He said Siddhartha's destiny was to become the king and he had to be in court to learn how to manage the kingdom. Siddhartha had a ninth-house Sun, so his father's response may have appeared to be an incredible obstacle. To be a good king, he had to understand the context of the position. What was he responsible for? How could he be a good ruler if his subjects were afflicted with aging, illness, and death? He needed to know why this happened and what he could do about it. Siddhartha's response is in harmony with a ninth-house Sun and a third-house Saturn-Moon conjunction.

Siddhartha's life was unreal up to this point. He was overindulged and lived in a dream of illusions about the real world. What is interesting is the effect this had on him. The outcome is that Siddhartha became a Buddha, which is not an easy attainment. He needed a strong catalyst to start the fire of spiritual inquiry. Perhaps if his life had not been controlled, he may not have responded as he did. His father tried to make him a world leader. Siddhartha ended up with a huge need for spiritual context. He had a perfect, worldly context for life. Siddhartha was wealthy and lacked nothing on the physical level, but his deeper spiritual side of life was impoverished. He had no context to understand suffering, whether it was his own or that of others. This dumbfounded him. He needed some answers to these questions. His father's refusal to let him study spiritually only strengthened his resolve to seek spiritual answers.

Mercury in the Ninth House

Mercury represents intellectual capacity. It is the ability to generate thoughts, concepts, communication skills, and a general inquisitive nature. Mercury refers to a wide variety of intellectual functions. The placement in the natal chart demonstrates the area of increased intellectual capacity.

Quietude meditation techniques are excellent for calming the mind and emotions. A quiet mind alone is not enough for deep transformation. Analytical meditations clarify personal context. Intellectual appreciation is like scaffolding that surrounds the core of our being. That scaffolding to some extent directs how the building grows. It is our intellectual understanding that clarifies motivation, the creator of what we become. The need for good intellectual intelligence is one of the many tools a spiritual seeker uses for both personal growth and for the benefit of other sentient beings.

Mercury in the ninth house increased Siddhartha's philosophical nature in an intellectual manner. He would question life in the search for context as a youth. His position in the palace explained the material context of life. He was the crown prince destined to rule the kingdom and he was being trained to take that position. His position automatically bestowed many comforts and luxuries. Siddhartha was an important person to the kingdom and everyone respected him. His intellectual mind could grasp the context of this quickly.

As Siddhartha grew up and gained maturity, he mastered all the material skills he required. He was a proficient reader and writer because of the need to compose laws and proclamations for the kingdom. He was good at strategic games and the use of weapons as he was a member of the warrior caste. He was educated to communicate well as he was destined to rule the court and kingdom. Mercury, which was conjunct his Sun, may have helped him master these areas of knowledge.

When Siddhartha married and the time to inherit the kingdom drew near, his naturally inquisitive mind started to look at responsibilities outside the palace. He went on four chariot rides to gain exposure to the subjects he was soon to rule. Mercury's need for intellectual understanding stimulated inquiry with the new experiences he had on those rides. He needed to format those experiences into an intelligent context. He saw people suffering from illness, aging, and death. He needed intellectual context to understand these sufferings. He observed that his people were not as happy and comfortable as he expected. Why? What could he do about it?

Siddhartha's father interviewed him after each excursion. He wanted to know Siddhartha's response. Because of Siddhartha's inquisitive mind, he posed questions to his father about illness and aging. He was concerned about the social programs his kingdom had in place. What was his father's position on these issues? If his father did not answer these questions adequately, Siddhartha might be in a quandary. He was soon to take responsibility of these people and these were areas his father would not address. Why was his father not compassionate toward his subjects? Why did these bad things happen to some people and not to others? These were truly the questions of a philosophical mind.

Siddhartha's departure from the palace took place shortly after the fourth experience of seeing the meditating monk. The monk deeply stimulated Siddhartha's interest to know what monks sought to understand. Siddhartha had five planets in the ninth house, so he was deeply contemplative. The monk represented an area he had not yet grasped. He didn't have a context for spiritual practice.

His entire life would be contextually investigated with five planets in the ninth house. As a prince, the context was clear enough. He was destined to become the ruler of the kingdom. The position of heir bestowed many luxuries. Because he was a contemplative man, he thought about these things. When he did become the king, what service could he offer his subjects? Was he to be a material supervisor or could he profoundly help them? What could a king really accomplish for his subjects?

The lifestyle Siddhartha experienced up to this point gave him every physical luxury. It avoided spiritual and philosophical questions because Siddhartha's father did not wish his son to become a Buddha. Life seeks balance, and perhaps this was the reason why Siddhartha reacted so strongly in abandoning palace life to seek deeper meaning. He needed balance, and his father had not supplied him with the circumstances to maintain a balanced life. His father ordered Siddhartha to be happy with the way things were. To ensure this, his father even put extra security in the palace so he could not escape. Siddhartha's father was a controlling man and Siddhartha was too old now to have serious issues ignored. Thus Siddhartha was driven from the palace because of his father's actions. Siddhartha's strong philosophical nature was obstructed and he needed answers.

The whole process to seek enlightenment was filled with intellectual and practical inquiry. After his escape from the palace, he sought spiritual teachers. He visited two great yogis. Siddhartha quickly mastered what those men had to teach. He needed a deeper answer than they both supplied. Possibly because he had left the palace, his wife, and newborn child, he had to take these issues seriously. He could not return to the palace with half-baked ideas about life. He needed depth and a fully transformational experience. He needed the transformation more than anyone else. The need to go deeper caused stress in many areas of his life.

Venus in the Ninth House

Venus represents the sensual response to the environment around us. It is the eye, ear, nose, tongue, and body sense doors responding to the stimulation from the sense objects of form, sound, smell, taste, and touch. Venus identifies the astrological area where one experiences pleasure, satisfaction, and fulfillment. Venus relates finally to affection, as it is through the body sense door that one shows affection.

To understand where fulfillment is found, it is best to consider first where Venus is placed in the chart. Venus' placement in the lower hemisphere of the natal chart generally means that fulfillment is more personally oriented; in the upper hemisphere, satisfaction comes from working with others.

Venus in the ninth house in Siddhartha's early years may have stimulated him to seek meaningful relationships. Siddhartha's father supplied him with many courtesans to satisfy his emotional needs. He had no shortage of women, but it appears that he did not show attachment to this aspect of life. The nonattachment could come from several sources, but if we look at Venus' placement, we get a few ideas. Venus seeks pleasure, but adjusts to where it falls in a natal chart. The ninth house seeks context, therefore pleasure and love cannot be arbitrary. Teenagers may respond to lust, but with maturity this will change. It would have been interesting to see how Siddhartha related to the courtesans as he matured. It might have been challenging for him to have meaningless, brief affairs from an astrological point of view.

The greatest impact on Siddhartha, related to Venus, manifested after enlightenment. He demonstrated his affection for the five yogis friends immediately. If he had been selfish, he might have passed his years in solitude and isolation. He kindheartedly thought instead about the yogis and sought them out in the deer park at Sarnath. This started his life as an instructor of a new style of spiritual practice. Venus stimulated deep satisfaction in Siddhartha as the years passed. He had the opportunity both to instruct thousands of people and to debate with other philosophers.

In India, it was tradition that if two differing schools of thought held a public debate, the philosopher who lost the debate had to embrace the ideas of the winner. Siddhartha made a name for himself within a few years of his enlightenment. He met with a popular guru who had several hundred disciples and convinced him of the superiority of the Buddhist path. This meant that all the guru's disciples instantly became Buddhist monks. Buddhism spread quickly because of this.

A group of yogis became jealous of the Buddha's success as time passed and demanded a public debate. They requested that the king of Banaras host it. The king was a disciple of the Buddha and thought it was a good idea. Other philosophers had not yet seriously challenged Buddha. The king contacted Buddha to request the debate. Siddhartha accepted, but when the date drew near he went away and missed the debate. This started a controversy about Buddha's capacity as a teacher. Could he meet the challenge of professional philosophers? Was he afraid of them?

A second time, Bimbisara, the king of Banaras, contacted the Buddha and set another date for the grand debate. Siddhartha again did not show up for the debate and the controversy raged. The Buddha must be afraid of these five yogis. Was Buddha a hoax and not a true saint? Even King Bimbisara was confused. He had great respect for the Buddha. Siddhartha, from his side, maintained that he was interested in meeting the yogis, but felt the timing was incorrect.

When a third date for the debate was set, there was heightened public interest. Many neighboring kingdoms had heard of the Buddha and his refusal to meet the five yogis. Many more people came to the debate now that interest was so high. The king of Banaras hosted the event and made a huge field available for the meeting. Buddha sat on one throne in opposition to the five yogis. The event was in the spring month of May, starting on the New Moon day.

Each day for fourteen days, one of the yogis would debate with Siddhartha and then perform a miracle. Buddha would respond to the debate and also perform a miracle vision. On the final Full Moon day, the yogis had not been successful in debate, so they tried to use their magical powers to defeat him. Buddha was unaffected by their magic and responded with his greatest feat. Having finished the lunch offered by Bimbisara, Siddhartha took a toothpick and stuck it into the ground. It started to transform into a huge bodhi tree that shaded everyone present. On each leaf of the tree appeared a Buddha. Each of these Buddhas then gave a different discourse. The five yogis were so humiliated that they ran from the event. Because they had been motivated by greed and jealousy and to avoid being converted, they drowned themselves in the Ganges River.

Buddha's Venus in the ninth house stimulated him to love debate and philosophy. The debate gave him deep satisfaction. That the five yogis committed suicide was unexpected. Buddha did not intend for that to happen, but the one event did convert a large section of India to his philosophy.

Uranus in the Ninth House

Uranus is revolution. It stimulates a sense of independence, originality, and spontaneity in positive environments. An analogy for Uranus is lightning that strikes suddenly with no warning. Uranus gives the individual spontaneous self-expression. The person may demonstrate this by being very independently minded. Another analogy for Uranus is a horse running free in a field. There are no fences or bridles to limit the horse's expression of freedom. That sense of power and unbridled freedom is what Uranus bestows to the chart.

A negative influence from Uranus, such as a square or opposition aspect, may stimulate a chaotic and unpredictable response. The person might appear disorganized and out of control because the energy is so unpredictable. The individual could feel that he or she is the victim of unexpected events if little mindfulness is exercised. Things might appear to never work out smoothly. The placement of Uranus in the natal chart may be an area of unrest and scattered energy. Short bursts of enthusiasm and effort are common aspects of Uranus' influence.

Tantric practitioners find Uranus' placement to be a wonderful stimulation toward spiritual freedom and bliss. This is because Tantric practice involves a more liberal view of reality. If an individual stubbornly holds to limiting ideas, it is difficult to approach the Tantric manner of expression. Tantra requires the abandonment of mundane attitudes about life, especially a mundane attitude about oneself. A Tantric practitioner sees the divine in everything. All beings, including themselves, are deities and all places are pure lands. To be able to accomplish such a vision, one has to be free of mundane recognition and association. Uranus bestows the potential for such a liberated view.

Generally, Uranus in the ninth house stimulates individuals toward liberal philosophical views. These people may have trouble joining large congregations or organized religions. They have far too liberated an attitude to agree with the congregation. This does not mean that they could never attend public teachings or be members of some spiritual group, but they may find conservative opinions to be constrictive to their self-expression.

Siddhartha definitely was a liberal thinker in his time. He abandoned the idea of caste and segregation. All beings could equally attain enlightenment and directly have spiritual experience. Siddhartha contradicted the control of the priest caste in India. One did not have to rely on a Brahman to do spiritual activities. His philosophy revolutionized Indian thought. This is so true to Uranus' placement in the ninth house.

Neptune in the Ninth House

Neptune is the spiritual pole that influences intuition and imagination. Intuition is the ability to know something without relying on intellectual knowledge. It tends to just know something directly by seeing the greater picture. Imagination applies to a broad speculative view about things. To be imaginative requires being open-minded and not concerned with small details.

An analogy for Neptune is to stand on the crest of a mountain with a 360-degree view. One looks to the vista and horizon, not directly in front. Both intuition and imagination rely on images for transmitting their understanding. This differs from the sensitivity of the Moon, for example, which relies on awareness of emotions. Individuals can develop inner awareness related to images and visions with Neptune. Wherever Neptune is found in a chart, there may be more of an emphasis on idealism and a nonmaterial point of view.

The intuitive and imaginative influences are beneficial for balanced spiritual people. They may understand something beyond the immediate physical reality that they perceive.

A negative influence with Neptune causes unrealistic ideas and speculation. Daydreaming and fantasizing are common negative aspects. An emotionally unfocused individual may experience Neptune's effect by being vague and unclear. The area of vagueness depends on where Neptune falls in the natal chart.

Neptune in the ninth house encouraged Siddhartha's spiritual interests. His spiritual side had an excellent intuitive component. Neptune's influence searches for the spiritual and idealistic side of things. The common effect of this placement is to have an open-minded approach to life and issues. The intuitive influence understands spiritual practice. Balanced individuals may see the validity of other spiritual traditions because of their open-mindedness. It is important to seek teachers and mentors with good qualifications if Neptune is in the ninth house. The intuitive side immediately understands the spiritual expression of such a teacher. This is because the individual intuitively responds to the presence of a realized teacher. Empathetic realizations can arise from such contacts.

Siddhartha had a practical side to his spiritual studies. His Saturn-Moon conjunction in the third house kept him grounded in logical, pragmatic discourses. Neptune ensured that he also looked beyond the small details. Buddha was an excellent teacher and was able to bring spiritual investigation to new heights. He gave teachings at different times to various individuals, matching the teachings to suit their unique needs.

This was the intuitive side of the Buddha's spirituality. When Buddha died and the whole of his teachings were reviewed, it became obvious that the subjects were vast and profound. The discourses cover mundane subjects such as karma and the benefits of a good heart. He expanded this to profound levels of truth by presenting the Perfection of Wisdom Sutras, which discuss the final nature of reality. He then complemented these teachings with expositions on Tantra. All these discourses were delivered at different times to different disciples. The vast extent of his views and teachings became evident only after his Parinirvana. Buddhist's believe that his capacity as a teacher came from lifetimes of spiritual practice and the current supportive environmental influences of planets like Neptune, Mercury, the Sun, and Uranus all placed in the ninth house.

Pluto in the Ninth House

Pluto influences the deep feelings and mood of the individual. It relates to the body's response to situations and "body intuition." Compared to the Moon and Neptune, which relate to emotional and intuitive sensitivity, Pluto is the body response to situations and people. The influence affects the body's feelings: comfortable in good environments, or uncomfortable and moody in negative situations. Pluto is the person's gut feeling about something. Pluto may affect the health of the individual because of its strong tie to the body. Awareness of Pluto's placement in the chart is important for understanding the effects it may generate.

Pluto in a positive environment stimulates sincerity and faith. The mood and temperament are in harmony with the environment. Pluto's negative influences incline individuals toward dark thoughts and moodiness. Decisions about residence and workplace should be reviewed if Pluto has stressful aspects. It is not simply Pluto that creates the problem; it is a lack of awareness of the internal and external environments.

Physical illness can develop easily with the negative influence from Pluto. The presence of illness can be stimulated from the ripening of past negative karma or a lifestyle not supportive of health. Pluto then becomes one of the circumstances to stimulate illness, though it is not the principal cause of illness. It is possible for people with stressful aspects to Pluto to live a healthy life, but they may require extra mindfulness to maintain their health.

Pluto in the ninth house stimulates deep faith. The nonintellectual influence of Pluto indicates that spiritual practice works on a gut level. The choice of a spiritual mentor is based on the presence of the teacher. This worked both ways in Siddhartha's case. He understood quickly that the teachers he relied on could not supply his spiritual needs. He had a gut feeling there was more to be found than what was offered to him. The other expression of this placement is that Buddha's disciples sensed his sincerity. Siddhartha exuded a confident feeling that comforted those in his presence. Pluto's influence aided Siddhartha to be an authentic spiritual individual. He deeply felt what he taught.

Aspects to the Sun

Sun Conjunct Mercury—7° 50' Applying Orb

The sense of self and the intellect are together. This aspect can contribute to an excellent intellectual capacity. The sense of self and the ability to think about things are synonymous. These people are curious and inquisitive. Anything that is interesting to them naturally brings forth their desire to know more about it. This beneficial aspect suggests the ability to use the mind competently.

Sun Opposite Saturn—7° 16' Applying Orb

The sense of self and conservatism are in opposition. An opposition is like a pendulum swinging back and forth. One can look at the two planets to get a sense of the dynamics that will influence the individual. There is, on the one side, the central sense of self (Sun), and on the other side is the need to be practical and reserved (Saturn). This aspect could cripple an individual from accomplishment if he or she weighed and judged situations too seriously. Hesitating and the desire to control activity could be the interference. The ability to be critical and discerning is strong on the positive side. This influence could make a person a solid source of wisdom and support.

Sun Conjunct Uranus—7°00' Separating Orb

The sense of self and revolution are together. This may stimulate a liberal point of view. The person may never be a conformist. This aspect makes one independently minded. These people might see themselves as unique. The negative side of this aspect may contribute to being an eccentric and odd individual. A beneficial aspect of Uranus is the possibility of liberation. Free of social dictates and norms, these people are able to do uncommon feats. If these individuals lack self-esteem, they might feel like social misfits and develop an inferiority complex. This is the product of a negative attitude. These people can equally be very liberated if they see the positive side of themselves.

Aspects to Mercury

Mercury Conjunct Venus—3°52' Separating Orb

The intellect and sensuality work together well. These individuals are able to think with both motif and analogy. The sensual world and thoughts combine harmoniously. Some of this aspect stimulates affectionate speech and a manner of dialogue that moves others emotionally. The golden speech of Manjushri, the Buddha of wisdom, comes from this aspect. Artistic ability with both the mind and hand are available. The placement of Venus in the chart can demonstrate where greater fulfillment is available. Mercury's conjunction to Venus may bestow the ability to express emotions fluidly.

Mercury Conjunct Uranus—0°50' Applying Orb

Intellect and revolution are well aspected. The intelligence of Mercury's influence is brilliant with this aspect. Uranus is similar to the sudden school of enlightenment in Zen Buddhism. That school says that reality reveals itself in sudden revelations. Uranus similarly, in this aspect, gives sudden realizations to the intellect. The effect is brilliant, startling ideas. Because of the beneficial aspect, the mind is spontaneous and liberated in its point of view. Mercury's placement in the chart can benefit from the spontaneity of Uranus.

Mercury Conjunct Neptune—0°30' Separating Orb

Intellect and the spiritual pole are well aspected. The inquisitive influence of Mercury mixes with the imagination and intuition of Neptune. This aspect makes the mind imaginative. It is said that Buddha's thought was vast and profound in content. Many obscure points in his teachings may have been aided with this aspect. If an individual meditates regularly, he or she can do visualization practices easily. Neptune is an antenna to draw in realizations. Dreams can be prophetic and knowledge of other people's thoughts is possible with good meditation skill.

Mercury Conjunct Pluto—4°07' Separating Orb

Intellect and the instinctual pole are well aspected. Deep feeling combines with thought. This can stimulate great sincerity and the expression of faith. The person can understand the deeper meaning of Tantra with this aspect. Meditations dealing with the body are quickly mastered. A positive attitude guarantees that the baser influences of the body are transformed. Pluto is not communicative, and people with this aspect may not be openly expressive of their feelings.

Aspects to Venus

Venus Trine Mars—3°53' Separating Orb

Sensuality and willpower are well aspected. This may give extra power to taking pleasure from life. The ability to pursue and satisfy desires is easy. The sexual response will be strong and healthy.

This aspect does not benefit someone pursuing a Hinayana style of practice. Hinayana Buddhism and faith traditions with similar beliefs see desire and pleasure as a distraction. Mars and Venus well aspected stimulate the pursuit of desire. Pleasure can be easily experienced. Individuals with this aspect may have to deal with frustration if their spiritual path prescribes abstinence. Siddhartha had the Saturn-Moon conjunction to balance the Venus-Mars aspect.

A Mahayana approach to practice may be more beneficial with this aspect. This is because the pleasures of the world can be used productively. Mars and Venus well aspected stimulate the wish to give pleasure to others. The practice of Tantra is excellent because of the power and sensual mix of Mars and Venus. The placement of Venus is important regarding where fulfillment and satisfaction are found. Mars facilitates striving for that attainment.

Venus Conjunct Uranus—4°43' Applying Orb

Sensuality and revolution are well aspected. Uranus tends to make a person very spontaneous wherever it is placed. The sense of freedom about love will be strong with this aspect. When this person falls in love, he or she feels love for everyone. The individual can be playful and artistic with this aspect. The art forms may be nontraditional, but they will have a strong aspect of individuality and charm. Spontaneous love toward others is combined with a liberal attitude.

Venus Conjunct Neptune—3°22' Applying Orb

Sensuality and the spiritual pole are well aspected. This aspect can bring forth the true romantic. The imaginative and intuitive aspects of Neptune influence the sensual realms of these people. This can produce individuals who love the anticipation and atmosphere of a love affair. The physical involvement of lovemaking may not interest them as much. A beautiful dinner on the side of a river with special people is much more appealing. The other side of this influence is the spiritual dimensions of love. Love transcends to the ultimate. Meditation can produce profound experiences of being one with the universe, and that the universe is love. The imagination works well with affection and pleasure. Neptune might also cause them to intuitively know when someone is feeling attracted to them.

Venus Conjunct Pluto—0°15' Separating Orb

Sensuality and the instinctual pole are well aspected. Pluto is the body's response to situations. With the affection and love of Venus conjunct Pluto, falling in love is a physical event for this person. It could almost be called biological love experienced on a cellular level. To love and not feel a strong attraction to the other would almost be impossible. In Buddha's case, this aspect generated deep affection from both the Buddha and his students. Disciples of the Buddha would have felt the depth of his love and been inspired. Buddha did not only inspire faith, he uplifted people with his sincere presence. Considering that most of Asia at one time was Buddhist, his presence was profound and people responded powerfully. One doesn't affect people throughout centuries of time without being charismatic.

Aspects to Uranus

Uranus Conjunct Neptune—1°21' Separating Orb

Revolution and the spiritual pole are conjunct. The spontaneity of Uranus stimulates intuitiveness and imagination beneficially. The sudden school of enlightenment suits this aspect perfectly. Sudden realizations and profound insights are experienced in a flash. These individuals can get ideas, visions, and insights in abrupt ways.

Uranus Conjunct Pluto—4°57' Separating Orb

Revolution and the instinctual pole are united. The spontaneity of Uranus may stimulate the mood and deep feelings to shift quickly. A positive attitude can energize the person on a physical level. The *chi* (*prana*, or energy) will have a great deal of power. Buddha was able to perform many miracles during his life. His energy was liberated and expressive.

Mars in the First House

The first house demonstrates influences on the personality. It describes the personality from an astrological point of view—or how one sees and projects oneself to others. It can also describe the physical appearance. First-house planets generally represent the person during initial meetings with others. Once the individual feels comfortable with a situation, then the rest of the chart's dynamics might gain expression. Planets in the first house, for a spiritual seeker, give a strong sense of personality. In terms of altruistic activity, the wish to benefit sentient beings, planets in the first house enhance presence and character. These people can project personal charisma. Although the Ascendant is important, the planets placed here give the first house stronger impact.

Mars represents willpower and determination. Mars fuels the ability and capacity of an individual. Negative influences of Mars demonstrate anger and aggressiveness. An analogy for Mars is two strong arms, giving the ability to accomplish a task well. Another analogy for Mars is an axe or sword. An axe cuts best when it has something solid to bite into, such as a tree or firewood. When Mars' influence is coupled with a positive attitude, it has excellent capacity to get jobs done. If it is weakly positioned in the natal chart and coupled with an unenthusiastic attitude, Mars' influence becomes less effective.

Clear-minded spiritual people could use their energy effectively. Decisiveness is a quality of strong willpower. Decisiveness on its own can be aggressive and destructive to success. Compassion and kindheartedness soften that effect. The best motive for action is skillful means joined with wisdom.

Power is embodied in the Tantric deity Vajrapani, who represents the complete self-control of enlightened beings. Self-control is power, power to act just as desired in any situation. Buddhas have no limitation to their willpower because they live in self-realization. Spiritual growth is assisted with a well-placed Mars. If an individual has a poorly placed Mars, it means they don't have astrological support for their willpower. It does not mean they are ineffective in what they do.

Mars in the first house generates a strong capacity to accomplish any task. Siddhartha was forthright and direct in what he did. This beneficial placement assisted him in accomplishing great tasks. His personality demonstrated a strong sense of willfulness and empowerment.

Pluto and Venus act in a supportive manner to Mars' influence. The Pluto-Venus conjunction generates a feeling of deep love and faith. Those aspects empowered Siddhartha's first-house Mars to act with positive emotions. Once Siddhartha had set his mind on a task that he deemed emotionally important, his will became insurmountable.

Aspects to Mars

Mars Trine Pluto—3°38' Applying Orb

Willpower and the instinctual pole are in a beneficial aspect. This can make these people emotionally powerful in any activity they pursue. Pluto, which stimulates deep feeling and mood, sits in a supportive position to willpower and determination. If these people are in the mood, so to speak, they are deeply motivated in that action. That feeling arises naturally for them. The stronger the belief in the activity, the more determined they are. This aspect could make individuals obstinate or overzealous. When the activity is positive, this aspect gives great power.

Jupiter in the Eighth House

The eighth house identifies the astrological component of the chemistry in relationships. It refers to a deeper connection and rapport with others. The eighth house increases the depth of relationships. Rapport is the key word here. This can be rapport on a basic emotional level or a very deep connection even including intuitive insights. The eighth house is the area of personal relatedness with others. A spiritual aspirant strives to develop sensitivity and clairvoyant powers as tools on the path. Those powers mostly involve a relationship with others, thus an emphasis for the eighth house.

The example of chemistry in the eighth house works well to demonstrate what can come from a strong rapport with another. Two chemicals when mixed together create something new. The same principle applies to people. Any occasion during which two people deeply interact can have a profound effect on both of them. This is demonstrated strongly with the Mahayana Buddhist principle of love and compassion. These feelings are expressed in the ideal of bodhicitta, the wish to attain enlightenment to benefit all sentient beings. This attitude has an effect on everything in life. The altruistic feeling brings harmony to everyone. Even if someone is negative, the person with bodhicitta can skillfully try to help. Planets placed here may also bestow a natural capacity to be interactive in a personal manner. That effect, if mixed with an attitude of loving-kindness, stimulates positive results for everyone. Close association with one's guru exemplifies the idea of receiving blessings and inspiration on the path, an eighth-house activity.

Jupiter represents expansion. It is the second largest object in our solar system and has a very fast rotation. Jupiter even has its own luminosity. Jupiter's influence in the natal chart generates optimism, goodwill, and enthusiasm. The influence stimulates a sense of what is possible. One moves toward the area where Jupiter is placed in the chart as if seeing a light at the end of a tunnel.

Jupiter fuels a sense of generosity. Generosity is an optimistic relationship with material objects. As a negative influence, Jupiter can make one busy with desires to accomplish too many tasks. The negative effect can also cause the person to project unrealistic expectations on others, even though the expectations may seem beneficial. This is because sometimes the sense of goodwill can be too enthusiastic.

Jupiter in the eighth house inspires the practitioner with a generous attitude. Allowance for other people's shortcomings and a generally positive approach toward them are the principal influences. Siddhartha saw the Buddha nature within everyone, plus their positive potential to attain enlightenment. The ability to inspire and support others is strong. The positive approach of Mahayana Buddhism is a natural response in this case.

Chiron in the Seventh House

Chiron is an asteroid and part of a newer form of astrology now being practiced. Chiron represents a personal challenge, but it is also a source of power. Individuals can grow and learn through any challenge and gain mastery over that area. The issue increases their sense of self-esteem and confidence. If a challenge defeats them, then they live with a sensitivity that may repeatedly obstruct success. Chiron is an asteroid that says, "Deal effectively with this situation or be obstructed."

The seventh house relates to people close to us. This can include the immediate family, spouse, and relatives, plus broader areas of relationship such as friends and work associates. This house refers to how important other people are in our lives. A spiritual aspirant is aware of others and strives to benefit them. Planets placed here stimulate this quality. It is important to develop skillful means in these relationships.

Skillful means in relationships starts with the ability to define boundaries concerning responsibility. Boundaries define what we are personally responsible for and what others are responsible for in a relationship. Practitioners are responsible for their personal karmic accumulation and how they present themselves to others. They are not responsible for how someone reacts to positive interaction. Spiritual people strive to benefit others the best they can. That is their main responsibility. If responsibilities are not defined properly, then boundaries are ignored and attachment and suffering can follow.

The lack of wisdom in a relationship may cause an individual to express only emotional compassion. That type of compassion can cause more trouble than benefit. Spiritual aspirants with planets in this house are naturally inclined toward thinking of others. The real capacity to be a friend comes from the ability to understand another compared to projecting one's own needs.

Chiron in the seventh house gave Siddhartha challenges from family and friends. The first major challenge was the death of his mother. Although he had no control of this situation, it was the first event that had a strong impact on him. He was lucky that his mother's cousin took over the position of mothering him, but he had to deal with the loss of one of the most important people in his life. This may have developed into his interest in becoming a celibate monk. His Moon-Saturn conjunction could have made him shy and reserved emotionally with women. He was stimulated to assume positions of authority with women. Saturn likes to be in control; in this case, emotional control of women.

The biggest challenge from women that Buddha faced was admitting them into ordained life. Ananda, his main attendant, lobbied long and hard for Buddha to accept women into the ordained spiritual community. Buddha finally accepted women, but it was an issue not quickly decided.

The second challenge in Siddhartha's life was his father. His father was controlling and manipulative. Granted his father gave Siddhartha everything he wanted, but with strings attached. His father wanted him to become the new emperor of India. Siddhartha had to deal with huge expectations from his father's side. This is a massive challenge for any son, especially if you are a crown prince.

Siddhartha dealt with this challenge by getting married and giving his father a grandson. He had many discussions with his father over the issue of his spiritual aspirations. His father always held over him the responsibility of being the next heir to the throne. It seems that Siddhartha was not able to personally defy his father. He gave his father a grandson who could take the mantle. Siddhartha's son was in line to take the throne after Siddhartha passed away. Siddhartha would let his son fulfill this princely role.

Later, when Siddhartha was enlightened and finally did return to meet his father, wife, and son, he ordained his son and wife. They became a monk and a nun and renounced worldly life. Thus he totally thwarted his father's wish for a long and powerful dynasty.

The final area of challenge for Siddhartha related to the seventh house came from a close family member, Devadatta. He was Siddhartha's cousin. Devadatta grew up in the palace and was constantly competing with Siddhartha. Siddhartha seemed to handle the challenges in the palace quite well. On one occasion, Devadatta shot a swan in the wing with a bow and arrow. Siddhartha saved the swan and was trying to protect it. Devadatta became furious and brought Siddhartha and the swan to the court. He demanded that the swan be returned to him, as he had shot it. The ministers of the court heard his argument and agreed. Siddhartha then interjected, "Who should have ownership of the swan, the person who would kill it or the person who would save its life?" The ministers agreed with Siddhartha and he kept the swan.

Later, when Siddhartha became the Buddha, Devadatta joined the spiritual community. He continued to be competitive and refused to see any positive qualities in Siddhartha's attainment. He constantly tried to undermine the Buddha's authority and even attempted to have the Buddha killed by a rogue elephant. Buddhist historians cite many stories of Buddha dealing with Devadatta fairly and justly. He never hated him or got angry with all that Devadatta did. Devadatta died a sad and lonely life in the end.

Siddhartha had an excellent astrology chart. The strong placement of six planets in the ninth house guaranteed that he would search for deeper meaning in life. His Saturn-Moon conjunction in the third house bestowed authority and compassion on his teaching technique. The first-house Mars bestowed power and effective abilities to lead one of the biggest religions in the world. Siddhartha's chart integrated the other factors of his life to create the person he became, the Buddha.

Three

The Wisdom of Siddhartha

There are three aspects of wisdom a Buddhist utilizes for practice. They are impermanence, interdependence, and voidness. Siddhartha's enlightenment is the source of that wisdom. Western chart interpretation, from a Buddhist point of view, offers a refreshing addition to traditional astrology.

Siddhartha's first wisdom came through seeing impermanence. The first motivational image for his spiritual life was a funeral procession. Siddhartha was twenty-eight-years old and on a journey to inspect his father's kingdom. The corpse was open for all to see. The grieving mourners carried it above their heads. Siddhartha had no contact with death in the palace. His father protected him from the suffering aspects of life. He knew of death as a concept but not an actual experience. No one from his group of associates had died yet. To see the pain of the mourners and a corpse forced him to question life. Death is a great shock to anyone and death is final.

Nothing in this world is permanent. Everyone knows this but tries to ignore it. People generally grasp after permanence. They want life to last forever. Siddhartha may have had similar feelings. He lived a life of incredible luxury. Now he was aging and his experiences revolved only around palace entertainment and preparation to take over the kingdom. It had been that way since his birth. His life was not challenging. He was raised a spoiled child and given little to challenge him as he grew older.

Siddhartha did not fully understand his father's objectives. The king tried to protect Siddhartha from suffering. He was afraid that Siddhartha might seek a spiritual life, but he wanted his son to become the ruler of all India. This paternal care pressured and smothered Siddhartha. The king's ambition, though, resulted in the completely opposite outcome. Siddhartha's search for realism was a response to the control his father applied constantly on him.

Siddhartha's natal chart demonstrates these events. One gets a wonderful view of the play of astrology within his life. The natal chart rectified here for Siddhartha shows the effect of his Saturn Return. A Saturn Return is a significant astrological event that individuals experience some time around age twenty-eight or twenty-nine. It often stimulates a time of critical reevaluation. Siddhartha's Saturn Return opposed a large group of planets at his Midheaven. This event is a perfect call to realism for Siddhartha.

If we follow the historical account of Siddhartha, we know that he married at age twenty-five. He fathered a son within a few years of marriage, at about age twenty-seven. That year he experienced transiting Saturn opposite his natal Venus. This is a call for responsibility in issues of affection. Saturn's influence in opposition to Venus asked Siddhartha to be truthful. This transit weighed on Siddhartha's heart, his emotional sense of duty and responsibility. Saturn in a conjunction or opposition causes stress. The stress generally deals with responsibility and reevaluation. Chart 2 represents these stimulating transits.

History says that shortly after the birth of his son, Rahula, Siddhartha started to look outside the palace. He made four excursions into the kingdom with his faithful attendant, Channa. This coincided with the first transits of Saturn in opposition to his Neptune, Mercury, and Uranus. Siddhartha experienced three astrological effects. Saturn's transit opposite Neptune caused questions to arise about spiritual life. Saturn's transit to Mercury made him reflect on life. The transit of Saturn to Uranus challenged him to do something bold. The end of these first transits marked his twenty-eighth birthday in May. Saturn then began a second (retrograding) transit of Siddhartha's Uranus, Mercury, and Neptune. This influenced him to make decisions about his revelations. He was motivated to do something intelligent and powerful about the things he had seen. This is a perfect example of Saturn in retrograde, which can stress individuals to the maximum. My astrology instructor, Michael Layden, said that a Saturn Return either effects personal change or stimulates some form of compensation. A common form of compensation is substance abuse. One wishes to escape the pain of self-analysis.

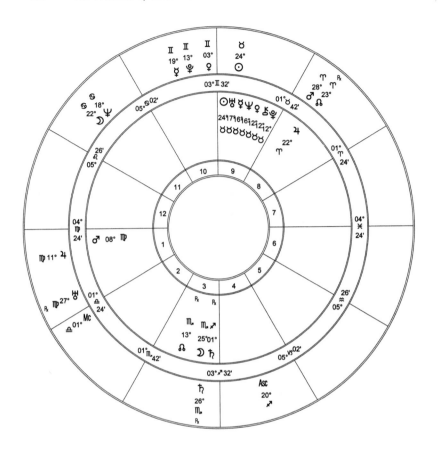

Chart 2
Inner Wheel—Siddhartha's Natal Chart
May 23, 575 B.C. / 12:30 P.M. LMT

Patna, India / 25N36 085E07

Geocentric Tropical Zodiac / Placidus, True Node

Outer Wheel—Siddhartha Renounces Palace
May 23, 546 B.C. / 8:30 P.M. LMT

Patna, India / 25N36 085E07

Geocentric Tropical Zodiac / Placidus, True Node

If we return to the wisdom teachings of Buddha, we get some idea of Siddhartha's spiritual evolution. His four excursions outside the palace exposed him to four realities of life. The first reality was illness, seeing a sick person. The second reality was aging, seeing an old, crippled man. The third reality was death, seeing a corpse en route to the cemetery. The fourth reality ignited spiritual determination. He saw a yogi in meditation. The first two experiences are part of the wisdom of detachment. They led Siddhartha to become disenchanted with his current life. Life includes illness and old age. Siddhartha could see his unconscious desire to live forever. The third experience was the reality of death. Later in life, Siddhartha, as the Buddha, said, "All that is born must die." If there is birth, death is the other side of that coin. Death makes a powerful call for everyone to review life. The death of a friend or relative shocks and awakens the unaware. This deepened Siddhartha's realization of mortality.

Siddhartha's Saturn Return

Siddhartha had all the circumstances to become a great ruler. He was destined to be either a ruler or a saint. The circumstances were organized for him to ascend his father's throne. He was a strong man, an excellent warrior, and highly intelligent. He had a beautiful wife, a son, and a luxurious life. What more could he want? This is the stage upon which his personal drama played. The fabric of his life was woven with many threads of influence. Some of those were astrological threads. All this played together to create his situation. It was the time of his Saturn Return.

Siddhartha looked at his material situation and had questions. A Saturn Return feels as if a mirror is placed in front of one's face. One must look at whatever is reflected. The image might not be fully appealing. The reflection shows just what is there. Dissatisfaction with the image often leads to a time of dynamic change. Siddhartha had a new vision of himself in relation to recent experiences. The experiences were a new awareness of illness, old age, death, and spirituality. Saturn added to these events and the effect was powerful. This was a strong call to take his life and actions into account.

Siddhartha was a powerful and motivated man. His Uranus-Sun conjunction inspired him to be a spiritual rebel. Mars in his first house inspired him to make powerful decisions. His Saturn-Moon conjunction gave him the emotional control to establish a worldwide religion. His Saturn Return is a perfect example of what Saturn can precipitate in life. Saturn Return cycles indicate a time in life when many question their current concept of reality.

A Saturn Return is a wonderful teacher. The mirror of reality shines. The image reflected is one's personal reality. If the person does not like what he or she sees, something has to happen. One option is depression. Depression for a healthy person is a good experience. My teacher Lama Yeshe often said, "Check up." Constantly review what is transpiring. The experience of a depression may be a call to check within.

Depression is generally perceived as being bad in Western culture. Even a short bout of depression is often dealt with by taking medication. My experience with astrological clients shows that depression is a wake-up call that something is wrong. It is a healthy response to a difficult situation. Saturn stimulates depression if there are unskillful areas in one's life. People are directed by Saturn to reflect with greater discrimination on their existence. Siddhartha had a wonderful life, but no emotional reality. The Saturn Return reinforced this and possibly was a causal factor for depression. Siddhartha did become depressed. His depression was so strong that he decided to leave the palace, his wife, and his newborn son. He needed a deeper meaning to life. Siddhartha's departure from the palace also had a compassionate motivation. He felt that life must be more meaningful than what he had experienced to this point. He wanted to understand so that he could help his son and family. He had seen through the veil his father had placed over all their lives.

The necessity to seek a more realistic view coincided with Saturn transiting in the third house in opposition to his natal Venus, Pluto, Neptune, Mercury, and Uranus all in the ninth house. To be motivated strongly enough to leave his palace and all its luxuries required a powerful emotional catalyst. Siddhartha's Saturn transits increased the power of his resolution. They made him reevaluate his life. The final Saturn transit was with Uranus in December of 547 B.C. Saturn and Uranus in opposition is a strong stimulation to do something powerful, to make bold decisions. He decided to leave the palace and seek spiritual illumination.

History says that Siddhartha left the palace when he was twenty-nine. His twenty-ninth birthday was in May 546 B.C. During this time he had transiting Saturn conjunct his Moon. This transit suppressed his feelings. He became cold, hard, and determined. Saturn conjunct the Moon is a beneficial natal transit for someone trying to leave a luxurious life and become a monk! This transit was in orb from December 547 B.C. until September 546 B.C., just enough time to get away from the palace and not lose heart.

Siddhartha lived in the forest as a beggar from age twenty-nine to thirty-five. He studied initially with two learned Hindu saints. He saw them at different times and quickly mastered what each one had to teach. The second guru actually saw Siddhartha's greatness and asked him to become his principal disciple. Siddhartha refused the offer. He had no feeling for power and prestige any more. He was a crown prince. He had experienced respect, wealth, and pleasure, and he was tired of it. He wanted to experience truth and the real nature of life.

Siddhartha traveled from the last guru's ashram to outside Gaya, Bihar State. He took residence under a tree beside a river. Here he began ascetic practices to discover reality. The five ascetic yogis joined him as he practiced. Historical texts say that

Siddhartha was an impressive sight, a man endowed with dignity and prestige. These five yogis instantly recognized that he was someone special. Siddhartha had the bearing of a crown prince.

Siddhartha met two Hindu gurus several months after leaving the palace. He had to learn their doctrines and then move to Gaya. This coincided with the final transits of Saturn to natal Saturn, which took place from September 546 B.C. until January 545 B.C. Saturn's cycle reflected the determination that Siddhartha set in place for the next six years of life. Saturn did not do this independently; rather, Siddhartha had all the prerequisites for realization. The Saturn cycle merely helped the process mature. Siddhartha's life was the play of many facets of stimulation and interdependence.

The Wisdom of Impermanence

Impermanence manifests in coarse and subtle ways. The idea of impermanence is obvious, but comprehension may be simplistic. The recognition that things change is naturally what everyone sees. This is excellent, but Buddhists seek to see the implications of impermanence in their lives. Impermanence properly understood creates a greater appreciation of personal mortality. Everyone will die one day and nothing can stop this process. What are the implications in relationship to the world? To evaluate death's implications, three things are reviewed from the Buddhist perspective. These are property, friends, and the physical body.

There is a story of a lay practitioner in Tibet. He was a member of the Kadampa tradition that flourished in the eleventh century C.E. The Kadampas were famous as pure devotees to the Buddha's message. This fellow had practiced the Buddha Dharma all his life. Toward the end of his life, he would go on walks through a small village. One day he fell into a ditch and started rolling around crying and shouting. When some villagers came to his assistance, he stopped shouting but continued to cry. The villagers offered to help him and asked what was the problem?

He responded, "I realize how empty my life is of real spiritual practice! I've understood this only now when death is so close. I'm upset because I now truly grasp that my life is impermanent, but the time to do something is almost gone!"

The villagers were shocked, but did not take the old man too seriously. His whole life had been spiritually focused. They thought he might be acting this way to set an example for them. Kadampa masters are famous for uninhibited and outrageous behavior to spiritually motivate others. This Kadampa master revealed the need to be conscientious during one's life.

The point is to avoid making property, friends, or the body the sole focus of this life. A materially focused life can ignore the higher qualities of human expression. Buddhists believe that a clear realization of personal impermanence can improve the quality of life. Buddhists develop internal acceptance that the world is in constant flux instead of thinking that nothing changes or grasping after materiality. They balance life with wisdom.

Impermanence Related to the Material World

There is a cutting expression on the subject of material attachment from Shantideva, a great Indian Buddhist of the sixth century C.E. He said, "One is merely the watchdog of possessions." Everyone wishes to protect and guard possessions. The limitation of this material focus is that one becomes a caretaker. One just ensures that the next owner receives an object in good condition. Just as a watchdog guards the possessions of the owner, a person becomes the watchdog of what he or she presently owns. The person growls and barks if others get too close to the precious objects. Buddhists believe that it is better to be the owner of possessions, rather than being owned by them. The unenlightened attitude grasping after permanence, in Buddhist terms, is a source of unnecessary suffering.

To own a possession wisely is to be detached from it or be in control of it. When an object breaks and the owner gets upset and angry, it means that the possession owned him or her. It had more control over the individual than the person had over himself. The individual unconsciously believed that the object could last forever. The attachment created a dependency on the object. The object takes on the illusion that it is the creator of happiness, not the person. The object becomes more important than the individual's self-esteem. The object dictates the person's state of happiness or sadness.

A sense of impermanence gives control to life. One owns possessions and can be more generous. All objects in life are impermanent. They come and go as time passes. Buddhists strive to understand that nothing returns to them but the nature of the relationship. The effect of the feelings generated is all that returns. One may experience fear, craving, and unhappiness in this life because of grasping attachment.

If there is a belief in future lives, the same applies. One receives the karmic residue of attachment, nothing more. Buddhists believe that it is better to collect good karma in relation to possessions than to collect karmic imprints of unhappiness. The relationship established with the object, never the object, stays with the individual at the end of life.

The Astrology of Impermanence

Astrologically, this wisdom helps immensely. For example, let's examine a planet that loves security and possessions: Saturn. Saturn stimulates a desire for security. Saturn's influence hates insecurity, vulnerability, and a lack of knowledge. The example works best when applied with a natal Saturn in the second house. The second house deals with material possession, including one's place of residence, the furnishings, and any other material assets such as clothes and money.

An unaware individual with Saturn in the second house may desire to build a fortress and seek material security. It is reasonable to assume that Saturn's influence will grasp after possessions because of its desire for stability. The person may feel the need to solidly possess and control what he or she owns. The stress is felt as a need for material security. Saturn's negative impact can stimulate an emotionally brittle response to everything material.

Lama Thubten Yeshe, my Buddhist teacher and one of the founding Tibetan lamas of Buddhism in the West, used an expression to exemplify this type of material grasping. He would say to someone who was, as he said, "freaking out" about material problems, "Oh my dear, your ego is broken."

This refers to one's ego having a fragile position in relation to one's attachments. Saturn can stimulate individuals to grasp after security. In other words, Saturn hates insecurity. Saturn stimulates one to seek a conservative and secure position. Anything less than strong grasping and control is too fragile, impermanent, and brittle. The concept of impermanence can be initially unsettling to individuals with a strong Saturn influence in their chart.

Saturn develops wisdom as time passes. Saturn is the wisest of all the planets when it comes to a practical approach to life. My experience from years of astrological counseling is that Saturn may not bestow wisdom until one is quite old. I have repeatedly found, in my client work, that the Buddhist wisdom of impermanence speeds up the process of realizing the wisdom of Saturn. If one learns to be reflective and contemplative about life, Saturn starts to bestow insights quickly. Saturn stimulates one to go slowly when looking at a new situation. Saturn hates insecurity, so a mindful person tends to harmonize with Saturn's point of view. Mindfulness and Saturn get along perfectly. They increase the positive qualities of contemplative realism. A wise attitude views what is transpiring on the material level and softens the individual's approach to life.

Impermanence Related to Friendships

The wisdom of impermanence applied to friendships helps diminish the tendency to grasp and cling. Most people are nice to others because of what they receive in return. One gives love because one gets support, affection, and a sense of comfort from others. People treat others with kindness to ensure continued acceptance. Friendship changes immediately to distrust with even a small disagreement. Without thinking, people may suddenly lose a friendship because of a few cross words. Most people deny this fickle nature and feel they are reliable. In contrast, many Buddhist saints say, "Friends of the morning easily become the enemies of the evening." This is because most friendships are based on personal need. Friendships are often not based on true caring for the other.

Test this theory. For example, let's say a friend of yours hears that others spoke poorly about him. How might he feel when those individuals are present? What happens when he inquires as to the truth of the matter? What happens when those people maintain their criticism of him? What does your friend do in response? Most likely his response is defensive as he tries to explain himself. He may take offense and just retaliate. This exercise is not to demean one's friends, but it does show how most people respond to unpleasant words.

Buddhists believe that wise people take time to respond to criticism. They reflect on what was said and think about the causes for it. If the criticism is true, they endeavor to change. If the statement is false, a wise approach is to express compassion. Wise people realize that everyone can have unrealistic projections about life. People grasp after something and then say horrible things. It is the nature of life in many cases.

Few people think in an enlightened manner. They simply retaliate or become defensive. Unaware people are quite predictable in their response. Often the basis for friendship is weak. Even if a problem is resolved, most still hold the other in distrust. These responses are due to attachment and clinging.

Another area of relationships that suffers the disruptive effects of grasping at permanence is unconscious association. The object of love is lost in projections. The unaware mind thinks, "Oh, my partner is here forever. I will find time for him (or her) tomorrow." This attitude embodies the words that John Lennon sang: "Life is what happens while we are making other plans." People with this attitude believe that time is endless and opportunity will always be there. It is easy to see how valued relationships are enriched with the awareness of impermanence.

The wisdom of impermanence makes life more dynamic. The awareness of impermanence draws on an inner set of guidelines when dealing with friendships. Individuals seek others who are attractive to them physically, emotionally, or intellectually. This type of attraction is natural. What the wisdom of impermanence changes is the attitude and manner of interaction. Relationships exist for brief periods of time and then change. This is what impermanence is all about. Even if one succeeds at living with a partner for an entire lifetime, at some point there is separation. Buddhists believe that all we receive from a relationship of any duration is the karmic role we played. Nothing more accompanies us into the future. Buddhists ask, "What do I want to take into my future? An attitude of clinging attachment, or a warm and supportive association?"

If you exhibit possessiveness, grasping, anger, and jealousy with friends, that is all you take with you at the end of life. Buddhists believe that your emotional output is the karmic luggage you take into your future life. This is the karmic continuity of actions within the mind stream. How can you expect to be different if you don't make yourself different in each present action? Astrology interpreted from a Buddhist standpoint operates actively within this context.

Those with love, kindheartedness, and wisdom for friends take that luggage into the future. Those karmic imprints are the qualities these individuals express now and as time passes. Buddhists believe that these effects grow in this life and even gain expression in the next rebirth. His Holiness the Dalai Lama says, "My religion is compassion, as this fulfills all that any religion would ask of us. If one has compassion, then all the requirements of Buddhist practice are fulfilled."

The realization of impermanence helps clarify the outcome of relationships. We see the effect of karmic activity in a personal way. We only get back what we put into the relationship.

Impermanence helps us recognize the boundaries between ourselves and others. Attachment likes to see people as possessions. If our friends act as expected, then we are happy. When our friends act outside of our expectations, then upset feelings, anger, jealousy, and resentment begin to surface. This is the karmic product of attachment and grasping. We want relationships to last forever and to always be good. Most people desire relationships that are a fantasy. Real life is not like a fairy tale. Relationships require dedication and compassion.

The wisdom of impermanence is a wonderful asset to help live a more fulfilling life. One enters into relationships realizing that time is not infinite. A person enjoys friendships while there is time. Impermanence keeps one in the here and now. Impermanence helps stop or slow down an unconscious way of relating to others. The wisdom of impermanence reminds us that we only get back what we put into a relationship. This wisdom positively stimulates authentic love, compassion, and communication.

Buddhists believe that to act in this manner contributes to a peaceful death. The wisdom of impermanence shows its face when death arrives and asks us to account for our actions. Impermanence is the first and most profound wisdom to realize from the Buddhist perspective.

Relationships in astrology relate to the upper hemisphere of the chart, principally the seventh or eighth houses. The seventh house shows the influences to those close to us, including spouse, friends, family, and business associates. To exemplify this, let's again put Saturn in the seventh house and see the effects. Lack of wisdom might cause Saturn here to be overbearing, attached, controlling, and stubborn. It takes awhile for Saturn in the seventh to become attached to someone. Its influence stimulates hesitation and shyness.

Once an association with another is established, then Saturn starts to create different influences. Saturn may stimulate the desire to make family and friends permanent. Strong insecurity may be felt if a friendship starts to deteriorate. The general response from Saturn here may be to assume a stubborn position of authority within relationships. Saturn wants to pressure the person back into compliance. Saturn in this house can also stimulate the desire to make the partner feel emotionally guilty. The seventh-house placement of Saturn may influence an individual to never forget anyone who was in his or her life.

The wisdom of impermanence helps ease the tendency to criticize others. A critical attitude arises when friends don't act as expected. It is hard for some people with Saturn in the seventh house to ever see how rigid their judgments or expectations are of others. Self-righteousness is common with this placement of Saturn.

My work as an astrologer helps me see that most Saturn problems lie with insecurity. Insecurity is based on grasping for permanence. Impermanence is the ultimate insecurity. To know that things will change no matter what one does causes great anxiety. It is this fear of change that stimulates a seventh-house Saturn to unconsciously cling to friends and associates. If only the person affected by Saturn could resolve the issues around impermanence, then wisdom develops easier.

Once people with Saturn in the seventh house start to see the wisdom of impermanence, they start to be reflective. The judgmental side of Saturn becomes a deeply contemplative consciousness. No planet can match the depth of thought that Saturn can generate. Thus a wise person with Saturn in the seventh house can become a great source of support for all friends and lovers. A wise Saturn moves slowly in response to issues.

This is Saturn's stubborn influence, but with wisdom, the influence moves the individual in a deliberate and consistent manner. The power of Saturn's wise influence is to be practical, reliable, and realistic.

Impermanence Related to the Body

The final area of grasping or fixation relates to the body. It is amazing that people think life will go on forever considering how fragile our bodies are. Everyone is potentially one inhalation away from death! People never see their impermanence that way. They feel death happens to everyone else. Even if one appreciates that death will occur, the time of death is a vague concept in the distant future, never close at hand. The mind may ask, "How can death come when there are so many things to be done?" This attitude ignores reality and is close-minded when it comes to thinking the body will die. Grasping and the desire to control things are hard concepts to soften. The insightful side of impermanence, though, is an asset to living an invigorated life. Impermanence is not a problem; it helps fulfill life.

Let us use an example of a trip to show the wisdom of personal impermanence. A guest is a short-term visitor. As a guest, one never takes situations too seriously. When something breaks or the accommodations are uncomfortable, one reflects that "This is a brief event." The normal serious attitude and expectations relax. This relaxation of attitude is based on the perception of a short-term set of circumstances.

Increase the length of the visit. Discomforts start to become bothersome. The longer one sees a relationship to a situation, the more the attitude changes. One takes the situation seriously and desires to control it. The issue is not the desire to change the situation, it is grasping at stability. The grasping attitude desires long-term stability and security.

Most people perceive the body to be attractive. Without appraising the real situation of the body, they identify with it as a fixed asset. They groom it, feed it, and clothe it with the best items available. Most people base their personal self-esteem on the body.

People get caught up in vanity by seeing their body as physically desirable. They put extra time and effort into maintaining its beauty. They want physical attractiveness to be as permanent as possible. If the body starts to show signs of aging, such as wrinkles, it causes distress. The body naturally reveals its impermanent nature, but no one likes that. People suffer impermanence as aging takes place. They start putting extra time into coloring the hair, polishing the teeth, and making the skin's color appealing without thinking about the real situation. They might seek expensive gurus to transform them with miraculous treatments and cosmetic aids. This fascination with the body can become obsessive. One is no longer in control of the situation, but ruled by the body's appearance.

The health of the body is generally ignored, provided it functions well. Some people generate fixed attitudes about the health and power of the body. They put time and energy into increasing and perfecting the attributes of the body's form and health. The body becomes a strong focus associated with its shape, power, and capacity. When it starts to show signs of impermanence, the individual experiences anxiety. This grasping attitude establishes an unbalanced relationship with the body that causes suffering. The suffering mind instantly raises its unhappy head when there is a loss of power or health.

The most incredible fact is that the body will be the source of death in all these cases. It is as if one placed all resources in a stock that is destined to fail. The body is definitely going to die. There is no other option. As Buddha said, "That which is born must die." Birth and death are the two sides of the same coin. The issue in all of the previous cases is not the object of the delusion, the body, but the unrealistic attitude. Everyone can still groom and take good care of themselves, but Buddhism suggests a balanced attitude, which includes the awareness of impermanence. The wisdom of impermanence does not abandon common sense, rather it fosters a more realistic approach to life.

There is no point in pursuing the recognition of mortality until one becomes paralyzed with fear. That response is a negative perception of the situation. To become paralyzed or dysfunctional is not the objective of realizing personal impermanence. The invocation of wisdom makes life more bearable and comfortable. External things are not the real source of happiness. If so, rich people would always be happy. Wealth, friends, and health would then guarantee happiness and be the only source of fulfillment. Everyone knows wealthy people who have a miserable existence. Some people have many friends but are unhappy and dissatisfied. Those who are healthy and strong may have complex psychological problems. None of this guarantees happiness. Something else is the creator of happiness. In Buddhist terms, it is the mind; the attitude is the creator of happiness, not the objects.

The mind creates the view of the world, and an enlightened attitude is an asset for a happy life. Seeking permanence in the impermanent is a mistake, but the mind constantly does it. This is because the attitude fails to see the benefits of incorporating the wisdom of impermanence. The correct view of personal mortality is not depressing. Rather, it is closer to reality and cools a mind hot with grasping and delusion.

Look at which house relates to personality and body to see the implications of this wisdom. For instance, the first house stimulates personality and appearance. A strong first house without wisdom may contribute to an overbearing and self-centered attitude. The self and everything related to the personality are emphasized. Little space and time are given for others and their needs. Egotism may reign supreme, depending on the attitude of the person.

Egotism may include not only the personality, but also vanity and pride of the body. If someone is a true egotist, a misapprehension of impermanence can inflame the sense of self and make things worse. A self-indulgent attitude may validate hedonism by seeing that life is fleeting. The stronger the sense of ego grasping, the more pride and arrogance can destroy the attainment of true happiness. The sense of self overemphasizes the personality and appearance.

Personal mortality can help release some of the pressure of a self-centered attitude. Most people diminish ego grasping and embrace a more realistic attitude toward life when impermanence is clearly understood. A compassionate approach softens the ego as well. As for pride, one can realize that there are people who are more beautiful and intelligent than oneself. Attractiveness and intelligence do not benefit the situation if they are flaunted. Things are impermanent and today's pride can be tomorrow's embarrassment. Nothing stands forever and as supreme. Think of all the great empires that once ruled the world and are now nonexistent. The higher people think they are, the farther they fall.

Buddha talked of four things that always bring their opposite. The four pairs are birth and death, meeting and parting, accumulating and dispersing, and rising and falling. Birth will bring the experience of death. Meeting with others naturally entails separating from them. Amassed goods will finally be scattered, and whatever rises will have to fall. These four things are two sides of the same coin.

One should never be too serious about these issues. A sense of humor is important. His Holiness the Sixth Dalai Lama, who lived in the eighteenth century, had a different opinion on one of these four points. The Sixth Dalai Lama was renowned for his love of women and wine. He was a realized being; the problem was that the office of His Holiness found him a bit too late in life. He was found as the incarnation of the Fifth Dalai Lama when he was nine or ten years old. Historians say his delayed discovery allowed worldly pleasures to become mixed with his spiritual interests. This did not stop his incredibly perceptive mind. He commented on the Buddha's saying that all must part with, "Ah, but everything that parts can therefore look forward to meeting again!" He lived only a short life, was never a monk, and was famous for his poetic reflections on life and love. He still showed the genius that is exhibited by all the Dalai Lamas. He is beloved by the Tibetans for his profound understanding of the joys and sorrows of falling in love. His poems were translated into English. They are wonderfully insightful and playful.

A story may illustrate how the wisdom of impermanence can make life more bearable. There was once a Jewish king who asked his group of spiritual advisors for a magic ring to help him deal with all problems. The wise men finally gave him a gold ring with a special inscription on it that read, "This too will pass." That became all the magic the king needed. He could always invoke this wisdom to help deal with the problems of state. This wisdom helped keep his ego in balance. He had less cause to suffer what Lama Yeshe referred to as a brittle ego. The king's attitude was flexible. Impermanence is an asset to living a successful life.

Consider what happens when something affects one's personal time and space. An open attitude accepts the change. This is because there is space to accept change. The attitude flows with the constant changes. When one gets upset, it is because of a dislike for the present situation. There is an attachment to the previous situation. One wants it to remain the same, granted maybe not forever, but at least for a little longer. This is the issue of grasping after permanence.

People have conscious boundaries between realistic and unrealistic expectations. Everyone creates expectations for different situations. New items should last longer than used things. Friends should be more consistent than people one knows only briefly. All these are based on ideas of reliability. When upset emotions are felt, one has gone past these expectations and enters the realm of uncertainty. Issues around what is acceptable are quite central to the basic concept of happiness.

The idea of expectations and projections is a central pillar of Buddhist practice. If people are open to what is happening around them, they handle things better. If expectations are few, they are more flexible. If this is applied to personal space, people are better prepared to deal with whatever comes their way. They don't lose their equilibrium in a changing environment. The situation will change, so why get upset? It is people with brittle attitudes that suffer the most when things change unexpectedly.

Lama Yeshe used the expression "Oh, your ego is broken." It is an apt expression for getting upset. If something rattles one's cage and one becomes upset, it could be said that the "ego got broken." Whether people get upset or angry, freak out, or get their ego broken, it all amounts to the same thing. A situation arrived to change the present circumstances. They were attached to the stability of the existing situation, and sought permanence among the impermanent.

No matter what astrological aspects are in a chart, one has the option to deal with them effectively. There is also the option to suffer if one is not skillful. It is not a question of changing the astrological influence; it is one of changing the attitude. Even astrologers often miss this point. There is the recognition that a harsh aspect will change its effect as the person matures. It is not that the planetary positions changed, it is because the person adjusts his or her response. Astrology does not have a special power to create the situations a person meets. It has to work through who the person is and a vast accumulation of developmental dynamics.

This presentation is concluded regarding the wisdom of impermanence related to possessions, friends, and the self. This discussion focused on a few of the important houses related to these three objects. The second house was covered in relation to impermanence and material possessions. The seventh house covered impermanence relating to friends and associates. Finally, the first house looked at our sense of self and the wisdom of impermanence.

The key points to draw from the Buddhist wisdom on personal impermanence are the following:

1. All conditioned phenomena are subject to coarse and subtle impermanence.
2. Death is definite; all that is born must die.
3. The time of death is uncertain; no one can predict when death will come.
4. A materialistic attitude about possessions, friends, and the body does not help at the time of death.

These subjects are for reflection and contemplation. If one gains insight into them, then the following realizations should arise:

1. One doesn't look for permanence in the impermanent.
2. One appreciates mortality, incorporating an attitude that is appreciative of personal impermanence.
3. One doesn't procrastinate, because time is moving constantly.
4. One shifts to a skillful attitude regarding possessions, friends, and the body. One can use possessions to benefit the world, friendship to benefit others, and the body as a vehicle to express positive action.

The last point, a shift in attitude, is the most important. One reflects on the first four points about personal mortality, which gives power to the last four points. Without a solid foundation, one will not maintain the proper shift of attitude or resiliency. Even Don Juan, in Carlos Castenada's book *Journey to Ixtlan*, refers to death as one's best friend and advisor.

The Buddhist use of impermanence is to enhance existence. It should eliminate unrealistic projections about reality. Obviously one will not become the Buddha by just intellectually understanding impermanence. Siddhartha's change in life was stimulated by real suffering and impermanence. These realizations motivated him to seek deeper wisdom through inner experience.

Buddhists look to the Buddha as a source of inspiration for their own liberation. Liberation frees people from deluded responses. Liberation makes them skillful, irrespective of what dynamics played on them in the past. Thus liberation frees everyone from unconscious negative influences, including those from astrology. Wisdom, love, and mindfulness are what liberate us from suffering and delusion.

Four

The Deeper Wisdom

"With the heavenly eye, purified and beyond the range of human vision, I saw how beings vanish and come to be again. I saw high and low, brilliant and insignificant, and how each obtained according to his karma a favorable or painful rebirth."
—*The Historical Buddha*, p. 55

Karma

Buddhist astrology enters the realm of deep and profound wisdom. Although we might consider the law of cause and effect—*karma*—to be simplistic, it actually lays the foundation for all higher wisdom. Cause and effect are the processes of any action. Astrology makes greater sense when the law of cause and effect is understood. Without it, no relationship between the planets and life could exist, as we know it. The Moon's movement could not relate to the ocean's tides or the growth of plants. Karma means connections between objects and actions. Karma is the dynamic force of interdependence.

Cause-and-effect relationships between phenomena span the spectrum of knowledge from simple physics to quantum mechanics. Karma might be considered to be a mystical force, but it is actually the relationship between phenomena. Whether it is the growth of a seed into a sprout or the intellectual-emotional effects of past actions on our present state of mind, all this is karmic activity. Karma translates into the word *action*. Actions relate to the immediate preceding moments; this is karma.

Buddhism presents a very practical set of rules about karma. These fall into four categories:

1. Karmic actions inevitably ripen in accordance with their cause. A chili seed produces chili plants and a strawberry seed produces strawberries. Positive human emotions lead to happiness, and negative thoughts and actions lead to suffering.

2. A karmic act creates many effects. One grain of rice produces many seeds, just as the storehouse of karmic actions is constantly increasing.

3. If a certain cause is not produced, its result will not be experienced.

4. Karmic seeds never lose their potency. At some point, all karmic action will ripen.

Phenomenal activity is a tremendous interplay among numerous causes and circumstances. Astrology, which is a karmic force, is part of that interplay. It is not the primary factor of influence, but it does play a role in the production of any action. It is an error to consider planetary influences to be more important than the immediate birth situation of the individual. To give the planets a primary level of influence on anyone delegates too much power to them. The planets are a circumstance into which we are born. Astrology is a secondary influence in the hierarchy of what has an impact on the moment of birth.

If human existence were like a plant, with few factors of choice, then astrology could be a primary influence. Plants respond to the environment and have no free will to change where they grow. Plants flourish in good environments and are weak and unproductive in bad environments. Plants are versatile, but they do not think about what they are doing. Buddhists believe that plants have life force but no ability to make conscious decisions. Plants do the best they can wherever they are. The life force they have can be wonderfully adaptive, but it still is only a response to the immediate environment.

Conscious beings have more options than the simple response of a plant. Human beings have the unique ability to learn. Uneducated humans are less able to see possibilities, but even a little education quickly changes the situation. Educated humans can see many more options of response when dealing with new situations. All beings with both awareness and knowledge become the principal creators of who and what they are. The outside environment, which includes the planets, falls into a secondary category of influence. The planets and the physical environment are circumstances of influence.

Any attempt to reverse this role takes responsibility away from the individual. This view would say that external objects and events are responsible for all actions. People often try to blame others for their woes. An unskillful action is not their responsibility. For example, an abusive person could claim that Mars squares his or her Moon. This makes the person angry and easily upset. They are therefore free of personal responsibility for any disruptive action. The idea of being unconscious and without judgment could apply to everything. People's actions would simply be the product of stimulation.

Life is the product of many complex factors. One component is personal volition. Individuals have a number of choices depending on their perspective. That perspective can be positive or negative. Buddhists define positive and negative attitudes in a particular manner. Positive attitude or karmic action is that which does not harm oneself or others. It can either just not cause harm or it can bring benefit to oneself and others. Both definitions work in regard to positive actions. Negative motivation or karmic activity causes harm or suffering to both oneself and others.

A positive response to a situation accumulates karma similar to the cause, the first point. The results are positive physical and emotional effects. If we enjoy being positive, we increase the karmic effect because of the enthusiasm joy creates, the second point. If we fail to act on our positive intentions, we cannot expect new growth in positive directions, the third point. Finally, no matter when we did an action with positive intention, the effect will never be lost until it ripens into some form of joy or happiness, the fourth point.

One component of karma that requires emphasis is that intention is the creator of action. As long as one has good intentions, one will accumulate positive karma. One may get a mixture of results, both good and bad, if a good motivation is not skillfully enacted. The issue of being intelligent and skillful with good intentions is important. Good intentions alone can be quite harmful. The definition of good intention is the wish to benefit oneself and others. Said in reverse, a good motivation avoids harm and suffering to oneself and others. Karma manifests through the actions of body, speech, and mind. The definition of negative karmic action is a motivation with harmful intention. It causes physical, verbal, or mental harm and suffering.

The law of cause and effect is helpful to understand the dynamics of action. People expect external physical events to be produced from supportive physical causes. This is a natural and realistic expectation. What is interesting is that some people do not expect emotional events to relate to any cause. Somehow human experience is unrelated to its karmic factors. I once heard a teacher say that if one experiences emotion during an event, then that person has a karmic relationship with that situation. Some individuals believe that they have no relationship to the events they experience. They are innocent of involvement, just bystanders in life's melodrama. If that were truly the case, people would not respond to anything that transpires around them. This belief is not reasonable when one considers that a response indicates a related cause within oneself. Any situation stimulates internal karmic seeds to ripen. An emotional response means that some seed is producing an effect, thus reproducing itself. The effect can be positive or negative, and that depends on the current attitude and disposition. Everyone is in some part responsible for how they feel and act in every moment of existence.

Valuable insights will be gained by taking this wisdom into account in future chapters that deal with the natal horoscope. Planets in aspect to each other may mean a stimulation of our body, emotions, and mind. That stimulation is definable from the point of view of what causes and circumstances create it. There are various physical, intellectual, and emotional seeds lying within everyone that wait for the right circumstances to ripen. The person with Mars square the Moon may understandably be emotionally impulsive or expressive. This is a factual aspect of this particular square. The manner in which the inner karmic seeds ripen is dependent on the attitude and the past actions of the particular individual. If the person was raised with few supportive factors to help deal with strong emotions, he or she could become an abusive individual. The negative attitude is not the fault of astrology. The abusive attitude is the product of a wide variety of things. The square of Mars and the Moon could become emotional courage if the right attitude and awareness were in place. The wisdom bringing that transformation could come from several sources. These include a supportive set of parents or even just the person being aware that abusive feelings do not produce happiness. There can be many sources for wisdom to grow. The main source is being aware of the effects of past experiences.

Siddhartha's life is full of examples of karmic interconnectedness. Buddhists believe that in his past lives he accumulated a vast store of positive actions. This gave him one of the causes to be born into a royal family. Siddhartha's physical prosperity ripened from past actions of generosity, an attitude of sharing prosperity. He was the owner of his possessions and used them skillfully in past lives. He was not owned by possessions, by the delusions of miserliness and attachment. Another expression of those karmic effects was the establishment of huge monasteries and meditative gardens after his enlightenment.

Siddhartha's spiritual life was also the accumulative product of vast stores of wisdom and compassion. The previous birth stories *(Jataka Tales)* of the Buddha tell of his accumulation of all manner of virtues and qualities. Occasionally he was born as a deer or a monkey that helped other forest animals. In some rebirths he was an elephant that helped local villagers earn a livelihood. He lived numerous human rebirths as a humble villager who simply collected firewood or worked the fields. He mastered one virtue or another in each case, thus culminating in his attainment of enlightenment.

Karmic relationships with various people show up in the life stories of the Buddha. Five yogis joined him as associates during the six years of his ascetic practice prior to attaining enlightenment. They were impressed by his presence, determination, and asceticism. Among the six of them, Siddhartha was the most severe in his asceticism. He maintained long periods without food and had the deepest meditation. When Siddhartha decided that asceticism was not the route to enlightenment and started eating again, the five yogis become discouraged with him and left the Gaya area. Siddhartha carried on meditating, but with a more balanced attitude toward asceticism.

The date of his enlightenment is placed on May 15, 539 B.C. in this analysis of Siddhartha's chart (chart 3). This was the Full Moon day in May, which coincides with historical accounts. Astrologically that was a powerful day for him. Siddhartha had Jupiter and Uranus in direct opposition from the third house to the ninth house, respectively. That was an incredible amount of spontaneous energy directed to areas of understanding, revelation, and insight in his chart. His ninth-house Sun was naturally in opposition with the third-house Moon. This added to the power of insight and coupled it with idealistic compassion. These aspects were not the sole source of his realization; they were part of the circumstances that set the stage for him to become enlightened. His enlightenment took place during the middle of the night, and by dawn he was omniscient. He had the complete understanding of life.

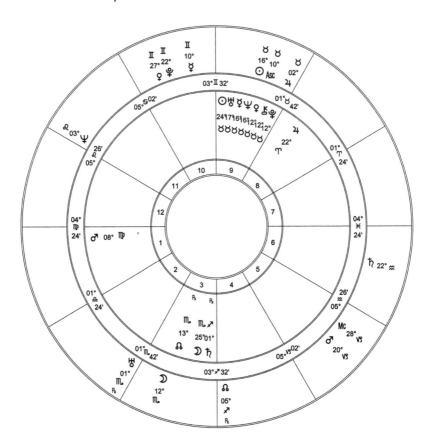

Chart 3
Inner Wheel—Siddhartha's Natal Chart
May 23, 575 B.C. / 12:30 P.M. LMT

Patna, India / 25N36 085E07

Geocentric Tropical Zodiac / Placidus, True Node

Outer Wheel—Siddhartha Achieves Enlightenment
May 15, 539 B.C. / 5:00 A.M. LMT

Gaya, India / 24N47 085E00

Geocentric Tropical Zodiac / Placidus, True Node

Historians say that Buddha sat in meditation for seven weeks after enlightenment reflecting on what to do with his profound revelation. He reviewed his past lives. He saw that he and his five yogic associates shared a strong karmic relationship. Buddhists believe that in several lives Siddhartha had even given his body to the five yogis as food. They were five cannibal spirits causing great harm to other beings in one such rebirth story. Siddhartha stopped their negative actions by donating his body for them to eat. As he died, he offered a prayer, saying, "Due to the generosity of offering my body to these five spirits, may I in all future lives be connected to them and finally lead them to enlightenment."

Buddhists believe that during the most recent life, prior to Siddhartha's enlightenment, the five yogis were born as tiger cubs. The mother tiger was ill and starving to death. She could not feed her offspring. She was so ill that she even thought of eating her cubs. Siddhartha was a prince in this rebirth and was with his siblings playing in the forest. When they saw the tiger, he immediately perceived her plight, even realizing that she was on the verge of eating her cubs. His compassion, cultivated over thousands of rebirths, was so strong that he decided to do whatever he could to save her life. He sent his younger brothers back to the palace and went to where the tiger lay. The tiger was so weak that she could not even kill him, so Siddhartha cut his body and made it bleed. This aroused the hunger of the tiger and she attacked him. During the attack he offered a prayer to establish a positive karmic connection with these animals. The prayer was: "I am offering you this body to physically sustain you and the cubs. May I in future lives be able to feed you the unsurpassed Dharma to nurture you into supreme enlightenment."

When Siddhartha became an enlightened being, his many rebirths and the karmic connections all ripened. He had karmic imprints to spontaneously benefit others, to not only help them in mundane ways but to benefit them with spiritual insights. He walked to Sarnath's deer park and found the five yogis. He had established a karmic relationship with these five yogis in several past lives and each time had offered a prayer that in all future lives he would benefit them. They were karmically destined to be the first to receive his teaching because of those prayers.

Historians say that the five yogis saw Siddhartha approaching and agreed to ignore him. He was no longer an ascetic. He was not worthy of any respect. Siddhartha's presence changed that immediately. Three of the yogis instantly realized that he was different and within minutes attained nirvana. The remaining two yogis gained realization as Buddha gave his first discourse, the Fire Sutra. This was his first discourse describing the nature of *samsara*, the confused and suffering nature of cyclic existence.

Interdependence

Interdependence is the third wisdom to be introduced. Interdependence helps develop deeper appreciation of karmic action. If we understand karma correctly, it is a presentation of linear actions. This result was preceded by that action and so on. We label a seed the cause of a plant. This is correct from a karmic perspective, but it has limitations when you consider interdependence. This is similar to Newtonian physics compared to quantum mechanics. Both describe the physics of any action, but quantum mechanics describes aspects not presented in the ideas of Newton.

For example, the seed is not limited to being the primary cause for a new plant. A seed can also be labeled a result. It is the result of the ripened plant. The labels we apply to things are merely relative designations. It all depends on one's point of view as to how things are labeled.

To expand karmic appreciation into interdependence means that the seed is not the only cause of a plant. There is the timing of the seasons, the weather, and the soil as supportive circumstances for the growth of the plant. Every product has innumerable causes and circumstances for its production. Interdependence opens the mind to a multifaceted viewpoint, supportive of karmic interrelatedness. Clouds require circumstances such as wind, sunshine, and dust to form. Emotions have their related causes and circumstances within the actions of the past. Attachment requires the motivation of desire, the attractive object, and the circumstances facilitating activity for it to be created. If the desire is successfully attained, then it is possible for emotions such as attachment to form. This is both the effect of previous attachment and the cause of new attachment.

The same understanding applies to harm. The action of harm may be caused by many factors. The motivation can arise from attachment, ill will, or ignorance. People harm each other from attachment when loved ones do not meet expectations. Although there is love, they lash out in anger because of clinging and grasping. They harm others with ill will because of anger at other people's success or qualities. Finally, harm is created because of ignorance and wrong views of the nature of reality. Animal sacrifice is a good example of such beliefs.

Looking deeper into the law of cause and effect, it becomes self-evident that many factors play a role in any karmic production. No one aspect has more power than any other component. They all have to interact together in just the right proportion for some phenomena to be produced. This is the interdependence of all conditioned phenomena. Conditioned things are produced from their circumstances.

This philosophy is called being "other powered" and is drawn from the Cittamantrin school of Buddhist thought. The

Cittamantrins expand this point with the idea that the world is a reflection of the mind. The world's appearance depends on how one understands any object. That view creates how the objects appear to one's consciousness. If one is unenlightened, then things appear as isolated and independent phenomena. If a more enlightened attitude prevails, then the world appears as a reflective play of interdependent causes and circumstances. The application of labels is not taken as seriously. Another Buddhist school of thought, the Madhyamika, uses the term *merely labeled* to affirm this point of view. For example, at one time cigarettes were labeled acceptable, but now they are labeled differently. This demonstrates just how fleeting designations can be. They are the product of the current social attitude. Everything is relative and interdependent with the circumstances that create them.

The world is nothing but a reflection of the mind. Each person only sees what he or she understands of phenomena. How else could things exist? How would it be possible to see something that one doesn't understand? The unenlightened mind sees the external world as permanent, causeless, and independently existent. The idea that permanence is found in an impermanent world was refuted in previous sections. The world is also not causeless because no one expects things to happen without some cause or circumstance. This brings up the final point in Buddhist philosophy. Phenomena: are they independent units or not?

One sees a house as a house, not as the product of many supportive factors such as building materials, carpenters, planners, and funding agencies. The house does not suddenly appear, but we often relate to the house as if it did. Therefore the unenlightened mind sees everything as real, isolated, existent, and independent.

This is why people get upset when the world changes around them. They feel upset initially with the world's impermanence.

There are even deeper implications though. People are attached to something because they believe it is isolated and exaggeratedly real. The object for the unenlightened consciousness is not as it appears. It is truly an impermanent product created by many circumstances, but it appears to them as a real and independent phenomenon. It is exaggerated into being overly real. Attachment sees the object of desire as isolated. Even though people intellectually understand that everything is changing and interdependent, they fail to apply that understanding to what they cherish. Why else would individuals get upset when their cars break down, friends abandon them, or their bodies start to age? Being upset is often due to the inner cause of grasping for permanence and independent existence. This is the causal relationship between an unenlightened attitude and suffering.

An enlightened mind does not see things in a fragmented manner. The image of a house is there, but wisdom relaxes the attachment to the image. The wise mind sees deeper into the object. Wisdom has the freedom of not grasping for permanence. The wise mind is more flexible. The enlightened mind has freedom of choice because of the liberty bestowed by wisdom. The view is produced with wisdom, the object appears in the light of that wisdom, and the response is supportive of true happiness.

This wisdom also applies to inner phenomena such as one's self-image. The self is not a permanent, isolated experience. The sense of self is an impermanent product of biological parents, upbringing, and education. Although our sense of self may appear as a singularity, it is the product of many dynamic phenomena. If one applies a superficial awareness to the sense of self, it may appear as self-existent. If one deepens awareness, it becomes obvious that the sense of self is an impermanent product of ever-changing causes.

The aware mind may see stimulating external or internal phenomena, but it does not cling. It reflects on the experience and makes a decision as to whether pursuing or identifying with the object is beneficial or not. A beneficial experience enhances happiness, liberty, love, empathy, and wisdom. If involvement causes more grasping, clinging, suffering, and ignorance, then it is not beneficial to have a continued relationship with that object, at least not in the manner that views the object so seriously. That is not a skillful way to live one's life. This applies to both external phenomena, such as possessions, friends, and the body, as much as to inner phenomena, like emotions and intellectual perspectives.

Buddhism is very realistic in relation to the process of enlightenment. If one wishes to be a wise soul, then that starts with exactly who one is today. The basis for transformation is the immediate awareness. The light of wisdom in that awareness shines on past experiences and makes them the source of realization and compassion. This is organic wisdom, wisdom that comes from the compost of personal experience. If the wisdom is applied skillfully, the fertilizer for enlightenment is created. The wisdom develops slowly and in a practical manner. A gradual evolution is necessary to truly compost experiences into the fertilizer of spiritual growth.

The process that generates the wisdom component of enlightenment breaks into two categories: the external world and the internal world. Understanding the external world as the product of many causes and circumstances generates a more relaxed attitude. Whatever happens has its causes, so why get upset? If it is not nice, then change the circumstances. Nothing has a fixed nature, so new dynamics can be applied to any situation. Those dynamics may not change things immediately, but they do effect a gradual shift. One may have to be patient about changing personal experience, but it will change. Shantideva, a great Indian saint, said, "Why get upset if something can be changed, and why get upset if it cannot be changed?" Although this is a simplistic statement, it does have beneficial implications. Essentially, if one can do something about a situation, why get upset? If there is nothing that can be changed, why get upset? The hard attitude of some people softens upon reflection of this truth.

Developing external wisdom leads to insight into the internal sense of self. This is inner wisdom. Inner wisdom generates greater freedom. It is based on the three wisdom aspects of this discussion. These are the wisdom of impermanence, the wisdom of cause and effect, and the wisdom of interdependence. The greater the internal awareness of these three wisdoms, the more one's consciousness experiences freedom. The normal, deluded response to situations slows down and finally stops. Inner awareness wisely reflects on past experience and unties the knot of grasping at a permanent and independent sense of self. The effect on conscious perception is the realization of the impermanent flow of consciousness. Images and thoughts are related causally to the attitude and past actions. If one does not grasp and exaggerate the sense of being, then one becomes open and flexible and transformation takes place.

The final realization of openness does not mean that one is out of control and subject to whatever stimulation appears. The awareness holds the realization of openness and the sense of self does not grasp and exaggerate itself. The individual does not respond to stimulation in the old habitual manner. It is an issue of being conscious and aware. If one fell back into unconsciousness, then one would be subject to a wide variety of influences. That is the actual situation as it stands right now. Often people are out of control because they don't exercise inner awareness. They use only a small amount of the wisdom they have available. This is called being "other powered," or motivated by external circumstances with little self-awareness.

Awareness and wisdom are the important factors in any situation. Everyone has varying levels of practical wisdom to help them deal with life. Generally the older people get, the more wisdom they have to make constructive decisions. Foolish people are the only ones who repeatedly act in a destructive manner. The discussion of wisdom, especially Buddhist wisdom, is not something outside the realm of practical wisdom. The Buddha's enlightenment is based on everyday experiences. It is not highly philosophical or impractical. To become enlightened does not make people useless. The movement toward enlightenment makes one more wise, compassionate, and liberated. All those experiences happen directly on the ground of the here and now.

Openness is a synonym for understanding interdependence. This type of open realization is actually freeing. It is called *voidness* in strict Buddhist terms. This voidness means the voidness of independent self-existence. This is the ignorance that Buddhism tries to eliminate. Ignorance holds all internal and external phenomena to be imbued with some sticky substance called *inherent independent existence*. This ignorant view creates all suffering and problems. To be empty, void, or free of this ignorance means to not exaggerate phenomena into something that they are not. Understanding the voidness of phenomena is to be open to all that is happening in a wonderful, liberating manner. It is open in the light of wisdom, not open and blindly stimulated. The realization of openness is liberating.

There are two emotional experiences related to this realization of voidness. Buddhist teachers say that a person of little merit will experience the understanding of openness with fear. That emotional response is related to feelings of insecurity and vulnerability. The person with a positive, loving nature gains an appreciation of voidness as freedom. Openness frees the mind of limitation. The inner awareness holds the nature of reality in the light of empathy and love.

To see everything as open means that there are options to any situation. Nothing one deals with is a fixed event. Events cannot be fixed, or they become separate and isolated. If an entity is fixed, it cannot change from its basic nature, and that makes it permanent. A phenomenon then could not relate to anything else, because if it did it would have to change. To be affected by something and to change contradicts the definition of having a fixed nature. The realization of impermanence, the law of cause and effect, and interdependence are all liberating experiences. The wise experience all external phenomena and inner perceptions in the sphere of wisdom.

There is no need for fear to be experienced when perceptions are based on a changing and open environment. A small-minded attitude and the related negative emotions are the real thing to avoid. The small, ignorant mind creates suffering constantly because of a lack of understanding. This is why Buddha referred to enlightenment as *tathata*, which means "suchness" or "thusness." It means that nothing has to change external to oneself; only the view has to change. The suchness of things, or the fact that things are just as they should be, is their pure, impermanent, casually related and openly interdependent nature.

Students of astrology may use this fundamental wisdom of reality to benefit their astrological practice immensely. Astrology becomes a factual influence validating wisdom. It is exciting to review the natal chart with an appreciation of the wide variety of influences. I think that Buddhist astrologers are like psychologists; in fact, possibly better than psychologists because of the depth of knowledge they bring into play when interpreting a chart. The coming chapters will discuss in detail each planet, its placement in the twelve houses, and the aspects to other planets. The future discussion will refer back to these preliminary chapters. This is to ensure the integration of the three facets of Buddhist wisdom.

Wisdom is a clear, pristine awareness. Pristine awareness gives the capacity to cut through ignorance and habitual patterns of thought. That awareness by itself is not complete. It must have love and compassion or it is dry and uncaring. Although the opening chapters did not touch on love and compassion in any detail, it is an important facet of enlightenment.

If Siddhartha had no love when he became enlightened, no one would have heard of the Buddhist path to enlightenment. It was his lifetimes as a bodhisattva, working for the benefit of others, that gave him a profoundly empathetic and loving nature.

Five

Love and Compassion

Love is the moisture that softens and expresses the wisdom of the Buddhas. Wisdom is cool, calm, and detached. Nirvana is called everlasting peace, and the wisdom that realizes nirvana cools the heat and passion of delusion. It releases the mind of aversion, miserliness, jealousy, and close-mindedness. Siddhartha attained enlightenment but wondered if anyone could understand this realization. It went against the practices of the day. Buddhism saw the equality of all sentient beings, and India was caste-oriented. It was finally love for others that motivated Siddhartha to walk to Sarnath to turn the Wheel of the Dharma. Buddhist love is the will acting to benefit others.

A good astrologer is wise and compassionate. The delivery of the astrological information requires skill. It goes beyond a description of beneficial and stressful aspects. A good presentation of the natal chart strives to increase the client's understanding of wisdom, love, and compassion. Wisdom imparts an understanding of why certain feelings and thoughts arise. Wisdom's understanding is detached; it cools the pressure and heat of deluded impulses. It is a view or perspective that provides distance from the intensity of emotional responses. Wisdom is a state of knowingness that understands a skillful response. Love and compassion are the response. Wisdom knows the right way to interact with others.

Siddhartha indicated that the first area of compassion is toward oneself. He found little benefit in his attempt to starve and emaciate himself. It was not a question of self-hatred. Siddhartha was a product of his time, and the prevalent belief was that asceticism was necessary for spiritual development. Yogis and yoginis of the day practiced asceticism to attract the attention and blessings of the gods and goddesses. Siddhartha reversed all that by saying that the practitioner is the creator of liberation. Gods and goddesses may bless the person, but the ultimate realization is only attained by personal effort. The avoidance of distraction is necessary to gain meditative stability, but there is little need to deprive the body of the necessities of life. Siddhartha said that one has to be compassionate to oneself first to gain functional realizations.

Siddhartha's first meal after his years of asceticism gave him physical strength. He walked away from the riverbank to start a new level of practice. He had never had any form of comfort in the six years prior. He found a grass mat and picked it up. He placed this mat under the bodhi tree near the city of Bodhgaya, Bihar State, and sat in a comfortable meditation posture on May 14, 539 B.C. That evening the Moon began a transit through the third house, opposite five of his natal planets in the ninth house. The transiting Sun was conjunct his natal Mercury and Uranus in the ninth house. This was a powerful and very compassionate moment for him. On this night, Siddhartha became enlightened.

Historical accounts say that Mara, the god who rules cyclic existence, understood that night that Siddhartha was close to enlightenment. Mara became concerned because he was the owner of samsara. In samsara everyone was under his influence and lived with delusion and suffering. If anyone escaped from cyclic existence, they were free of his control. This was not a happy situation for Mara.

To distract Siddhartha from his goal, Mara decided to send his three daughters to stimulate lust. Siddhartha had Pluto and Venus conjunct in his natal chart, which means that he had a component of strong physical love. Mara hoped to use that to his advantage. Siddhartha had enjoyed a pleasurable sexual life in the palace. Historians say that his father had kept 500 courtesans in the palace, so Siddhartha knew a great deal about physical pleasure and sex.

The daughters of Mara came to Siddhartha in a playful manner. They flirted before him with dance and sensual movements. At this moment the Sun was conjunct Siddhartha's natal Pluto and Venus. The physical energy that these goddesses generated was immense. They knew how to look seductively attractive. What Siddhartha did to counterbalance the vision of these beautiful goddesses was to imagine them twenty years older. The girls all started to age before his eyes and he perfectly understood the fleeting and impermanent nature of pleasure. The girls were in shock to see their magic fail and disappeared into the night.

Mara next decided to use force to scare Siddhartha from his state of meditative focus. As the night progressed, great armies of demons assembled all around Siddhartha. Some demons threw lightning at Siddhartha, some cast horrible curses on him, and other demons uprooted trees and boulders to throw at him. At this moment the Moon was opposite Siddhartha's natal Mercury, Venus, Uranus, Neptune, and Pluto. As all the weapons and negative energy fell upon Siddhartha, they became flower petals. This was due to his aura of love and compassion. Not one weapon intimidated Siddhartha to leave his meditative focus. Love and compassion transformed everything that Mara's hordes threw at Siddhartha into a shower of flowers upon his body. Siddhartha's mind turned all the seductive and angry actions of Mara into a victory for wisdom and love. Wisdom was the peaceful energy to keep Siddhartha's mind calm. His display of love and compassion was the action that made everything become flowers. This completely defeated Mara.

Siddhartha attained enlightenment at dawn. Dawn brought the Moon into full opposition to Siddhartha's natal Sun. At daybreak Mara came before Siddhartha the Buddha and asked him who he thought he was. Siddhartha replied, "I am the Buddha, the Tathagata, the Fully Enlightened One." Mara asked if someone could witness the fact that Siddhartha was enlightened. Siddhartha then touched the earth with his right hand, and the goddess Bhumi, Mother Earth, appeared and testified that Siddhartha was a Buddha. Feeling dejected, Mara disappeared into space.

Strictly speaking, Mara is the deluded mind. The story of Siddhartha's defeat of Mara is an analogy of the inner journey spiritual people must travel. The power of Mara is the illusion everyone has about reality. This power can also be increased by an astrological transit. It includes strong habit patterns on which illusions are created. It is hard to cast aside illusions and old habits. The habits do not like to lose their grip on the mind. When a particular delusion starts to lose influence, a series of events takes place. First the illusion demonstrates how pleasurable it is. One cannot live without it. These are Mara's daughters. They say, "I am wonderful and will give you pleasure." If the person manages to go beyond the attractive qualities of the illusion, then fear and anxiety arise. This is Mara's army. The anxiety says, "How can life exist if this fixation no longer exists?" Any illusion that is deeply ingrained will manifest these stages. This will include both positive and negative illusions about reality.

Siddhartha's story of enlightenment is an excellent example of how one needs love and compassion to deal with life's hardships. Everyone is assailed daily by challenges that stimulate delusion. Experiences become distorted by the illusions people carry. Each day one has an opportunity to defeat those illusions and the delusion related to them. Wisdom bestows detachment from deluded responses like fear, attachment, and jealousy. Love and compassion offer a variety of positive responses in contrast to delusion. Buddhists consider love and compassion to be active. Love is the wish to give happiness to others, and compassion is the wish to release others from suffering. Wisdom understands the situation; love and compassion do something about it.

Love, in a more detailed explanation, is the wish to give both relative and ultimate happiness to others. Relative happiness includes pleasurable things like gifts, love, support, and protection. To give a material gift to another is quite simple. Love, support, and protection require time and energy to help others in need. One has to be wise with love or the support can be disabling. Wisdom needs to be present with the expression of love. Unwise love causes more problems than benefits. Love without skillful means is just an emotional response. It may not always be beneficial to help another person.

Ultimate love is to help others become enlightened. To give wisdom and skillful advice to others accomplishes the ultimate purpose of life. One can intervene repeatedly in a situation, but may not ultimately benefit another. An individual can be a great friend if he or she showers love and support on a loved one, but is this person really helping anyone in the long run? Ultimate love wishes for others to become enlightened, realized beings. Wisdom is necessary if this wish is to be successful. One must skillfully intercede in another's life to help them. This is why in Buddhism one seeks enlightenment first. How can the unenlightened help others when they can't even help themselves? First one becomes skillful relating to oneself and then one can start to help others. The ability to help others successfully requires experience, which is another name for skillful means. Buddhists have great devotion to Lord Buddha because of his skillful love and compassion. They feel he is an ultimately skillful person, because he made the world a better place. Buddha loved everyone equally. Whether someone is a Buddhist or not, the Buddha works equally for the benefit of all. This is universal love, universal skillful means. It strives to bring happiness and the causes of happiness to everyone. To be devoted to the Buddha is to admire his life and actions. It is an example of the way to become enlightened. The Buddha cannot give enlightenment to anyone. What the Buddha can do is show the path to enlightenment and be a spiritual friend as one walks on that path.

Being a spiritual friend is exactly what an astrologer needs to be. Astrology is a specific expertise among many areas of knowledge that people can use to approach enlightenment. Astrology is not the cause of enlightenment. It is an external phenomenon that stimulates the fabric of who and what we are. Astrology can be a basis to gain understanding. The astrologer's job is to realize and interpret the interdependent dynamics of particular planetary placements and aspects.

The astrologer's role is to describe the astrological influences for the client. This bestows a basic understanding of what is going on, but the presentation can be more profound. If the astrologer has personal realization of the nature of reality, then he or she is in a better position to share information. Realizing the ultimate nature of reality brings a more profound understanding to astrology. Looking at the planets and seeing them as impermanent, interdependently related, and finally empty of inherent existence releases the astrologer's mind. Understanding astrology correctly opens the mind to the interdependent play of reality. Astrological influences are void of having an inherent nature, just like everything else. There is a wonderful play of interdependence demonstrated by astrology. This realization avoids the presentation of astrological influences as a predetermination of life's events.

An unrealized astrologer and client may feel that astrology predicts many events that have transpired. This does not mean the whole life is predetermined or predictable. Rather, the predictability of past events merely demonstrates what level of awareness was present for the individual. It shows how interdependent that moment was with the world around the individual. It is not a statement of predetermination and inherently fixed existence; in fact it demonstrates exactly the opposite. Nagarjuna, the most famous Buddhist saint to expound on voidness, presented the correct understanding of reality. In chapter 24, verse 18, of *Mulamadhyamaka Karika*, he said, "For some scholars the appearance that things affect each other means those objects have a true existence. These scholars assume interdependence establishes self-existence. For me, interdependence demonstrates the exact opposite. Because phenomena are interdependent, they have no true existence at all. Interdependence allows phenomena to interact and function. To be truly existent would completely contradict the meaning of interdependence."

How can something that is truly existent affect anything else? Buddhists say that true existence means that a phenomenon has a nature that is not produced from causes and circumstances. True existence is independent and has a self-expressed nature, a truly existent nature. This cannot be true, as no object has a self-existent nature. Everything depends on a wide variety of other phenomena for its existence. Even supporting phenomena depend on others yet again. The universe is a play of interdependence and nothing more. Everything is wide open to the interplay of change and transformation. Nagarjuna called interdependence the *king of reasoning*. It defeats any idea that phenomena have a real or self-existent nature.

The higher the level of self-awareness and wisdom people utilize, the more choices they have at their disposal. Every experience they meet has some level of choice. Whether the event is an internal experience of feelings and ideas or an external situation, all of these are dealt with equally. Awareness and wisdom bestow detachment from the event. This allows choices to be available for an individual. The person's experience and wisdom expand the variety of responses available. The more wise and aware one becomes, the more possibilities are seen in life.

This wisdom can be personally focused or based. A person may be wise, but utilize that just to fulfill personal needs. People who care about others have even more possibilities. This is because love and compassion naturally expand horizons. That is wise love and compassion. This is how a bodhisattva, an altruistic person, functions in the world. Bodhisattvas look to benefit all whom they meet.

There are wise people who manage their lives skillfully, and there are bodhisattvas. The wise make few mistakes, but may be only personally focused. Bodhisattvas expand the focus of life to include others. Just as the bodhisattva does not want to suffer, the same applies to others. Bodhisattvas want to be happy, both relatively and ultimately, and so does everyone else. Even if others do not understand what ultimate happiness might involve, they unconsciously want it. Ultimate happiness is everlasting fulfillment.

Bodhisattvas use wisdom to understand themselves and others. They work to bring both relative and ultimate happiness to fruition for everyone. Think of the options available for people who only think for themselves and compare that to people who think for the benefit of everyone. There is quite a difference between these two groups. Both are wise, but the people with love and compassion have a larger perspective. This is the meaning of Mahayana Buddhism and the bodhisattva vehicle.

Siddhartha was from a long lineage of bodhisattvas. He spent many lives cultivating love and compassion. This is why he felt motivated to benefit the five yogis at Sarnath. It is why

Mahayana Buddhism took root in most of northern Asia. The altruistic idealism of Siddhartha is contagious. If one understands the nature of reality as completely interdependent, how is it possible to not work for the benefit of others? Someone would have to practice close-mindedness to avoid that conclusion. The bodhisattva's altruism is an expression of the realization that nothing is a closed system. In *Bodhisattvacharyavatara: Guide to the Bodhisattva's Way of Life*, Shantideva, a great Indian saint, referred to this realization in this manner: "The hand alleviates the suffering of a thorn in the foot because of being part of the body. How can one not work to alleviate the suffering of others once they realize they are part of reality?"

Lama Yeshe refers to loving-kindness in a slightly different manner. He said, "If you wish to practice being gentle and kind with others, you have to first practice being gentle with yourself. It is not possible to be a kindhearted person if loving compassion does not pervade your whole being." If this is true, then you have to even be kindhearted toward your own suffering.

Giving and Taking is a meditation teaching in Buddhism. The practice of giving and taking enhances loving-kindness. This meditation links one's inhalations and exhalations with compassion and love, respectively. As one inhales, one wishes for everyone to be free of suffering. The meditator feels that all sentient beings' sufferings are taken away. This is inhaled into the heart. As one exhales, one wishes for everyone to have happiness. The meditator, from the depth of his or her heart, feels that all sentient beings receive happiness. This is the meditation of giving and taking.

Geshe Rabten, the teacher of Lama Yeshe and myself, said that one might begin this meditation focused on personal suffering. The meditator has to look on his or her sufferings and feel the inhalation draw that into the heart center. At the heart center one feels these sufferings, which one visualizes as black smoke, absorb into a hard black stone that resides there. This black stone is the self-cherishing attitude. It creates all suffering and misery. This is the principal obstacle to the realization of loving-kindness. The absorption of personal suffering into that hard black stone in the heart cracks the stone wide open.

The exhalation sends out happiness. The happiness is drawn from all the positive things one has ever done and is exhaled upon oneself. This stimulates the desire to be more positive. The exhalation breath is seen as white smoke or energy as it leaves the heart.

Geshe Rabten said that one may visualize a mini-self image seated directly in front of oneself, the meditator. This mini-self looks sad and pathetic. The meditator inhales and draws black smoke out of the mini-self seated in front. The exhalation sends white energy that flows into that mini-self and that image starts to appear more and more happy. The meditation continues until the mini-self seated in front of the meditator appears more wise, skillful, and compassionate. At the end of the meditation the meditator absorbs the second mini-self into his or her heart and rests for a short while in that reintegration. Everyone has a dualistic view, even in relation to the body. It is referred to as "my body." The subjective and objective poles are established. This meditation utilizes that dualistic view in a constructive manner. One starts to see oneself as improving and becoming happy.

Everyone wants wisdom and skillful means to deal with life's various trials and tribulations. If the attitude is unenlightened, then there is suffering. This is the nature of samsara, existence mixed with delusions about reality. If there is delusion, there will be suffering. What differentiates an ordinary being from a practitioner is the ability to deal effectively with life. The Sakyapa lineage of Tibetan Buddhism refers to this as the base, path, and result. The base situation is being a samsaric sentient being. The path is realized when someone starts to practice meditation and gain insights. The result is the attainment of Buddhahood. All three of these are based on one stream of consciousness. The three designations describe how one looks or experiences life. Ordinary beings see the world and themselves as mundane and suffering. Practitioners see that everything has positive potential and can be transformed. Enlightened beings have realized the highest positive potential possible.

It is important to look at things in the light of their positive potential. It affects the vision of how other sentient beings appear. If one's self-image appears in a positive manner, then one will naturally look at others like that, too. If an individual sees no positive personal qualities, it is similar to self-hatred. The issue is self-image and positive potential. Everyone has a wide variety of sufferings and issues. This is the samsaric quagmire they are presently in. There is potential for transformation if the correct view is established.

All Buddhas sit on a lotus seat. The lotus is a beautiful flower that blossoms above the water. This is symbolic of where the roots of a Buddha are to be found. The roots of a lotus are in the dark mud and slime at the lake's bottom. The lotus cannot grow without those roots. The same is true of a bodhisattva, the source of a Buddha. Bodhisattvas grow from their roots of suffering. How can people be compassionate if they do not look at their own suffering first? There can be no empathy, the source of compassion, if there is no relationship to one's own situation. People need to look at themselves in a loving and compassionate manner if they want to see positive potential.

Trungpa Rinpoche, the Tibetan who established the Shambhala Centers, had an excellent expression for this. He said that everything is a matter of perspective. For example, when you look at a pile of excrement, you may see it as filthy and disgusting. If you are open-minded and creative, you might see the potential of the excrement. It can make excellent fertilizer if it is composted properly. It is just a question of time and skill. If one likes beautiful flowers, the need for powerful compost is there.

This is similar to how people look at themselves. Presently, some may see their situation as simply miserable. They want to escape. This is because they are motivated by a fear and loathing of suffering. If those people were to open up and accept what they are dealing with, they could see it as an incredible source of growth. Suffering is the fertilizer of spiritual practice. If people deal skillfully with suffering, they compost it into deeply empathetic love and compassion. It is a question of perspective as to how one experiences suffering.

Take this example and expand it. The lotus is one of the most beautiful water flowers that exists. It is above the quagmire but has its roots in the quagmire. This is like the enlightened beings. They were once ordinary beings like us, but by the practice of wisdom and loving-kindness they evolved into a Buddha. Now they are glorious and open to everything. This is made possible by empathetic compassion. This evolution makes them able to share their sweet essence, like the lotus flower. Spiritual seekers are the bees that want the essence of enlightenment. What is the essence of enlightenment? It is wisdom and compassion. Enlightenment views all situations with quiet, peaceful wisdom and skillful, loving compassion.

Siddhartha began his spiritual practice many eons ago. He first became inspired to become a Buddha when he saw a previous Buddha named Drum Sound. Siddhartha saw the Buddha Drum Sound approaching a small stream. He was awestruck by the majesty and presence of the Buddha and decided to help him across the stream. The meeting gave birth to his desire to emulate this glorious and peaceful man. That moment awoke in Siddhartha the wish to become enlightened, the wish to become a bodhisattva and move toward enlightenment.

That moment of altruism started Siddhartha on a journey of millions of rebirths. It was the start of his spiritual practice.

His strong motivation was related to the desire to benefit all sentient beings. The glory and presence that Siddhartha saw in Buddha Drum Sound was inspired by that Buddha's supreme love and compassion. This made him so attractive to Siddhartha, and inspired Siddhartha's practice of universal loving compassion. By the time he got to within one rebirth of being Siddhartha, he was a deeply wise, loving, and compassionate man. He had no attachment to or grasping about himself or his body. His only wish was to benefit others completely. The body of that second-to-last rebirth was donated to the mother tiger and her five cubs. This action is seen as the ultimate physical offering. Siddhartha's final rebirth was the manifestation of the supreme spiritual being, the Buddha, which was an offering of wisdom and compassion to all who contact him or his message.

Love and compassion are completely necessary to balance spiritual practice. Astrologers can first develop personal wisdom and compassion by dealing with their own issues and then expanding that to help others. An open and empathetic heart develops with self-transformation and that creates an excellent mentor. No one can bring another to enlightenment. If this were possible, then the fully enlightened beings would have done so already. What compassionate person would not alleviate the suffering of another if it were possible? Enlightenment is the product, the interdependent product, of personal enthusiasm. Once people see how hard it is to transform their mind, they understand just how difficult it is to help another. Mentors in any form of discipline are best positioned if they are wise, compassionate, and supportive. Siddhartha was an inspiration and guide for how to practice. In teachings I (Jhampa) attended, His Holiness the Fourteenth Dalai Lama said, "We should strive for enlightenment as if we might get it in the next moment, but be without expectation as to when that moment will come."

Six

The Houses

The astrological houses are areas where action is emphasized for the individual. Buddhists believe that action results in a consequence. Planets in a house in the current natal chart would attract karmic imprints from the individual's past life. This emphasis continues into the present existence of the person. The nature of the past action and its implications for this lifetime can be determined by looking at the aspects a planet makes to other points in the chart.

Each house represents an area of life. The first six houses represent areas of personal expression. The final six houses represent areas of greater interaction with others through relationships, career, and contributions to society.

First House

The first house influences the *personality*. It also represents the quality of willpower and determination a person may naturally express. It describes the personality from an astrological point of view; first one's self-image and then one's presentation. It can also describe characteristics of physical appearance. Planets and placements here stimulate the individual when initially meeting others. Once the individual feels comfortable with a new situation or person, then other planets may predominate from alternate positions in the natal chart.

Planets in the first house increase personal presence for the spiritual individual. This can manifest as a style of spiritual practice. The development of bodhicitta, the altruistic wish to benefit sentient beings, places an emphasis on personal presentation. Each house will emphasize a different manner of expression when benefiting others. Here the focus is personal charisma.

If no planets fall in the first house, then personality and presentation are not as emphasized. The focus might be stronger in other areas of the chart.

Second House

The second house is one's relationship to the material world. Having established a personal presence in the first house, the individual begins to accumulate material resources. This house relates to one's place of residence, the objects that furnish it, one's clothing, how one manages money or assets, and most importantly one's approach to *survival*. It also includes one's sensual response to the physical environment. Planets in this section of the chart indicate where one's abilities focus strongly in the material world.

A Buddhist astrologer can advise those with this arrangement to be thoughtful about their physical environment. What do they create around themselves? People with planets in the second house could have a natural tendency to identify with material objects; therefore, they may need to be aware of the effect those objects generate. For example, one might reconsider collecting certain objects if these generate vanity and pride. Granted, the attitude toward those objects is what creates such delusions, but the objects can help create delusion, too. The number and type of planets in this section could be reflective of what kind of physical environment is created.

Buddhist practice is divided into six *perfections*. These span the areas of spiritual development that one requires for enlightenment. The first perfection is the *Perfection of Generosity* and relates to the second house. If an individual has a strong placement of planets in the second house, it can be advantageous to study this perfection. Generosity includes both material sharing and also giving one's time, energy, and advice.

Third House

The third house is the astrological influence that stimulates the learning process. It also represents the qualities of the *intellect* and linear thinking. It can be divided into two areas: the early years of exposure to educational situations, and sharing knowledge in the mature years. This house indicates how one best learns, not the level of intelligence.

When an individual is young, planets in the third house represent the subjects toward which one naturally gravitates. It can also demonstrate what type of teacher could have the strongest impact. This is because the learning process involves both instructors and subject material. A negative example of this interplay is to dislike a subject because the instructor is not skillful. This astrological information may be of assistance to the parents. An awareness of the planets could help the parents choose the child's school or course of study.

When an individual matures, this house indicates an instruction style; how the person could, from an astrological point of view, share information with others. When spiritual practice becomes an interest, a review of the third-house planets may be useful. A review might be related to the teachers best suited for the individual's personal growth. Some teachers instruct students in a strict manner and others with affection. All spiritual mentors are valuable, but in regard to personal growth, some teachers may be more valuable than others.

Buddhists believe that planets in the third house bestow a good capacity to master the Buddha Dharma. Naturally, there are other factors to take into consideration, but good planetary influences increase the capacity to study. The Dharma is the teachings of the Buddha. If more than one planet is placed in this house, a bodhisattva can easily master and share the Dharma.

Fourth House

The fourth house relates to one's *roots* during two different phases of life. The first phase relates to young children under the guidance of the birth family. The second phase is after maturity when the individual establishes a personal home. The fourth house also indicates areas where one may naturally express the soft emotions of empathy, compassion, and receptivity.

Planets in the fourth house may influence who is attractive within the birth family in a child's early years. This may cover a wide spectrum of family members, from those who project power and authority to those who are warm and loving. Planets in the child's fourth house indicate which of these people are more attractive. The child's planetary influence reflects or projects onto these family members. This identification fosters the child's viewpoint in the mature years.

The fourth house extends to identification with the family name, status, and lineage. One might tend to put an emphasis on the home, the family lineage, and even the spiritual lineage of practice if there are planets in the fourth house. The individual's roots and where the person comes from mentally and emotionally are the emphasis of the fourth house.

When mature, an individual creates a home according to a variety of values. This naturally relates back to the experiences in the birth home. The effects are felt in both the physical and emotional environments related to house and home. Astrology will play a role in the view of the home.

Spiritual practice in the fourth house relates to lineage. It is both personal lineage and the external lineage one identifies. Planets here may indicate what spiritual motivation seems most natural. The way people motivate themselves about their spiritual practices differs from individual to individual. Some people can be strict, self-disciplined, and self-controlled while others may be freer and approach their practice easier with joy and enthusiasm. Fourth-house planets may play a role in developing this inclination. Planets in this house may show what lineage may appear more attractive to the individual. It is similar to the personal level of motivation except that it is seen as being mirrored in a particular teacher or spiritual group.

Fifth House

The fifth house covers areas starting with procreation and extends to all forms of *creativity*. When the individual is young, there is no interest in offspring and the influence is more focused on nurturing qualities. As one matures, the focus shifts to the desire to procreate, and child-rearing capacities manifest.

Occasionally astrologers attempt to predict the number of children someone might have. Buddhist's view this as a difficult prediction. This is especially true in the twenty-first century.

Women in the modern world have options. Even if they have planets in the fifth house, the desire for childbearing is not definite. This is because of the options available to a woman in a modern social and cultural environment. Women nowadays have options because of education, birth control, and career possibilities. One hundred years ago, many of these options were not available. Procreation for the modern woman may not be a focus compared to a woman in an underdeveloped country, where few options for education and birth control exist. These women have fewer life choices. Modern society offers more possibilities and therefore may diminish the importance of astrological factors related to parenthood. Astrology contributes to the development of each individual. Astrological influences adjust relative to the impact of cultural and family conditioning.

General creativity relates to personal interests. The more one's interest grows in any area, the greater the potential for creative expression. This can be creative expression beyond just physical interests. It can relate to creativity with people and even emotional and spiritual creativity. For example, emotional creativity might be the desire to have and nurture children. This may move to people outside the family circle and include emotional support for others. Spiritual creativity is the desire to bring about transformation.

Spiritually minded individuals with planets in this house may generate creative interests on either a personal or social level. If altruism is emphasized, this may generate a feeling to share their spiritual experience. This approach differs from the first-house attitude because it stimulates the desire to reach enlightenment together with others. It is like being an oars-person among other passengers on a boat. They are all crossing the ocean of samsara, cyclic existence, at the same time.

Sixth House

The sixth house progresses from the creativity of the fifth house and seeks to make it a livelihood. This house generally indicates how one relates to *work* and employment. It does not strictly have to be employment; it can mean the way work is accomplished. Spiritual practitioners with planets here draw on the specific influence of those planets to give context to what work or activities attract them. Planets with a feeling-based influence may tend to make them choose more humanitarian jobs. Planets related to energy influence might direct the individual toward active, dynamic work environments. Planets related to intelligence and structure may attract individuals toward intellectual work and large organizations.

The spiritual individual with planets here may be on the path of *karma yoga*. Karma yoga is work or service for the benefit of others. Spiritual individuals with sixth-house planets naturally seek out a spiritual context for work. The idea of service for others is the easiest expression of this desire. Even if the direct environment is not seen as having a spiritual feeling, if it benefits others, it qualifies as good karma yoga.

No matter what work is undertaken, for spiritual individuals the simple phrase "May I help you?" can be their spiritual context. Although they may start by selling a customer a shoe, down the road they could help that customer become enlightened.

Seventh House

The seventh house relates to people close to oneself. This can include immediate family members, such as the spouse and relatives, to broader areas of *relationship*, such as friends and work associates. This house refers to how important other people are in one's life.

A spiritual person naturally focuses on others and strives to be supportive when planets are placed in the seventh house. It is important to develop skillful means in these relationships or one could become meddlesome. Skillful means starts with the ability to define boundaries. Boundaries define where one's personal responsibilities lie and where another's responsibilities start. Wise people are responsible for their personal karmic accumulation and how they present themselves to others. The emphasis is on motivation and presentation. Spiritual people are not responsible for how someone reacts. If an action was undertaken with kindhearted consideration, karmic responsibilities reach fulfillment. One strives to love, support, and benefit others as much as possible. This is the main responsibility in Buddhist terms. If the recipient of one's attention is similarly minded, the relationship can be powerfully engaging. Both parties enjoy each other and yet are not responsible for each other.

If responsibilities are not defined properly, then boundaries are ignored and attachment, expectation, and suffering come about. A lack of wisdom in relationships causes one to express one's needs without consideration for the other. A relationship is not what we can get from another, it is what we bring and give to a relationship. Spiritual people with planets in this house naturally think of others before they think of themselves. The real capacity for companionship comes from the ability to see friends for who they really are, not how one expects them to be. Spiritual people strive to see others outside the framework of personal need. It is a direct and clear vision of the person. This view may not be totally factual because of personal needs and desires, but spiritual beings attempt to see friends and associates in a positive light.

Among the six Buddhist perfections, the *Perfection of Morality* and the *Perfection of Patience* apply to this house. The Perfection of Morality is to avoid intentionally causing harm to others. Harm can be caused physically and verbally, but morality includes abandoning harmful thoughts as well. The Perfection of Patience translates into the ability to resolve hardship. Patience may include doing difficult spiritual exercises such as having to meditate early in the morning. It also means dealing with complicated people who challenge one's personal boundaries. Patience means bringing skillful resolution to all these hardships.

Eighth House

The eighth house identifies the astrological component called the chemistry of relationships. It refers to a deeper rapport with others. One met and associated with others in the seventh house. The eighth house seeks depth in those relationships. *Rapport* is the key word here. This can be a basic emotional intimacy or a far deeper connection, even including psychic insights.

The eighth house is the area of personally relating to others. A spiritual person strives to develop sensitivity and clairvoyance as tools to benefit others. The example of chemistry works well to demonstrate what can result from a strong rapport with another. Two chemicals, when mixed together, create something new. The same applies to two people interacting. The ideal of bodhicitta is the wish to attain enlightenment for the benefit of both oneself and others. It has an effect on everything in life. Buddhists consider this altruistic attitude to be an excellent attribute to add to all relationships.

Planets in the eighth house may give the individual a natural capacity to be charismatic. That warmth, if mixed with bodhicitta, will stimulate positive results for everyone. Close association with a guru exemplifies the idea of chemistry. Receiving blessings and inspiration on the spiritual path are definite eighth-house activities.

Ninth House

The ninth house deals with a deep investigation into the world around us. It is an *expansive* view of what is happening. A good word for this curiosity is *context*. Context strives to view things with the idea of understanding them better. The search for context leads people to philosophy and finally to spiritual and religious expression. The ninth house is the area of vast and profound thought. This is the sixth perfection of Buddhist practice, the Perfection of Wisdom.

Whenever planets are placed here, the individual might become a Buddhist to satisfy the need for a coherent life context. Because Buddhism emphasizes logic and investigative insight, planets here influence the person beneficially. Spiritual individuals seek perspective to clarify what is important to them. If they are truly altruistic people, the ideal of universal responsibility comes naturally. Organizing personal context clarifies how one wishes to deal with life and relationships. Studying spiritual teachings is a technique to bring that clarity to one's existence.

Tenth House

The tenth house is the direction in which one is moving. The fourth house is where one is coming from; the tenth is where one wants to go. There are many variables to be considered concerning goals when there are planets in the tenth house. Goals are not just ambitions on the material plane, such as career and financial success. This house can refer to what one sees as personally fulfilling.

Planets in the tenth house clarify people's understanding of their personal vision. This can also influence the expectations they have about their life direction. Ambition, even in spiritual practice, is a necessity. Spiritual goals are directed by motivation. Skillful individuals need to take time to clarify their motivation. A badly identified goal can cause unnecessary stress in life. A poorly thought out motivation limits the possibility of success. Intention and motivation set the stage upon which experiences manifest.

The Buddhist *Perfection of Enthusiasm* relates to the tenth house. This enthusiasm is defined as joyous energy moving in a positive, virtuous direction. Joy is an important factor of enthusiasm. To be enthusiastic does not mean to push oneself. Joy ensures a deep dedication to the task, and that is true enthusiasm. Spiritual effort has a positive objective, which is the second requirement of the Perfection of Enthusiasm. This means the endeavor brings benefit to both oneself and others.

Eleventh House

The eleventh house is the public or social arena for the natal chart. It can extend from an individual's relationship to the immediate neighborhood to the city or country around the person. This includes any organized group in those areas, such as schools, medical-care facilities, government bodies, corporations, and even spiritual groups. All these areas involve situations where one meets the public, socializes, or contributes to innovative change in society.

The eleventh house does not have to explicitly mean being social, but can refer to one's *attitude about society*. Fire planets in this house suggest that the individual might become a good social activist. Water planets stimulate an individual toward social and humanitarian issues.

Altruistic spiritual individuals do not have to be social activists. Eleventh-house planets do demand the recognition that one is interdependent with society. Spiritual practitioners seek to benefit or enhance society by their presence or activities. Even if they are in retreat, they could satisfy the influence of planets placed in the eleventh house. This is accomplished by having a strong sense of caring for the welfare of others. The practitioners are in solitary retreat, but their meditation strives to gain realization for the benefit of all. This is a socially responsible activity because in the long run it benefits society. Generally, with planets in the eleventh house, a bodhisattva will have a natural orientation toward social improvement.

Twelfth House

The twelfth house is the astrological influence on the individual's *private unconscious thoughts, feelings, and intuitive awareness*. Any planet placed in the twelfth house may exert an unconscious influence. The average busy person, active from the time they get up until they go to bed, may have little time for inner contemplation. A busy lifestyle may cause one to be motivated unconsciously by whatever planets are in the twelfth house. For example, if the Sun is placed in the twelfth house, these people may unconsciously seek privacy. Their job may demand meeting the public on a daily basis, but as soon as that requirement is over they disappear. The unconscious effect is to withdraw from social situations as soon as it is possible. Often such people disappear on weekends to private, secure environments. The expression "I need personal space" is common.

When an effort is consciously dedicated toward a downtime activity such as meditation, this unconscious influence changes. A downtime activity can be as formal as meditation, but even just sitting quietly in a chair qualifies. The planets in the twelfth house become part of one's conscious awareness with a little meditation. This does not mean that the planets stop affecting the person, rather one has better control or awareness of the energy generated by them.

The spiritual individual with planets here has a strong inner life. The importance of finding the balance between inner needs and outer work is the deciding factor. A balance means good social skills; an unbalanced attitude makes one antisocial.

Most people are caught up by outer demands so that their inner world is seldom touched. Some people put great emphasis on personal space and withdraw into their inner world at the expense of being social and friendly. A Buddhist tries to find the balance, the middle path, between these two extremes. This is why a Mahayana Buddhist is called a bodhisattva. This person is a spiritual warrior establishing the balance between outer activity and inner quietude. This house can be related to the Perfection of Meditation because of the natural desire to go within and find inner peace.

Seven

The Planets

The planets in astrology embody unique qualities that stimulate certain components in human consciousness. The relationship is one of interdependent stimulation. The energy of the planets is filtered by the individual's conscious and unconscious tendencies. It is not a question of predictable stimulation; rather the planetary influence is personalized by the individual's interests, attitude, and past habits.

Moon—Empathy/Compassion

The Moon and the Sun exert the strongest influence astrologically on an individual. This is because they are the closest and largest objects, respectively, in our solar system. The Moon represents soft emotions: *empathy, compassion, and receptivity*. It also represents emotional sensitivity to the immediate environment and relationships with women. The Moon, for a woman, represents her self-image. The Moon can affect both genders' relationship to mother, sisters, female relatives, and women. The Moon, although mainly related to the feminine, is not limited in its expression to that gender. The Moon demonstrates a strong influence in compassionate men.

The Moon empowers compassionate meditation practices. When well aspected in a natal chart, it stimulates the expression of both sensitivity and compassion. A Moon with stressful aspects will express compassion with a higher sensitivity. The stress can be beneficial in developing empathy and an open heart. This follows the Buddhist perspective that one has to experience and accept one's own suffering before compassion has a solid foundation of empathy.

A spiritually motivated person needs both wisdom and loving compassion to be an effective spiritual entity. These are the two legs that carry one to enlightenment. Wisdom often comes from the experience of suffering. Suffering is a great motivator. To actualize compassion, one appreciates the equality of oneself and others. No one wants to suffer and everyone desires happiness. Everyone is equal in this way. This recognition awakens an empathetic compassion and altruism.

Sun—Sense of Self

The Sun is the largest body in the solar system and clearly the greatest influence in astrology. It represents the influences central to oneself. The Sun demonstrates the astrological influences to the sense of self. The sense of self comprises one's primary identity. These are the core beliefs one feels and knows. The Sun indicates where one's greatest interests lie, or where one will tend to put greater emphasis.

Buddhists see the sense of self as an interdependent phenomenon. Meditation on the self reflects the many factors that create it. These include the birth family, the education, the social or economic structure, and finally the cultural and ethnic environment of the birth country. All of these things, and other subtle factors such as astrology, create the holistic total of self. Buddhists do not recognize a soul that is independent from the self. The self is a stream of consciousness that flows from lifetime to lifetime. It carries the karmic imprints of all the various existences. The Buddhist's view of the soul is an impermanent flow of consciousness and imprints.

The Sun's placement in the chart identifies the astrological influences on the self. Buddhists include astrology in the grand picture of the self. The self has no capacity to exist as an independent sense of being. It may feel that it is independent, but reality does not support that belief. It is an illusion that the self may create to feel it exists. The vision of interdependence plays a central role in Buddhist astrology. A Buddhist meditates on the Sun's placement in the natal chart to understand the self astrologically. The meditation draws on a reflective wisdom that creates a big picture of the self. This means the sense of self is seen in a network that includes astrology. No facet of the self stands apart in this vision. It is a play of interdependence.

The job of any spiritual person is to take whatever circumstance they find themselves in and "turn it to the path." This central practice is called *attitude transformation* in Mahayana Buddhism. All situations and influences integrate as grist for the mill. This expresses the Mahayana attitude that all situations and experiences transform into components of spiritual realization. The sense of self is a multifaceted play of dynamic factors, and a positive attitude is one of the more important factors. The Sun's placement may reveal where one's greatest interests and unique *creativity* may find fulfillment. A positive attitude further stimulates positive expression of those interests.

Mercury—Inquisitive/Intellectual

Mercury represents the influences related to the *intellect*. It is the ability to generate thoughts, concepts, communication skills, and a general inquisitive nature. Mercury stimulates a wide variety of intellectual functions. It is the astrologically stimulated component of intelligence.

A spiritual person requires an intellectual capacity to function well. Quietude meditation techniques are excellent to calm the mind and emotions. The quiet mind is helpful but it is not enough for deep transformation. Buddhists believe that analytical meditations clarify the context of the self and the larger world. Intellectual appreciation is the scaffolding that surrounds the core of one's being. That scaffolding directs how the building takes shape. It is the intellectual understanding that clarifies motivation, the creator of what one is and will become. The need for a good intellect is one of the many tools a spiritual person uses for both personal growth and to benefit others.

Venus—Sensuality

Venus stimulates the sensual response to the external environment. It is the eyes, ears, nose, tongue, and body sense doors responding to the stimulation of the sense objects form, sound, smell, taste, and touch. Venus identifies the astrological area where one seeks to find pleasure, satisfaction, and fulfillment. Venus also relates to affection, because it is through the sense door of the body that one shows affection.

Consideration of Venus' placement may determine what is deeply satisfying to an individual. Venus' position offers a strong indication of where to seek fulfillment. Venus' placement in the lower hemisphere of the natal chart generally means fulfillment is more personal. An upper-hemisphere Venus stimulates satisfaction working in the world and with others.

Mahayana Buddhism has a unique view of Venus' qualities of sensuality and attraction. Many spiritual lineages cast a negative light on sensuality and sex, seeing it as a distraction to be avoided. It may indeed be important for some individuals to suppress physical affection. They may have little capacity to deal with their sexual emotions. One solution is to avoid sexuality.

Spiritual practitioners vary in their personal abilities. All experiences can be the ground for transformation. If strong physical feelings exist, it may become more of a distraction to try to suppress them than to just work with them. The objective of love and attraction is to share feelings and pleasure. Granted some individuals are licentious, but for most, physical love is a shared experience. The Mahayana motive to benefit others may offer a technique to transform the more confusing aspects of this attraction.

If one truly wishes to benefit others, as a bodhisattva does, then one can apply this altruistic attitude even to encounters of love. Giving pleasure is an offering. There are relative offerings and ultimate offerings. On the relative plane one can assist others to be happy, comfortable, and satisfied. This can even include making love very well. That is an offering as much as anything else.

Buddhists believe that all offerings need an aspect of the ultimate. The ultimate is not an external entity, but the appreciation or realization of the ultimate nature of reality. This can manifest as a wise and reflective relationship to another. The more skillful the wisdom one brings to a relationship, the more both people benefit. All phenomena are interconnected; it is possible to make love one avenue of realizing that interconnectedness. If the attitude behind affection is unskillful, then affection causes problems. Those problems can be the signposts that indicate areas requiring personal growth. The Mahayana offers constructive possibilities to apply to any area of life.

At the time of the Buddha, there was a wealthy young man who dedicated his time to sensual pleasures. Once, on a picnic with some women, he met the Buddha meditating under a tree. The fellow was deeply moved by the Buddha's presence and requested some teachings. The Buddha understood his attraction to sensuality and did not mention the First Noble Truth of Suffering. Instead he explained the pleasures of the higher realms. Buddha focused on teaching about the god realms and the high level of pleasure found there. The young man asked how one could go to those realms and was told it was possible with meditation.

Motivated with strong inspiration to have even higher experiences of bliss, the man meditated diligently. He attained a high state of consciousness and was able to travel to the god realms. There he experienced profound pleasures. At a later date, the Buddha met this man again. He asked about his meditation experience. The man was ecstatic with his new abilities and the power of his mind. The Buddha then explained the more factual nature of existence. Due to the young man's meditative capacity, he was able to understand the emptiness of only seeking pleasure and expanded his horizons. The affection he had previously experienced shifted and became heartwarming love toward others. The change of attitude made him a famous meditation teacher.

Mars—Willpower/Determination

Mars stimulates willpower and determination. The positive side of Mars affects the ability to accomplish tasks. Two synonyms for willpower are *ability* and *capacity*. Negatively the placement of Mars indicates where anger and aggressiveness may manifest. The aggression relates to the intensity of the desire. Mars also represents physical and sexual energy in men and women.

The are several analogies to describe Mars' capacity. One is the image of two strong arms; they can accomplish any task quickly. Another analogy for Mars is an axe or sword, which represents the power and decisiveness of Mars. The axe works best when it has something immediately present to bite into, like a tree or firewood. When Mars' influence joins with a positive attitude, the person has an excellent capacity to get jobs done. Mars with a weak position in the natal chart does not mean the person is ineffective. Rather, effectiveness and skill in action require other sources of inspiration. Astrologically, Mars is only one facet of an individual's power and determination.

Spiritual individuals aim for a clear-minded and effective use of energy. If they are not skillful, they may become exhausted easily. Decisiveness is a quality of strong willpower. Decisiveness on its own can be aggressive and destructive. The spiritual person requires a compassionate motive and wisdom to best accomplish any beneficial action.

Buddhists believe power is symbolized by the Tantric deity Vajrapani. He represents the complete self-control of enlightened beings. Self-control is power. This type of power can act just as it desires in any situation. Buddhas have no limits to their willpower because they live in self-realization. A bodhisattva, one aspiring to become a Buddha, with a strong Mars placement can quickly develop willpower. Buddhists consider this a blessing from Vajrapani.

Jupiter—Expansion

Jupiter represents *expansion*, growth, and enthusiasm. The physical size of Jupiter makes it the second largest object in the solar system. It has the fastest rotation of all the planets and possesses its own luminosity. Its astrological nature is reflected in these physical attributes. Jupiter's astrological influence generates optimism, goodwill, and excitement. The influence stimulates a sense of what is possible. Individuals move toward Jupiter's position in the chart as if they see a light. It is attractive and exciting.

Jupiter generates a sense of generosity because sharing is an optimistic relationship with material objects. As a negative influence, Jupiter may make one too busy with desires and ambition. The negative effect may also cause the person to project unrealistic expectations. Although the expectations may be positive, they may be inappropriate for the situation. One final negative tendency of Jupiter is to overemphasize the positive. Things are seen in too optimistic a light, which may obscure the potential flaws of a project.

Saturn—Conservative

Saturn astrologically stimulates a personal desire to be *conservative*. Saturn's placement influences a person to be practical and pragmatic, and take a reasonable approach to issues. Positive aspects related to Saturn may make new projects develop slowly. It stimulates a desire to move gradually in a new direction. Saturn creates a sense of hesitation. The individual might feel a lack of confidence in a new situation. Saturn may seek safe or secure situations.

Negative Saturn influences can stimulate stubbornness, resistance to change, fear, and insecurity. A negative aspect in a natal chart may cause Saturn to be an anchor to the other planet, dragging it back with fear and insecurity. It is the sense of insecurity that is the main issue. This might be expressed by introverted or extroverted behavior. The particular expression depends on the individual's attitude and other secondary factors of upbringing and social pressure.

Introverts feel Saturn's stressful aspect and might identify with a sense of weakness. These people identify with the sense of Saturn's hesitation and accept it. They could feel useless and have low self-esteem. It is a negative, disabling relationship with oneself.

Individuals with an extroverted personality could express the negative influence of Saturn as aggression. These people experience insecurity, but due to their extroverted personality, they hide behind a show of aggressiveness. If these individuals have little self-awareness, they may appear stubborn and resentful toward others.

Saturn's spiritual influence is a great asset. Saturn supports the development of profound wisdom because it bestows deep insight. Saturn has a reflective, calm, and constructive influence when coupled with a positive attitude. The Buddhist development of wisdom is benefited tremendously with Saturn's positive influence.

Uranus—Revolution

Uranus is *revolution*. Positively, it stimulates a sense of independence, originality, and spontaneity. An analogy for Uranus is lightning; it strikes suddenly with no warning. Uranus inspires spontaneous self-expression. Another analogy for Uranus is a horse running free in a field. There is no fence or bridle to limit the horse's expression of freedom. Uranus bestows a sense of power and unbridled freedom.

A negatively positioned Uranus stimulates chaotic and unpredictable responses. These people may appear disorganized and out of control. They might feel that they are the victims of unexpected events. Things never seem to work out smoothly. Uranus' placement in the natal chart could highlight an area of unrest and scattered energy. Short bursts of enthusiasm and effort are common manifestations of Uranus' influence.

Tantric practitioners experience Uranus' placement as a wonderful asset to spiritual freedom and bliss. It inspires liberated feelings.

Neptune—Spiritual Pole

Neptune is the *spiritual pole* that influences intuition and imagination. Intuition is the ability to know something without relying on intellectual knowledge. It tends to just perceive directly without thoughts. Imagination applies to a broad, speculative view about things. It sees the bigger picture of interdependence. To be imaginative requires being open-minded and not concerned with small details. The view has to be from many directions for imagination to function at its best.

The analogy for Neptune is the crest of a mountain with a 360-degree view. It looks at the vista, not at small details. Both intuition and imagination rely on images for transmitting their understanding. Dreams are a good example of this. The sensitivity of Neptune differs from that of other planets. The Moon relies on an awareness of emotions. Pluto is the body's response to a situation. Neptune is visions and images. Neptune's intuitive blessing requires that the person develop an inner capacity to see the visions. Meditation offers great assistance in developing this capacity. Wherever Neptune is placed in a chart, there will be more emphasis on a nonmaterial perspective.

A spiritual practitioner might utilize Neptune's intuitive and imaginative influences to establish a greater vision of life. The individual is able to understand things beyond the immediate material existence.

A negative aspect with Neptune stimulates a lack of realism. Daydreaming and fantasizing are common expressions. Individuals with a weak attitude may experience Neptune's effects by being vague and unclear. They feel they are in a fog and cannot clarify their intentions. It is like looking through a camera that is out of focus; everything appears fuzzy and unclear.

Pluto—Instinctual Pole

Pluto influences the deeper feelings and mood of the individual. It relates to the body's response to situations and therefore can be called *body intuition*. There are three planets that stimulate sensitivity. The Moon and Neptune relate to emotional and intuitive sensitivity, respectively. Pluto heightens the body's response to situations and people. The body feels comfortable in good environments or uncomfortable and moody in negative situations. Pluto gives the person a gut feeling about something.

Pluto may affect the health of the individual because of Pluto's strong tie to the body. Pluto's placement in the chart may indicate where to look for physical problems. If one consciously creates a positive environment related to Pluto's astrological location, one stimulates consistency in mood and temperament. The balanced spiritual person feels Pluto's stimulation as sincerity and strong faith.

Pluto in a negative aspect can incline the individual toward dark thoughts and moodiness. The bad feelings can be increased due to an unsupportive environment. If decisions about residence and workplace are not wisely considered, there is a high possibility of added stress from Pluto's influence. The effects may be felt as pessimism and despondency.

On a physical level, a challenging aspect to Pluto can produce illness. In Buddhist terms, illness is not simply a bad aspect or transit involving Pluto. Illness can arise from the ripening of past negative karma or a lifestyle that is not supportive of health. Pluto could become one of the circumstances to stimulate illness, but it is not the principal cause. A person with a badly aspected Pluto can live a healthy life. Pluto's influence can merely demonstrate a vulnerability to illness. It is one factor among many in the greater picture of health and well-being.

Eight

The Moon and the Sun in the Houses

The two main planets in our solar system are described in this section. These planets have a strong impact on an individual's personal focus. This focus is structured by attitude and so references concerning attitude will be repeated in each placement. Attitude is a crucial component of astrological influence. The current attitude being expressed is the ground or fabric where the astrological influence is generated. The planets do not create someone, they interact with what the person is manifesting presently. If the attitude is negative and selfish, then even a positive placement of planets will not benefit. A positive attitude facilitates potential success.

The Buddhist description of a negative attitude is a lack of awareness. It is essentially an unskillful way to deal with life's issues. It may manifest as insensitivity, aggression, attachment, jealousy, or miserliness. Buddhism recognizes these as the primary delusions and causes for suffering. They motivate unskillful and unaware responses and cause more complication than benefit.

A positive or skillful attitude works beneficially with life. It creates the causes for happiness. If a situation is problematic, the skillful person manages their negative feelings. They are positive or constructive in resolving difficult situations. A resolution can solve personal issues and it may positively affect others. There is no guarantee a resolution pervades to everyone, but it has the potential to help on a larger scale.

Buddhists see a positive attitude has two divisions. The first division is the desire to see people and situations in a good light. It spreads goodwill toward others. This expression of positive energy may manifest as generosity, emotional support, enthusiasm, and good advice. It can be focused on those close to the person or to larger sections of society.

The second good attitude has a spiritual basis. It wishes to benefit self and others in a deeper manner. This may still be a personally focused spiritual activity in some occasions. A Mahayana Buddhist incorporates universality and the concept of past and future lives, striving to establish long-term goals. The wish to benefit someone can spread over many lives. This attitude does not just look to alleviate suffering for the immediate situation, but attempts a deeper healing. It reviews the causes of difficulty and suffering. One repetitive factor that creates suffering is a negative attitude. In the following sections, references are made that exemplify the impact of positive and negative attitudes.

The Moon in the Houses

Moon in the First House

The Moon in the first house stimulates a compassionate, sensitive image. This placement moves one toward openness and sensitivity. People seeking a receptive listener might be attracted to such a person. The Moon may make these individuals a barometer of the emotional environment around them.

They respond quickly to any emotional pressure. The expression of joy comes easily. Individuals with an unskillful attitude may feel this sensitivity as being too stimulating. They could appear emotional and overreactive.

An emphasis on quietude meditation and detachment creates an excellent mixture of wisdom and compassion. The compassion exists and one adds cool detachment to improve it. The empathetic ability to understand emotions quickly is a natural quality. The compassionate face of the individual's Buddha nature shines openly with this placement. The Buddhist meditation of giving and taking found in the Seven Point Mind Transformation texts are beneficial to do regularly. These practices involve a shift of attitude, moving from a fixation on oneself to a kindhearted awareness of others.

Moon in the Second House

The Moon in the second house can indicate compassion expressed on a material level. There is emotional receptiveness to the physical world. The person might be attracted to locations that invoke peace and harmony. People with this lunar placement who live in a politically violent geographical area require a strong sense of self-confidence to deal with their sensitivity to the environment. This is because of their direct access to physical suffering. Individuals with an unbalanced attitude may find that they respond emotionally when dealing with material needs. A Buddhist can balance this with meditation on detachment and impermanence.

Balanced spiritual individuals may naturally feel compassion and empathy toward any sentient being's physical suffering. They might be motivated to alleviate it. Possessions containing emotional meaning or context are attractive to them. The home may be decorated with objects that contain important emotional history. One might be able to easily discern the emotional message reflected from decorations. The study of Feng Shui would be useful with this placement.

Moon in the Third House

The Moon in the third house stimulates an inclination toward educational subjects that have emotional content. Humanities, social sciences, and healing arts could be natural choices for such individuals. Teachers who have a strong impact on these people will generally be instructors with a compassionate and sensitive nature. If a person with a third-house Moon becomes an instructor, a compassionate relationship with students is easily established. The manner of instruction may stimulate **warm feelings, which for a spiritual instructor** can be beneficial. In terms of Buddhist or spiritual study, the texts dealing **with compassion, love, and** altruism are important. These studies could clarify how to use compassion in a constructive manner.

Moon in the Fourth House

The Moon placed in the fourth house establishes an affinity toward the female members of the family. This can include the mother, sisters, aunts, and grandmothers. It may also stimulate strong relationships with the male figures who exhibit a compassionate, sensitive nature. These people may find that the home is an important place to recharge their emotional batteries. The Moon in the fourth house commonly motivates people to feel responsible for the emotional harmony of the family. They might be the first to react to stress in the family.

When these people become interested in spiritual practice, they have a natural basis for compassion. This may be caused by an attraction to the emotional dynamics between family members in the early years of life. The mother may play a strong role in this person's life. Whether the relationship is positive or negative depends on various factors, not just astro-logical placement and aspects.

A well-placed Moon in the fourth house may increase ideal-ism. If the parents read the birth stories of Siddhartha or stories of saints, it could stimulate identification with their compas-sionate lives. Buddhist practice suggests that if the upbringing of this person was not emotionally supportive, then emphasis on transforming that pain is important. The compassion is there; it needs help to gain a positive expression.

The ability to turn harsh emotional experiences from one's early years into something useful comes from getting in touch with those emotions. Buddhists see the ability to touch hurt emotional content with compassion as the healing process. One learns to be gentle toward oneself. The transformed emo-tional response then increases empathy and compassion to-ward others who suffer similarly. Pain becomes the source of authentic compassion in this way.

Moon in the Fifth House

The Moon in the fifth house can increase a naturally compas-sionate creativity. These people will be good parents, or at least emotionally involved in the upbringing of their children. This placement stimulates empathetic, nurturing qualities. Women with this placement may nurture everyone they love. They are the heart of humanity.

This placement attracts one toward the emotional elements of creativity. This may show up as an interest in the emotional lives of others. As this interest develops, the healing arts such as psychology and counseling may come into focus. The sense of emotional empathy toward others is strong and will stimu-late a creative wish to assist or help. Buddhists study the Seven Point Mind Transformation texts of Mahayana Buddhism to develop greater skill in these areas. They strive to be skillfully compassionate with others. The skillful assistance offered is not just on a relative level, but includes an intention to benefit ultimately. This translates into helping others on the path to enlightenment.

Moon in the Sixth House

The Moon in the sixth house stimulates the desire for employment or work in any caregiving environment. If these people do not choose employment that involves compassion, they may create a work environment focused on their relationships with coworkers and clients. There is a natural desire to be supportive or interactive with others. A caring attitude is easily expressed.

The healing arts and nursing are common types of employment. Because the emotional sensitivity is strong, careful choice of the work environment is important. The modern world is capitalistic and competitive. The wrong choice of career might create emotional stress. Generally, people with the Moon in the sixth house are better suited to employment in a peaceful and harmonious environment.

Moon in the Seventh House

Compassion and receptivity toward others may arise with the Moon in the seventh house. These individuals might find that they have many female friends. They may naturally demonstrate empathy toward others and people can be attracted to them.

Spiritual individuals could have an excellent capacity to do meditation focused around love and compassion. In Buddhism, these meditations are taught extensively in the attitude transformation techniques of the Mahayana path.

One important facet to be aware of is codependency. If wisdom is not mixed with compassion, this placement expresses kindness for all the wrong reasons. The empathy toward others is strong and an unskillful individual could become emotionally overreactive. There is a need to balance compassion for others and compassion for oneself. This means understanding and maintaining personal limits. Unskillful compassion may be debilitating to everyone and cause more harm than good.

Moon in the Eighth House

The Moon in the eighth house stimulates a compassionate, empathic rapport. The focus is to attain an emotional interaction. If heartfelt communication is not established, these individuals may feel unfulfilled. Their sensitivity can cause anxiety if not carefully monitored. There is a strong ability to understand another's emotional response on an intuitive level.

Daily meditation practice is a tremendous asset for these people. Meditation can help balance and relax the emotional sensitivity experienced. The dream life of these individuals may easily absorb the influence of people with whom they relate on a daily basis. If the Moon is well aspected by Neptune and Pluto in this house, these people can develop clairvoyance. The ability to be accurately clairvoyant depends on the ability to detach from personal emotions and projections. Otherwise the insight is polluted by individual biases. If wisdom and detachment are well established, these people are perceptive of the emotional temperament felt by another.

Moon in the Ninth House

Emotional context is important with the Moon in the ninth house. The correct and appropriate emotional feeling may constantly be sought. Questions such as "Where am I coming from?" and "How do I relate to you?" are common for people with the Moon in the ninth house.

Religious or philosophical idealism may seek to express love and compassion. A Buddhist with this placement might emphasize bodhicitta, spiritual altruism working for the benefit of others. The Buddhist practice of the Four Immeasurable Thoughts encompasses this ideal. These are: "May all sentient beings have happiness and its causes. May they be separated from suffering and its causes. May sentient beings experience ever-enhancing joy and may they abide in equanimity, being unaffected by the bias of friend or foe." Of these four, immeasurable compassion gains the most impact with the Moon in the ninth house.

The Moon can represent the feminine components of an astrology chart. Therefore, the practice of female deities or Avalokiteshvara, the Buddha of love and compassion, would be excellent.

Moon in the Tenth House

The Moon in the tenth house can move the person toward compassionate goals. This placement is good for devotion to female deities such as Tara. Feminine or compassionate role models may be admired in this case. If this individual's mother personifies kindhearted qualities, the person may try to live up to the mother's standards.

Life choices in this case can be scrutinized from the point of view of emotional impact. A spiritual person with the Moon in the tenth house might emphasize feelings and compassion. The ideal manifests as the desire to be receptive, nurturing, and focused on emotional goals rather than the material side of life.

Moon in the Eleventh House

The Moon in the eleventh house stimulates a conscious awareness of society. These individuals are emotionally sensitive to the environment around them. Spiritual individuals may naturally feel compassion toward the world. The extent to which they express that compassion may depend on other factors of influence. A philosophy that promotes compassionate work and a confident personality are examples of this. If these people are not self-confident, they may seek to avoid contact because they are too sensitive to what is going on around them. The sensitivity of the Moon is extended toward the world. A Buddhist can use meditation such as Calm Abiding and love to counter the negative aspects of sensitivity. Calm Abiding settles the mind and promotes self-confidence. Love overcomes fear and complacency.

People with this placement may prefer to work in social areas. Working in large, humanitarian organizations could be deeply satisfying. The ideal of compassionate work is attractive.

Moon in the Twelfth House

The Moon in the twelfth house may move emotional sensitivity to an unconscious level. These people may respond to emotional situations more dramatically than others. Both men and women with this placement may feel called to situations where compassion is a necessity. They might quietly shed tears in the background rather than step forward to offer help. Compassion moves them, but they do not always understand why.

This placement may manifest as an experience of inner fear and anxiety. If meditation is done daily, the unconscious effects of oversensitivity are diminished. One is sensitive, but it is not overwhelming.

The Sun in the Houses

Sun in the First House

The Sun in the first house may create a strong sense of personal presence. The largest astrological body meets the world directly. One's sense of self and one's presentation are synonymous. The individual could be aware of being a key player in the game of life. The instinctive image or persona projected can be dynamic, so it is important to be conscious of what that image is.

The Buddhist presentation of selflessness, the interdependent nature of personality, helps one avoid the tendency to be overbearing. One could express opinions without sensitivity for others. There is little problem with egotism if the realization of the true nature of self is being developed. Spiritual practitioners can be inspirational for others because they project self-confidence and compassion. Study, contemplation, and meditation on the interdependent nature of all phenomena, especially the nature of the self, are essential investigations for people with the Sun in the first house. This assures that delusions such as pride, arrogance, and insensitivity do not have a foundation on which to stand. Love and compassion support a balanced approach to life. These qualities synchronize with the higher awareness that all life is interconnected.

Sun in the Second House

The Sun in the second house stimulates strong identification with the material world. If these individuals are not aware of the power of this association, they may express pride related to possessions. The material assets can become the defining objects for personal status. This does not have to be a problem for spiritual individuals because the physical environment becomes their mandala. The items they possess create a positive and stimulating influence on everyone. If an awareness of impermanence is not strong, then a limiting materialistic attitude can predominate.

Buddhists use meditations on personal impermanence and the suffering nature of attachment to counter grasping at the material side of life. This creates a balance between the spiritual and material needs. Once this realization is stabilized, one can utilize material possessions without fear of being deluded.

The use of ritual items and appreciating their meaning has a supportive environment. The spiritual life often manifests through physical symbols, and people with the Sun in the second house can utilize this understanding. Essentially, spiritual individuals make the material world a manifestation of their spiritual values.

Sun in the Third House

The Sun in the third house presents a natural inclination to study and investigate everything. The central sense of self is inquisitive. The whole life may be spent in the pursuit of knowledge. A spiritual individual might exercise extra mindfulness to avoid the pursuit of knowledge just to be a database of information. The spiritual individual can be an excellent teacher if humility is present.

There are many techniques available to make life meaningful, but one must take the time to study. A Buddhist with the Sun placed in this house is encouraged to set long-term study goals. The desire to study can be expanded to facilitate study groups, giving instruction, and the publication of meaningful texts.

Sun in the Fourth House

The Sun in the fourth house emphasizes the home and roots. A young person with this placement has a natural inclination to identify with the main family members. This can be to an actual member of the family, such as a parent, or it could be to a value system within the family. When these individuals leave the birth home, they will most likely seek to create a strong home base to satisfy their need for security.

Placements in the fourth house may help define and identify the principles, beliefs, and spiritual lineage a person might find most valuable. The family heritage or social position, going back to the grandparents and great-grandparents, may seem special to people with the Sun in the fourth house. Spiritual individuals might seek to know the details of their lineage of practice. What tenets are the central principles of their spiritual practice? Who are the people who have transmitted these techniques in the past? This can even extend to inquisitiveness about past lives. Generally, people with the Sun in the fourth house like to feel that they have somewhere to return to, where they can feel grounded.

Sun in the Fifth House

People with the Sun in the fifth house tend to view everything with interest and enthusiasm. They may want to change the world. Specific areas of creativity can vary depending on personal interest, which can be interdependent with upbringing and social factors. The current object of attention may generate a great deal of energy for them.

Nurturing qualities, especially with children, are often evident with this placement. This can expand to an interest in productivity and the creation of new ventures. The interest in something is what leads the creativity. Spiritual individuals with the Sun in this house may be creative with spiritual transformation. Work on spiritual projects could be a good way to express this influence. These individuals may demonstrate a naturally charismatic enthusiasm in all activities.

Sun in the Sixth House

The Sun in the sixth house may create a focus on work and activity. An unskillful individual could be a workaholic with this placement. One needs to be careful not to overidentify with one's profession. An example of this is using a professional label when it is inappropriate, such as introducing oneself as "Dr. so and so" all the time. The point is to make the professional persona and the leisure persona separate and distinct entities.

If a good balance is established between work and play, these people can accomplish great tasks. They have a natural interest to work hard at whatever they do. Generally, the establishment of clear goals helps organize life. The clearer the goal in work, the more one can structure leisure time.

Sun in the Seventh House

The Sun in the seventh house stimulates an awareness of others. The sense of self is there for others. Unskillful individuals may define their lives by their friends. The more balanced approach realizes that others are important, but one also needs a personal focus.

Self-definition improves the quality of what one offers to others. A clear set of personal boundaries stops the tendency to overemphasize lovers and friends. People with this placement can create a positive impact on others. Living with a sense of dignity and personifying admirable qualities may become a source of inspiration for their friends. A seventh-house Sun may have many friends and associates. The spiritual person can use this natural quality to positively influence others.

Sun in the Eighth House

The Sun in the eighth house stimulates the individual to seek involvement with others. The important point here is self-realization. Before one can help others, it is important to gain understanding about oneself. Individuals with an unbalanced attitude could have a tendency to get caught up in other people's lives. They feel the need to share and communicate, pushing themselves into undesirable situations.

The balanced approach has personal clarity and can implement a certain amount of wisdom in relationships. This placement often ignites the desire to be a psychologist or therapist. There is pleasure in experiencing a strong rapport with another. The depth of communication is important with the Sun in the eighth house.

Sun in the Ninth House

Individuals with the Sun in the ninth house may have a natural desire to be a philosopher. They may not see themselves this way, but they most likely ask many questions. People with this placement often want to understand the greater picture or scope of life.

Unskillful individuals could be lost in intellectual realms if they are not careful. In contrast, balanced individuals have a natural gift to put things into context. A Buddhist uses context to appreciate existence, such as gaining an understanding of the law of cause and effect and the ultimate nature of reality. The Sun, in this case, wants context. It seeks to put things into some form of personal order. This placement creates an excellent opportunity for the individual to be a teacher.

Sun in the Tenth House

The Sun in the tenth house generates feelings of goal identification. Ambition, whether personal or related to a career, is a common characteristic with this astrological placement. Individuals with an unbalanced attitude could be quite egocentric and demand personal recognition in everything they do. The pressure of personal expectations can cause unnecessary anxiety.

Skillful individuals choose attainable goals. The sense of accomplishment that comes from attaining a goal enhances self-esteem. This can be an inspiration for others when the individual has a compassionate attitude. Personal idealism could be central for these people. They often see themselves as key figures when striving toward a goal. It may be important to incorporate the realization that success is interdependent with others. Even if one is the source of a great idea, it requires others to appreciate the idea for it to be successful. A humble attitude is a necessity with the Sun in the tenth house. There is no success if there is no support from others. This realization balances pride and arrogance.

Sun in the Eleventh House

The Sun in the eleventh house manifests as a socially oriented individual. Work dedicated to the good of all might be a natural inclination. An unbalanced attitude may generate expectations that are unattainable. The person could overemphasize social standards or sit at a distance and be opinionated about others. There is an awareness of the larger community, but a judgmental attitude might predominate.

A balanced attitude tends to benefit society constructively. In Buddhist terms, this is the role of a bodhisattva. These people are part of society, hence they aspire to enhance it. They play a role that benefits the world.

Personal charisma can be strong with the Sun in the eleventh house, so it is important to have a positive motivation. Buddhists focus on the wish that others have happiness and freedom from suffering. This ensures that they work for the greater good. To be authentic about that wish, one has to understand personal suffering first. To appreciate personal hardships allows one to empathize with other people's suffering. Compassion is invoked with the perception of suffering.

Sun in the Twelfth House

The Sun in the twelfth house inclines one to be reclusive. These individuals might be reserved and private. The more active they are, the more they require personal time for themselves. An unbalanced attitude may constantly struggle between the demands of others and the need for personal time.

A balanced attitude makes time for personal needs and does not feel stressed or overextended when busy. A spiritual individual might consider a regular practice of quietude meditation. This harmonizes inner needs with outer demands. Meditation or downtime activities supply the inner nourishment these individuals seek.

Nine

The Inner Planets in the Houses

The inner planets consist of Mercury, Venus, Mars, Jupiter, and Saturn. These planets have a shorter rotation around the Sun compared to Uranus, Neptune, and Pluto. Astrologers also call them the *personal planets* because each one symbolizes areas of individual expression.

Mercury in the Houses

Mercury stimulates the intellect wherever it falls in the natal chart. This refers to the astrological component of intelligence, not the total possibilities of the mind. The ability to delve into something intellectually is enhanced with a good education. Buddhists feel that the mind can be used to help establish a strong spiritual practice. To rely on faith or dogma is not sufficient in Buddhist terms. A discussion about the ultimate nature of reality may only be considered speculation, but it is important to establish the framework of realization. If the ultimate is to be realized, it has to be expressed in some context or it becomes meaningless. There is nothing to talk about if it is beyond expression.

Mahayana Buddhists rely on the deity Manjushri to enhance the intellectual mind. These meditations focus on mantra and visualization to sharpen and expand conscious appreciation of spiritual matters. The mind is used to stabilize and strengthen practice.

Mercury in the First House

Mercury in the first house demonstrates obvious inquisitiveness. To search, investigate, ask questions, and communicate are Mercury's forte. Unskillful people may be too talkative, which disturbs their ability to hear what others have to say. A more balanced approach is the use of intelligence to inquire and understand what is happening. The development of good communication skills could enhance the influence of Mercury. The eloquent speech and intelligence of Manjushri, the Buddha of wisdom, could be realized if this deity practice is used on a daily basis. The meditation enhances Mercury's positive effect.

Mercury in the Second House

Mercury in the second house may aid in the development of intellectual skills that deal with the material world. This placement has little trouble working efficiently in the world and has excellent budgeting and supervising skills. Care is needed to avoid becoming fascinated with material pursuits. Spiritual aspirants may have an interest in ritual items used by religions. This can extend to a deeper investigation and understanding of their meaning and use. The balanced spiritual individual could use material items to help others. This placement carries the potential to mentally deal well with assets and property.

Mercury in the Third House

Mercury in the third house bestows a strong ability to study. These people may demonstrate innate intellectual qualities during the early years of education. When mature, they could instruct others from their wealth of knowledge. Generally, subjects that require an intellectual capacity are more attractive. This attraction can include subjects such as literature, writing, and philosophy. Spiritual individuals might want to spend time reviewing what teachers are available for their spiritual studies. They can benefit from a masterful teacher with a deep understanding. The practice of Manjushri can be beneficial as a daily practice.

Mercury in the Fourth House

Mercury in the fourth house stimulates inquisitiveness. Children with this placement may ask many questions. They try to understand their family dynamics and ask questions about why things are done a certain way. They could have an excellent mind, especially if their family values intellectual development. This is because they identify with their family as being well educated. The motivational forces could equally come from the opposite situation. If the birth family did not value intellectual capacity, the child may attempt to go beyond the family's intellectual limitations.

The choice of a spiritual mentor who is capable of embodying an intelligent and logical approach to spirituality may be of value. This satisfies the desire to understand the foundations of spiritual practice. The intellectual study of spiritual practice clarifies motivation. Mature spiritual individuals understand their roots and motives. They come from a confident and knowledgeable foundation.

Mercury in the Fifth House

Mercury in the fifth house helps develop flexible ideas and communication skills. The focus of interest and creativity is more intellectual. The inquisitive nature manifests wherever an interest is felt. An unskillful attitude may ask many questions in an attempt to understand a situation. Endless talk and speculation could be a distraction.

The balanced spiritual individual may develop wonderful creativity with meditation techniques to help others. This placement is good for therapists or psychologists. Intellectual creativity enjoys playing with ideas.

Mercury in the Sixth House

Mercury in the sixth house stimulates the ability to work intellectually. Any form of employment that involves focused mental application is a good choice. Those with an unskillful attitude may have a problem putting their ideas to practical use.

The positive effects of this placement can include skill in managing situations easily. This placement indicates that the person could be an office worker or a supervisor. This is because the mind desires expression in the workplace. Writing, teaching, and communications are excellent career directions.

Mercury in the Seventh House

Mercury in the seventh house stimulates the quality of inquisitiveness. Communication skills are easily developed and friendship could be based on the shared ability to enjoy meaningful discussion.

An unskillful attitude might develop negative activity such as gossiping and slander. The desire to know more than is necessary about others can become a problem. A balanced approach and attitude attracts others with eloquent speech. These individuals know how to ask questions and listen. Manjushri practice, which focuses on the Buddha of wisdom, benefits Mercury's placement here with enlightening conversational skills. Teaching and communication-related employment are excellent activities for these individuals.

Mercury in the Eighth House

Mercury in the eighth house increases therapeutic skills. The mind focuses on understanding interpersonal dynamics. Mercury placed here establishes a good basis for professional counseling, but it is not necessarily the only choice for employment. The individual truly enjoys a good dialogue. An unskillful attitude might use this to manipulate others to satisfy personal desires. Knowledge of how others think and feel is used for selfish purposes.

The spiritual individual can use this ability to gain skillful insight. This is an excellent aspect for therapists and psychologists. A practice of Manjushri, the Buddha of wisdom, and the study of psychology is a good mixture with this placement. A Buddhist is advised to pursue the traditions of Mahayana and Vajrayana practice, because Mercury in this house increases the capacity to understand the psychology of these styles of practice.

Mercury in the Ninth House

Mercury in the ninth house stimulates the desire for philosophical context. The mind is thirsty and may inquire constantly to seek understanding. This is a desirable placement for those involved with philosophy. Even if these people do not identify with the image of being a philosopher, they may unconsciously always look at the world with a question in their mind.

Those with an unskillful attitude may feel the need to debate small details. They are fussy and intellectually unsettled about everything they study. A positive attitude could master dialectics and debate. Buddhists would cherish this aspect, as they value the ability to intellectually validate spiritual logic. The practice of Manjushri, the Buddha of wisdom, is an asset. The mind seeks to philosophically understand what spirituality and religion are all about.

Mercury in the Tenth House

Inquiry and understanding about goals and their dynamics are part of Mercury's influence in the tenth house. If the mind cannot grasp the meaning of the goal, then there is little interest to go after it. Goals can also be intellectual. The intellectual mind strives for expression.

An unbalanced attitude could waste time fantasizing about attainments. An intellectual approach dominates activities. The balanced spiritual attitude is articulate about values and goals. There is potential to lead others on the spiritual path. Mercury in the tenth house could bestow excellent communication skills to inspire motivation in other people.

Mercury in the Eleventh House

Mercury in the eleventh house generates commentary and an intellectual interest in society. Social awareness is awake. An unskillful attitude might lead to excessive expression of opinions and personal bias. These individuals might have something to say about everything. The mind is extroverted. The balanced attitude may express the eloquent speech of Manjushri, the Buddha of wisdom. There is the ability to lead others with clear ideas of social value. This placement might be used to further social harmony as the mind articulates what is important and beneficial.

Mercury in the Twelfth House

Mercury in the twelfth house increases thoughtfulness. A spiritual practitioner can have profoundly reflective meditations. This is because the mind works well with contemplative thought.

An unbalanced attitude or a busy lifestyle can cause problems with this placement. If these people do not reflect on their desires, they can be sidetracked by many intellectual doubts and projections. This can keep them awake at night worrying about options they had not considered. A balanced attitude has an excellent ability to contemplate profound subjects. Mercury in the twelfth house for a spiritual individual is an asset in terms of intellectual clarity. The meditative lifestyle slows down the mind and makes it reflective. Rushing into decisions can cause mental anxiety, whereas a well thought out decision has confident conviction. A twelfth-house planet can penetrate deeply into personal areas that are normally below the threshold of consciousness.

Venus in the Houses

Venus is sensually oriented. That means that the sensual world of form, sound, smell, taste, and touch are related to Venus' functions. Venus appreciates beauty, the arts, and gracefulness. The issues that may negatively affect Venus' placement are attachment, craving, and indulgence. The Buddhist remedy for these negative emotions is meditations on personal impermanence and the suffering nature of cyclic existence. These help release the mind from the negative aspects of craving and obsession that distort the appreciation of beauty.

If individuals are obsessive about some realm of pleasure, they can use personal impermanence to realize that they are destined to die and that all the craved objects will pass away. Focusing attention on attractive physical objects does not guarantee satisfaction or happiness. The Tibetans have a saying: "The more one desires, the harder it is to find satisfaction." Desire and ambition motivate and give focus to life. Impermanence balances the scale between overemphasizing desires and being apathetic with no ambition. Even a spiritual life requires desire. The desire to practice a system of spirituality is a useful emotion. The implementation of impermanence bestows flexibility and inspiration to our goals. Nothing lasts forever.

The suffering nature of reality realizes that nothing in cyclic existence can be truly satisfying. The nature of phenomena is change. The general attitude for most people is to seek pleasurable experiences and extend them as long as possible. Reflections on the suffering nature of reality generate detachment. The mind does not grasp and cling to those experiences. No matter how pleasurable something may be, its nature is to change. If one does not understand and integrate this realization, one may suffer as time passes. The unsatisfied mind is a suffering mind. Reality is not the cause of suffering; an unskillful attitude is the cause.

Venus in the First House

Venus in the first house makes the sensual world immediately available. This can indicate a quick feedback loop seeking sensual stimulation. If the current activity does not stimulate the sense doors, then the individual loses interest.

This placement suggests that the person is attractive, with a colorful and engaging personality. Venus stimulates the desire to seek immediately pleasurable experiences. The ability to express affection directly toward others is strong.

Those with an unbalanced attitude might find obstacles due to craving and vanity. The sensual world and beauty could be viewed in a manner that creates a negative effect. The person might exhibit demanding and vain behavior. Meditations on impermanence are useful in this case. A more balanced approach generates the potential to give and receive pleasure gracefully. This is a good aspect for someone practicing Tantra. The stimulation of the sense doors is used in Tantra to heighten the experience of voidness, the ultimate nature of reality.

People with Venus in the first house are encouraged to seek a long-term study program of the Tantras. This ensures the correct understanding of bliss and voidness. Once the correct appreciation is established, Venus can be more directly incorporated into spiritual practice. There are many ways to appreciate bliss. Tantra uses blissful feelings to open and relax the mind. The nerves of the body are the basis for blissful feelings. The mind's spiritual appreciation enhances the understanding of voidness, the nature of reality. Buddhist commentaries indicate that one relaxes into reality, as it is ever-present.

Venus in the Second House

Venus in the second house stimulates pleasure with the physical world. The joy of a beautiful world and the fulfillment of attaining material success might become a central focus. Venus brings forth a strong appreciation of the beauty and the pleasure of the physical world.

Obstacles such as craving, grasping, and indulgence may be the negative effects of a second-house Venus. It is beneficial to meditate on personal impermanence or the suffering nature of samsara to calm the negative effects of these feelings. This is to balance the attitude and avoid the suffering caused by craving. The mind that is constantly full of desire is a very unsettled mind. This prevents the possibility of actually experiencing pleasure, as the craving immediately disrupts those feelings.

A more balanced spiritual attitude can experience beauty, affection, and joy in sharing material possessions. Buddhists feel that the experience of the world is a product of interdependence. This placement is not good for strong ascetic practice. Although these people could renounce material pursuits, they may always feel a lack of fulfillment. Satisfaction seems empty. This placement is better suited for a spiritual practice that expresses generosity and shares pleasure with others.

Venus in the Third House

Venus in the third house may create a sensual component to the process of learning. If a teacher uses example and analogy, people with this placement realize the subject matter much faster. Venus relates to learning as a sensual experience. There are two sides to an educational environment. One is the instructor, and the other is the subject material. Teachers who express a loving and affectionate nature have a greater impact on these individuals. Subjects dealing with feelings, sensual objects, and pleasurable experiences can naturally appear more interesting. Artistic expression can manifest in any of the five sense realms. This includes artwork, music, and dance.

An unbalanced attitude may be distracted from learning because of a need for sensual experience. The mind wanders to the external world and does not focus on inner growth. A balanced spiritual attitude includes the ability to share affectionately with others. This is a good placement for employment in massage therapy, exercise-related work, and all forms of artistic expression.

Venus in the Fourth House

Venus in the fourth house generates the desire for a warm and loving home environment. Individuals with this placement might seek out members of the family who are affectionate in nature. These people are inclined to create a warm and cozy home.

An unbalanced attitude could generate inappropriate attachments to family members. The need for warmth outweighs common sense. There could be a demand that others appreciate the warmth being expressed. A balanced spiritual attitude exudes a natural sense of love. There is a flow of give and take with affection and fulfillment, because Venus stimulates an appreciation for love and affection. The spiritual individual will feel endowed with innate qualities of affection.

Spiritual traditions that do not reject the sensual world are good choices for these individuals. Venus in the fourth house generates colorful, sensual roots and can express itself with spiritual ritual. Buddhists with this placement are encouraged to practice Tantra to enhance spiritual transformation. This is because a sensual and affectionate nature is in their roots.

Venus in the Fifth House

Individuals with Venus in the fifth house can express artistic qualities easily. The sensual world and creativity are in harmony. A good example is gardening. Venus in the fifth house loves the feel of the soil, the idea of a beautiful garden, and the colors of the flowers. Expression of creativity in a sensual and affectionate manner is the influence with this placement. Artistic expression can manifest through any of the five sense doors. These include the eye with form, color, and shape; music for the ear; cooking for the nose and mouth; and for the body, movement and dance.

People with an unbalanced attitude could have hedonistic tendencies. The pleasure of creativity may outweigh the creative process itself. They might indulge their feelings and become selfish. A balanced spiritual attitude focuses on inclusive and loving feelings. Love is a shared event. There is appreciation of other people's beauty. The desire to nurture and love comes easily with Venus in the fifth house. Spiritual practices that utilize form and image are attractive.

Venus in the Sixth House

Venus in the sixth house affects work and activities with a sensual component. These individuals generally seek employment that is stimulating to the sense doors. A good example is massage therapy because it involves direct physical contact. If the job itself is not sensually expressive, then expressions of flamboyance or being flirtatious might manifest. There is a desire to reveal affectionate feelings.

Venus is related to satisfaction and fulfillment. The sixth-house placement may stimulate spiritual individuals to see work as a source of accomplishment and pleasure. They may seek employment that involves people, which allows expression of their colorfulness. Jobs that involve any of the sense doors are attractive. This includes forms related to design, shape, and color, music, culinary activities, and finally physical activities like dance and body-related therapies.

Venus in the Seventh House

Venus in the seventh house enjoys the company of others and is playful and fun loving. Affection and pleasure are easily expressed and received. A wealth of pleasure comes from friendships. Any of the sense-door activities are part of this expression. This includes beauty for the eye, pleasant speech and music for the ear, and physical affection for the body.

The person with an unbalanced attitude can express a demanding nature. If there is not enough stimulation emotionally and physically, this negative attitude feels bored. This effect may arise because of a selfish motivation. There is a desire for personal gratification. Balanced spiritual individuals may naturally exude charismatic qualities. They could seek involvement to share spiritual experiences. A sense of beauty and warmth is carried naturally.

Venus in the Eighth House

Venus in the eighth house exhibits warmth. The general influence is affection with friends once the relationship is established. Sharing and generosity are some of the spiritual qualities of this placement.

Individuals with an unbalanced attitude may desire to avoid boring and lackluster people. They might only seek people who are fun. The mind can be distracted by desire. It is beneficial to meditate on the equality of oneself and others. This equality is the realization that all beings desire to be happy and avoid suffering. Everyone is equal in the desire to be happy. This understanding ensures that one does not focus on personal gratification to the exclusion of everyone else.

The expression of affection comes easily with a more balanced attitude. These people might express colorful and engaging qualities. The practice of a unbiased attitude is an important foundation. Empathy has a strong expression with this placement.

Venus in the Ninth House

Venus in the ninth house influences structure and context involving sensual activities. Love is structured around the meaning of the relationship. For example, these people may have trouble with a sexual relationship that is not meaningful. If the relationship has deeper context, then they feel more comfortable.

Problems can arise over the need to be loved. An example might be an obsession for a friend's attention. The context has become unbalanced and personally focused. A balanced approach realizes that love is a shared event. Spiritually, people with this placement may enjoy a more colorful style of religion, one expressed with pageantry and form. Tantra and visualization practices can suit those with Venus in the ninth house well.

Venus in the Tenth House

Venus in the tenth house may seek quick signs of success. There is a desire to experience fulfillment shortly after initiating a new activity. Goals become interesting if they are pleasurable. The desire for fulfillment is strong with Venus in this house. There can be obstacles if goals require a long-term effort. This is especially the case if there are few perks along the way. A sense of boredom is the main interference. A good balance for this placement might include work with others. Altruistic projects may bring a great deal of satisfaction. It is wise to choose goals that bring joy to others and have the possibility of quick realization. Even if the main goal is enlightenment, it can be staged with small projects to keep the interest high.

Venus in the Eleventh House

Venus in the eleventh house is attracted to work and pleasure in social settings. Essentially, the desire to go beyond personal goals is stimulated. These individuals seek to experience the larger sense of connectedness that society can offer.

People with an unbalanced attitude could seek public recognition and fame as a goal. Pleasure is equated with being in the limelight. The desire for social involvement has turned into a need for social recognition.

Balanced spiritual individuals might naturally seek to involve themselves in social activities to affect others positively. If they are spiritual teachers, they often are approachable and loving. Venus in the eleventh house may stimulate spiritual individuals to do public works and be socially responsible. They feel a strong sense of satisfaction with those goals.

Venus in the Twelfth House

Venus in the twelfth house creates the need for private time. If these people do not put time aside to be reflective, they could feel empty and dissatisfied. If they understand that satisfaction is experienced in quiet moments, they can have greater inner fulfillment. The issue lies in how busy they are in external activities. The more external the activity, the more satisfaction is evasive. Pleasure, love, and fulfillment seem to disappear even though the causes of these feelings may appear immediately present. There is a need to back away from being busy to find fulfillment. A regular meditation practice generates feelings of peace and harmony. This is because the threshold of consciousness is lowered to a deeper, quieter level with meditation and that allows fulfillment to surface consciously.

Areas of life such love and affection are very private events with this placement. If too many demands are experienced, such as requests for attention and love, these individuals may withdraw and become inaccessible. They need to be aware of their motives in order to feel confident enough to express affection. Such people often find that meditation brings great satisfaction. Meditation lets them access love and satisfaction as internal experiences.

Mars in the Houses

Mars affects willpower and determination. It relates to the ability to accomplish tasks and feel effective. Mars also represents physical and sexual energy in men and women. The positive side of Mars is willful and effective.

The negative side of Mars may include issues of aggression and assertiveness. The best relative opponent to anger is meditation on love and compassion. Engendering a compassionate attitude benefits Mars wherever it is placed in the natal chart. This Buddhist prayer encompasses this compassion: "May all sentient beings have happiness and the causes of happiness. May all sentient beings be free of suffering and the causes of suffering." The final opponent to anger is the realization of the ultimate nature of reality.

The Perfection of Patience, the ability to deal effectively with upset feelings, is an asset for the negative effects of Mars. Patience is not mindlessly submitting to difficult situations; it is the fortitude to deal skillfully with situations to bring resolution.

The old belief that anger is a steam engine building up pressure is now refuted in psychology. Anger is a destructive emotion. Expressing anger causes far more stress on the body than holding it in check. The important thing to learn is how to deal with strong feelings in a manner that allows individuals to resolve the problem, and not just ventilate their unhappiness.

Mars in the First House

Mars in the first house may create a strong desire to accomplish tasks. The person might feel forthright and direct in all actions. An unskillful attitude could manifest desires that are mixed with aggressive tendencies. The desire to get something done quickly overrides common courtesy. Mars' negative influence can be pushy and aggressive.

The skillful individual benefits from Mars' influence and can accomplish great tasks. The personality can demonstrate a strong sense of willfulness and empowerment. These are qualities that even spiritual activity requires on occasion. The upfront decisiveness of Mars becomes an asset when applied skillfully.

Mars in the Second House

Mars in the second house stimulates a strong determination to work with the material world. Mars enjoys accomplishing tasks, and in this case it manifests on a material level. The philosophy of *karma yoga*, service for others, enhances this placement. Effective capacity to manage assets and property resides with Mars placed in the second house.

An unskillful attitude may demonstrate aggressive and violent feelings toward attaining important goals. The focus is to get a job completed quickly. This may create a lack of mindfulness and become a cause for obstacles. The skillful spiritual individual has dynamic enthusiasm to manage assets and property. The Perfection of Enthusiasm appears on a material level with the blessing of Mars in the second house. The definition of this perfection is joyous interest in a positive direction. This translates into effectively manifesting material needs.

Mars in the Third House

Mars in the third house may promote learning skills mixed with discipline. If a course of study is presented in a structured and disciplined manner, this individual could master it quickly. Mars stimulates productivity when goals are clearly defined. Physical activity and martial disciplines like aikido and tai chi are excellent matches.

An unskillful attitude might generate arguments and confrontation with instructors. The relationship with the teacher can play a major role in how Mars affects the individual. Aggressive tendencies and frustration manifest in the classroom if the individual feels no respect for the teacher. An instructor who demands respect in a skillful manner suits individuals with this placement well.

People with a skillful spiritual attitude express a confident and disciplined ability to help others. That sense of confidence can pervade all actions in which they are knowledgeable. Discipline applied wisely benefits Mars in this house. Students with Mars in the third house can realize vast amounts of knowledge if their instructor skillfully motivates them. This ability could then translate to the student's capacity to inspire others.

Mars in the Fourth House

Mars in the fourth house stimulates the enjoyment of an organized home environment. Members of the birth family who demonstrate good work ethics may be attractive. Mars' effect can generate a desire to be motivated. When mature, these people naturally seek to keep their home in order. If the home is messy and disorganized, they could feel frustrated and angry.

The effect of Mars in the fourth house could create a strong, willful determination in the very roots of the individual's being. The power is drawn from a feeling of capacity. Spiritually, if an instructor walks their talk, this becomes very motivating for others. This is because the students feel inspired and enthusiastic.

An unskillful attitude might harbor dormant aggressive tendencies. These individuals may push to have their way. The motivation to see their goals realized becomes overbearing. Arrogance and pride may hamper their achievement of success.

People with a skillful spiritual attitude are empowered with this placement. They have the fundamental resources to get a job done. A compassionate attitude, which is central to spiritual practice, manages the power that Mars stimulates.

Mars in the Fifth House

Mars in the fifth house can stimulate pleasure when working on a demanding project. Mars' desire to act creatively generates these feelings. This is related to enthusiasm and the will to create. Parenting skills are more focused on action. Activities that involve the children are seen as important.

An unskillful attitude is demanding and reactive. Frustration is common when projects go too slowly. There is a need to slow down and wait for others to catch up.

People with a skillful attitude feel a sense of empowerment in whatever they do. They act decisively on their desires and do not procrastinate about projects. This is a good placement for those who see self-improvement as a creative goal.

Mars in the Sixth House

People with Mars in the sixth house enjoy clearly defined tasks. They might consider seeking out a well-organized company or style of employment as their work environment. This is because Mars performs best when goals are defined.

An unskillful perspective leads to becoming a workaholic. These individuals might exhibit anger and frustration when projects are not accomplished quickly. The desire to work hard becomes a demanding taskmaster and can manifest as intimidation of others.

A skillful attitude can manifest as confidence with this placement. A compassionate attitude ensures that Mars manifests as an agreeable expression that inspires others. Group projects are accomplished easily if several of the members have this placement. If such a person lives in a spiritual community, he or she could easily become the caretaker of a center. Karma yoga, the idea of service for others, is a good philosophy to adopt with Mars placed here.

Mars in the Seventh House

Mars in the seventh house can create an effective capacity to work with others. Anyone who is befriended by these individuals is uplifted and propelled forward. This is because Mars is a doer and an accomplisher. Mars in the seventh house can stimulate someone to become a catalyst and motivator. This applies to both work and play.

An unskillful attitude could manifest as a tendency to be pushy. This creates a hostile environment because of a lack of sensitivity. Some of the harmful aspects of Mars in this house are aggressive feelings and actions.

The skillful spiritual attitude inspires others. It all depends on generating a friendly sense of inclusion. This placement can create an individual who is a motivator and leader. A compassionate attitude plays a pivotal role wherever Mars is placed in the natal chart.

Mars in the Eighth House

Mars in the eighth house can manifest as people with a charismatic ability to influence others. Their desire for action can powerfully impact and encourage group dynamics. Mars' effects here are felt on an internal basis. These people are emotionally willful. For example, spiritual practice with Mars in the eighth house is decisive. The emotions are directed by strong motivation.

People with an unskillful attitude could feel frustrated if others do not agree with their point of view. Desires on a personal level naturally project to include others. Issues around codependency and unclear personal boundaries come into focus in this case. Anger is often experienced when others do not meet personal expectations. People with Mars in the eighth house may assume that everyone has the same desires.

Individuals with a skillful spiritual attitude can be attractive to others because of the sense of purpose this placement exudes. Strong personal determination and the ability to motivate others are attributes here. The establishment of a clear motivation is important to bring forth the best side of Mars in the eighth house. If the motive is kindhearted and skillful, then Mars benefits everyone.

Mars in the Ninth House

Mars in the ninth house may seek a sense of context before starting any project. The less defined the meaning of life, the less powerful these individuals may feel. Often such a placement stimulates strong motivation where spirituality is found. Suddenly there is meaning behind the tasks they wish to accomplish. Spiritual practices that involve strong and engaging meditation sessions may suit people with this placement.

An unskillful attitude could generate anger when these people feel they are made to do things that have no observable meaning. Context and structure are important motivators. Another aspect of this aggression might be to demand that others act in a certain manner. Fanatic dogmatism can be a product of this placement if there is little reflection.

A skillful attitude carries great responsibility with this placement. A strong expression of spiritual discipline is possible. This placement could stimulate a desire for repeated cycles of meditation practice. Attending regular meditation retreats can be attractive. These people have a need to act on what they believe philosophically. If the spiritual mentor offers them a challenge in their practice, they feel fulfilled.

Mars in the Tenth House

People with Mars in the tenth house are benefited by having clear goals. Ambition is a common attribute and is expressed by striving after goals with a strong work ethic. A good spiritual example for Mars in the tenth house is being a bodhisattva, someone who works for the benefit of others. When spiritual tasks are understood, these people feel motivated to accomplish goals that are for the highest welfare of all. If these individuals have a good education, they are deeply empowered. An unskillful attitude could produce unrealistic personal ambition. Goals become more important than personal well-being.

A skillful approach could accomplish whatever the mind has set as a goal. People with Mars in the tenth house actively pursue objectives, which are determined in part by personal interest and also by social context and peer pressure. Spiritual goals are possible provided the objective can be physically realized.

Mars in the Eleventh House

Mars in the eleventh house stimulates social activism. These people might benefit by working with people or within a structured social program. Their determination moves toward society. Even if such people are not social activists, they might express opinions about society.

Individuals with an unskillful attitude could experience anger and frustration over social injustices. An opinionated attitude could become a problem. Personal desires are mixed with what is going on in society. Mars tends to manifest unpleasant energy if compassion and empathy are weak.

The skillful spiritual attitude may see social problems as possible projects. People with Mars in the eleventh house can desire social change if there is personal interest to do so. Mahayana Buddhists encourage learning attitude-transformation techniques that take bad circumstances and bring them into the spiritual path. No event is a problem if the right attitude is in place. This teaching incorporates social activism and spiritual values. Mars works best when things are defined clearly. The Buddhist attitude-transformation techniques clarify personal responsibility when working for social change.

Mars in the Twelfth House

Mars in the twelfth house spontaneously generates a strong sense of determination that wells up unconsciously. A negative side of this is being close-minded when pursuing desires. The instinctual push of Mars in the twelfth house drives one to act constantly.

People with an unskillful attitude may experience a sense of always wanting to be busy, which can cause great agitation. This is because Mars stimulates the unconscious wish to act without foresight. The lack of a reflective nature shows up as a restless disposition.

A skillful spiritual attitude may be able to perceive the depth of inner fortitude that is available. These people know that they do not have to be busy all the time. This is because a downtime activity such as meditation counters the pressure of Mars in the twelfth house. There is a need to be mindful of the enthusiasm that Mars spontaneously generates, as it can set these people off in too many directions. The good side of this placement is the power Mars bestows in sustaining long-term projects.

Jupiter in the Houses

Jupiter is generally beneficial wherever it is placed in a chart. The negative influences of Jupiter are busyness and excitability. The enthusiasm of Jupiter stimulates an overreaction. It is beneficial to practice Vipassana or Zen meditation if there is too much energy or chi in the natal chart. This could include

Jupiter in a stressful position or mixed with predominate fire planets such as Mars, Uranus, or the Sun. Vipassana develops the discipline to sit peacefully, no matter what arises in the consciousness.

The beneficial meditations that enhance Jupiter deal with optimism. The positive meditation techniques in Mahayana Buddhism are good subjects to study. They work to establish a positive and skillful rapport with the world compared to the detachment that is promoted by the Hinayana traditions like Vipassana.

Jupiter in the First House

Jupiter in the first house generates energy for personal presentation. This could be expressed as overt enthusiasm toward the world or as a sense of busyness. People with this placement may radiate good feelings and energy toward everyone. They are often recognized as having a good attitude.

This placement could make these individuals too busy and appear to always be in a rush if an unbalanced attitude is generated. The balanced approach radiates abundant goodwill. This could manifest as a generous attitude that inspires others.

Jupiter in the Second House

People with Jupiter in the second house feel generous with material possessions. The basic feeling is abundance, so even if they are materially poor, they share what they have. An unbalanced attitude could create trouble because of attempts to manage many material projects.

These people may feel that they can do more than is possible. They could have an overly optimistic attitude that glosses over problematic situations. They believe their abilities can solve any sort of problem.

Those with a balanced attitude might feel generous and full of goodwill toward others. The principal influence is the ability to share and see material situations in many different and positive ways. Jupiter creates an optimistic and versatile approach to the material world.

Jupiter in the Third House

People with Jupiter in the third house might approach learning situations with abundant enthusiasm. Interest in a subject combined with this placement creates excitement. Flexibility and versatility with knowledge are the positive influences. If an unbalanced attitude predominates, then the possibility of being an overachiever presents itself. These people try to master too many subjects. They might spread themselves too thin and not gain any depth in one area. People with a balanced attitude may be particularly attracted to subjects that inspire hope and vision. The educational enthusiasm they feel can naturally inspire others. If these people become instructors, they attract many followers and students.

Jupiter in the Fourth House

Jupiter in the fourth house may stimulate generous feelings toward family and home. There is a natural idea that everyone can be part of the family. Many warm connections with a wide group of people may be a component with this placement. These children may invite the whole neighborhood to their house. The home may be a place of constant activity, and family members that exude enthusiasm help nurture this placement.

Those with an unbalanced attitude may always appear busy and never at peace. They feel a need to go places and do things. This is because Jupiter agitates them.

Individuals with a balanced attitude might experience Jupiter's influence as inspiration. They stand on positive ground. There is a sense of positive personal history in their roots. They move forward into life with a strong feeling of abundance and the support of many close friends. Family is defined in large numbers. In spiritual practice, people with this placement are attracted to lineages that promote a positive view about life.

Jupiter in the Fifth House

Jupiter in the fifth house presents the possibility of having many offspring. Even if these individuals have not personally had children, they may feel supportive toward children. This is a good aspect to have as an elementary schoolteacher. Their enthusiasm nurtures the young. There is an optimistic attitude that pervades anything of interest.

An unbalanced attitude could produce interferences because of trying too hard. These people spread their enthusiasm over too many projects. The more balanced attitude brings a great deal of energy to bear on whatever is undertaken. The key point with this placement is a keen sense of interest. This naturally inspires others to work, thus making these people a positive influence.

Jupiter in the Sixth House

Jupiter in the sixth house might manifest as the ability to do many jobs. Work and activity are a joy. Work is the creation of new possibilities. Flexibility in employment can be an influence here.

There is a strong possibility that an unbalanced attitude could create a workaholic mentality. Another negative component is to never accomplish a task properly or fully. These people might start the next job before completing the one at hand. Jupiter's influence could produce fatigue when its enthusiasm is unchecked.

A balanced approach stimulates flexibility, enthusiasm, and inspiration toward any work. The positive meditation techniques offered by Mahayana Buddhism could create supportive circumstances with this placement. Karma yoga, working for the benefit of others, is part of that presentation. The objective is to tie skillful mindfulness to employment.

Jupiter in the Seventh House

People with Jupiter in the seventh house may never lack friends and associates. They see all sentient beings as potential friends. They may naturally generate a positive sense of expansion and awareness toward others.

Those with an unskillful attitude might never achieve a deep level of conversation with others. They are too excitable and move quickly between many people. They may also find many things to do for others, thus never slowing down enough to be accessible for any length of time.

A balanced attitude creates a wide spectrum of friends. These individuals most likely know everyone in town and automatically include everyone in any project. Natural charisma is available for these spiritual individuals.

Jupiter in the Eighth House

People with Jupiter in the eighth house might experience a generous and inclusive attitude toward others. Allowance for other people's shortcomings and a positive approach toward friends are possible with this placement. The chemistry of enthusiasm and joy fills everyone.

An unbalanced attitude may produce an overly optimistic view, thus not seeing reality in a constructive manner. This placement stimulates the desire to do and be everything for others. This negative attitude creates a lack of wisdom that never understands when to stop helping.

The balanced approach to life may manifest as seeing the positive qualities of others. Flexibility to work with even difficult people is possible. The ability to inspire and support others is strong. This is a good aspect to have in healing or mentoring professions.

Jupiter in the Ninth House

Jupiter in the ninth house stimulates natural joy toward spiritual practices. Even if these people practice the Hinayana path (personal liberation), they put their spiritual practice in a positive format. Individuals with Jupiter here manifest a positive attitude about life.

Individuals with an unbalanced attitude might tend to be evangelical. They would simply see that everyone needs enthusiasm and their particular brand of faith to be successful. There might be a lack of sensitivity. The enthusiasm is not balanced with wisdom.

Those with a balanced spiritual approach feel good about their religious path. Flexibility in teaching and spiritual practice is available with this placement. Jupiter can bestow an open-mindedness that goes beyond dogmatism.

Jupiter in the Tenth House

Jupiter in the tenth house creates a set of limitless possibilities. Essentially, these individuals think of their future in bright terms. There are always other options if one goal is not realized.

An unbalanced attitude could stimulate overt ambition. This experience does not arise from greed, but rather from not wanting to miss out on anything. No possibility can be missed. These individuals become too busy and unbalanced.

A skillful spiritual attitude may sense that enlightenment is a real possibility. These people can see the possibilities for personal growth. They work toward their goals with joy. The ability to inspire others because of personal vision is present with this placement.

Jupiter in the Eleventh House

Jupiter in the eleventh house opens the possibility to public involvement. Even if these individuals do not work directly with the public, they most likely work toward the improvement of society. This is because Jupiter brings an openness and vision.

People with an unskillful attitude might create obstacles by being too opinionated. They might feel that there are too many options. It is possible that they could express their opinions with little sensitivity. They may be too busy with their own ideas to hear what anyone else has to say.

Those with a balanced spiritual approach can see the seeds of potential in society and want to help. Work in a public office or some socially visible activity can be highly attractive with this placement. These people consider large undertakings to be natural choices. They bring an optimistic inspiration to whatever they do.

Jupiter in the Twelfth House

Jupiter in the twelfth house stimulates a strong desire to always be busy. The more people are unconscious of their motivation, the more they are compelled to act and know little peace. The more conscious individuals are on a deeper level, the more they can draw on an inner sense of goodwill. The main issue is to realize that there is strong inner energy to help and be useful. The negative side of this can create the possibility of exhaustion. These people never slow down to rest. Jupiter in the twelfth house is beneficial; people with this placement feel buoyant about life and activities.

Saturn in the Houses

Saturn is a truly wise planet. The general influence is to be conservative and approach life in a gradual manner. This can manifest as pragmatism and rationalizations. Saturn has a strong sense of judgment about life. This can be a great asset for a spiritual individual. There is the ability to see things in a realistic light.

The negative side of Saturn is to be stubborn and resist change. New ventures and directions in life are not enjoyable for this planet. It prefers the status quo. Astrologers say that wherever Saturn is placed in the chart is an area of slow development. This is actually a good influence, except possibly in our society. Western society normally wants quick attainment, and Saturn may appear to create many stumbling blocks. It seems to get in the way of personal development.

What is beneficial with Saturn's influence is exactly what our culture may see as an obstacle. It offers slow gradual development. Personal growth should take the whole life into account. His Holiness the Fourteenth Dalai Lama once said in a private interview about the subject of personal growth, "For Buddhists, we look at personal growth on a scale of eons. To expect strong transformation in one rebirth may be unrealistic, rather think of your capacity to transform on a grand scale. That is more practical."

Although Saturn is not normally seen as a spiritual planet, it has the potential for great spiritual insight. This is because it draws on experience. It ruminates over past experiences. and provided there is a desire to learn from the past, Saturn can give deep insight into life. A strongly positioned Saturn in an astrology chart will normally mean the person becomes a source of wisdom in the later phases of life.

Saturn in the First House

Saturn in the first house generates a strong, stable personality. The persona of the individual is practical, conservative, and possibly even a little shy. This is because Saturn does not express itself quickly. Security is the issue, and as it develops with any new situation, the person will become expressive. Initially these people can appear shy or reserved. Age and maturity stimulate Saturn to assume a position or image of authority.

An unskillful attitude may stimulate difficulty with personal expression. A feeling of insecurity predominates in new situations. There may be a need to realize that people in positions of authority are not adversaries. This is caused because a negative influence from Saturn might create resentment over taking direction from others. The person could appear stubborn.

Individuals with a positive attitude exude confidence and wisdom. They can give emotional support to others because they are a source of quiet wisdom and reflection. This capacity becomes more evident in the later years of life.

Saturn in the Second House

Saturn in the second house generates a conservative attitude about material goods. Importance is given to the proper and appropriate use of the material world. There is an ability to manage material affairs well with this placement. These individuals tend to be conservative in their investments and make safe and secure choices when dealing with money. They also tend to pick a place of residence and furniture that are well built and reliable. Employment in a managerial position could be a good choice with Saturn here as these people can be responsible with other people's property.

An unbalanced attitude could create the dual interference of miserliness and arrogance. People with this negative attitude feel that miserliness protects their personal assets. They generate arrogance toward those who are not as successful. Saturn can be very judgmental. People with a positive attitude feel responsible about helping others. Their compassion softens the harsh perspective of Saturn. This type of compassion seeks a practical solution for difficult material situations. Saturn mixed with a positive attitude creates deep wisdom.

Saturn in the Third House

Saturn in the third house may foster a diligent attitude toward study. Children with this placement may have difficulty with school. They need time to become familiar with the subject matter. As time passes and they establish good study habits, this placement can bestow deep wisdom. It may be necessary to give structure and discipline to help these children develop.

An unbalanced attitude can stimulate opinionatedness. Students with this placement may fight with their teacher over small details. They may feel stubborn if the material is not presented clearly. The practical aspect of Saturn can become self-absorbed in the pursuit of perfection.

People with a positive attitude may master knowledge in a gradual manner, but once it is accomplished, then profound and deep wisdom manifests. This placement, for a spiritual individual, bestows honor in the senior years of life. This does depend on the pursuit of knowledge in a continuous manner. People with this placement relate best to teachers who are authorities in their subjects. They also appreciate an organized presentation. A course of study that is too open ended and unstructured is not a good approach for these people.

Saturn in the Fourth House

Saturn in the fourth house can stimulate the desire to find family security. Members of the birth family such as the father and mother are important to these people. If the actual members of the family structure are not reliable, this can transfer to inanimate things like the ethnic or cultural background of the family. When these people mature, they take their role in the family seriously. They desire deeply rooted security and a sense of stability in the home. These individuals often maintain a strong loyalty to cultural and family traditions.

Individuals affected by this planet unconsciously may demonstrate sectarian and close-minded opinions. They want to protect themselves and may do so with a narrow-minded attitude. If a negative attitude establishes itself, these people can be powerfully stubborn and inflexible. They dislike vulnerability.

A skillful attitude with a mixture of spirituality can develop deep and profound wisdom. Such individuals prefer a long-established spiritual group with ancient traditions. If their teachers emulate power and authority, they feel secure in their practice. The establishment of a strong family group, or at least a secure home environment, is naturally manifested. A stable and reliable spiritual mentor can be a good choice for people with this placement.

Saturn in the Fifth House

Saturn in the fifth house slowly nurtures creative activity. These individuals may initially desire to feel comfortable with a project before developing it. Generally there will be either few offspring or a careful plan of how and when they are conceived. Saturn takes the whole process of creative endeavors through the context of great responsibility.

Individuals with an unskillful attitude may suffer from being stubborn in a situation over which they have little control. It is not a question of being in control, rather it is a dislike of doing things quickly and then feeling vulnerable to failure. There could be a tendency to structure situations and be too authoritarian with offspring.

People with a more balanced attitude embark on projects they have initially studied. These people have the determination to follow through on projects until completion. The positive side of Saturn in this house is reliability in creative activity.

Saturn in the Sixth House

Saturn in the sixth house generates the desire to work for large organizations. People with this placement seek structure in the workplace for reasons of security. Large organizations like governmental bureaucracies, healthcare facilities, educational institutions, and corporations are all attractive forms of employment. If these people are self-employed, they may choose a reliable occupation that offers security.

A bad attitude may generate an inferiority complex and thus hold these individuals back from advancement. Another influence is to become a tyrant in the workplace. The stimulation causes anxiety and thus a desire to control everyone. This influence comes from focusing on insecurity.

People with a skillful attitude manifest authority in any workplace and create organization where it is necessary. Supervisory positions or becoming the owner of a business are good choices for individuals with this placement. The important component is a compassionate attitude and the desire to benefit other people. This ensures a congenial approach toward others. A compassionate heart is not as vulnerable to fear as someone who focuses on authority.

Saturn in the Seventh House

Saturn in the seventh house can stimulate a sense of responsibility toward others. It helps establish long-standing dedication and attachment to family and friends. Saturn generates the desire to give others stability and wisdom as the relationship develops.

An unbalanced attitude can create obstacles with control issues and faithfulness. Friends and associates may find these people insecure and demanding in relationships. These people generate attachment toward others because they feel vulnerable. Once a friendship is established, this negative attitude may show a very stubborn face. Any desire by the friend for change stimulates resistance.

Those with a more balanced attitude can become a rock of stability for others. The wise side of Saturn shines through, and these people can offer wise counsel. The development of friends is generally slow with this placement, but once a friendship is established, it lasts a lifetime.

Saturn in the Eighth House

Saturn in the eighth house might create a great resource of wisdom. Saturn enjoys self-inquiry and analysis, which naturally expands into most relationships. This aspect becomes beneficial provided that one is first aware of one's personal suffering. This awareness ensures that empathy for others is established. Unskillful people without compassion may be judgmental and biased when relating to others. This is because of the rigid approach they can take.

A positive attitude can produce people who are a great resource. Saturn's practical wisdom in this house can stimulate profound insight when focused on the nature of the mind. Professions that offer counseling and mentorship are excellent choices. Individuals with Saturn in the eighth house can benefit from seeking a mentor who is available on a consistent basis. The relationship developed with their mentor helps them develop greater personal wisdom.

Saturn in the Ninth House

Saturn in the ninth house creates a philosopher. This influence does not have to become a professional interest, but it could manifest as an investigation into the meaning of life. Saturn seeks practical context for life. There is a desire to have a secure view of the world and to organize life in a manner that is structured and safe.

People with an unbalanced attitude could suffer from being opinionated and stubborn about ideas regarding reality. There is also the possibility of being bitter or pessimistic if there have been hardships in life. Saturn likes to judge situations, and when suffering predominates, the judgments become cold and factual.

A skillful attitude manifests as practical appraisals of life. There is a tendency to join orthodox faith traditions and tow the party line. A solid, levelheaded approach to life with little pageantry is common with Saturn in the ninth house.

Saturn in the Tenth House

Saturn in the tenth house might seek realistic goals for this life. The choice of direction may often appear to be taken slowly, but in the end, these people exhibit great dedication. This placement is good for individuals who wish to be leaders. They enjoy the power and prestige such positions in society offer. The positive side of Saturn in this house can stimulate a wise view of life and goals.

The negative effect of Saturn in this house is a tendency to be critical of other people's attainments. These individuals may suffer from arrogance and pride. If there are stressful aspects to Saturn in this house, they may cripple their chance for success by hesitating and having low self-esteem. Saturn moves slowly toward a goal, but with negative inclinations, it obstructs personal growth and becomes stubborn.

A positive attitude stimulates life choices based on a solid progression of sound judgments. Spiritual mentors who have worked hard to attain their goals are inspirational to people with this placement. This is because such mentors inspire similar qualities in these individuals. There is an attraction to people who exhibit authority. These people feel inspired by meeting such people. This placement normally bestows deep wisdom about life and goals as one matures.

Saturn in the Eleventh House

Saturn in the eleventh house is attracted to the structure of society. Saturn dislikes insecurity and therefore chooses stable situations. An organized social setting is attractive for this reason. This can extend even to employment options. Although the eleventh house does not deal with work and employment, it affects an individual's choice about social position. A secure administrative position within a large bureaucracy is common with Saturn in either the sixth or eleventh house.

Individuals with an unbalanced attitude may have the need to view society from a distance and be opinionated. These people withdraw into isolation. They fear the confusion of social activity.

Those with a positive attitude seek an organization or structured work environment. Choices of employment could be with nonprofit organizations and other groups that work for the benefit of others. Spiritual individuals may feel drawn to work within boundaries that are clearly defined. An unstructured environment is not comfortable. Great works in society can be accomplished over a period of years with this placement.

Saturn in the Twelfth House

Saturn in the twelfth house stimulates privacy issues and the desire to withdraw. The inner life is quiet and peaceful because of Saturn's conservative influence. This placement is extremely beneficial for a contemplative lifestyle. Saturn seeks to reflect deeply on important issues in this house.

People with an unskillful attitude can seek inner knowledge, but via a series of close-minded investigations. This placement may adversely affect them when they are feeling insecure. People with Saturn in the twelfth house withdraw to a stubborn position if they feel threatened. The worst characteristic of this placement can be inflexible stubbornness.

A positive attitude with Saturn in the twelfth house is a source of great inner wisdom. Regular meditation practice or some similar inner activity can generate the capacity to structure inner experiences. Meditation styles that stress quietude are generally better for these individuals. It is important not to limit meditation to just quietude. A good education in conjunction with quietude meditation creates a powerful set of assets. These individuals tend to be deep thinkers.

Ten

The Outer Planets in the Houses

The house location of any planet indicates the area of life where that planet may have the greatest expression. The outer planets move slowly through the signs, so many people may share the same sign for Uranus, Neptune, or Pluto in their charts. The variables widen depending on the house in which each outer planet is located. For example, Neptune in Libra placed in the tenth house of career indicates a different emphasis from Neptune in Libra placed in the seventh house of relationships. This chapter explains how each of the outer planets may find expression through the houses within a Buddhist context.

Uranus in the Houses

Uranus stimulates originality and spontaneous ideas. This can be a blessing or a curse depending on one's attitude. If self-esteem is low, then fear of change and a sense of victimization due to unforeseen circumstances may dominate. It is the attitude that establishes this experience. Uranus bestows a wonderful sense of freedom wherever it lies in the chart. It needs a liberal attitude to have expression.

Buddhism suggests two tools to create a positive attitude. One is to be mindful of the current negative or debilitating attitude. It is not possible to stop negative thoughts totally, but mindfulness can limit their grip on consciousness. This ties together with the second tool, a positive motivation. Motivate each day with as positive a perspective as possible. Buddhist instruction offers many motivational thoughts that can help develop a good attitude.

Uranus generates a high potential for liberation when mixed with a positive attitude and self-confidence. This can be expressed as a liberal point of view, uninhibited behavior, or as a deep, internalized sense of spiritual liberty. Someone with a good spiritual practice might start using unconventional wisdom when interacting with others. This is called "crazy" wisdom in some Tibetan traditions and it openly abandons social norms to shock others into a higher level of awareness. Care is necessary when exhibiting outrageous activity so as not to be misunderstood and thus not benefit anyone.

If Uranus plays a strong role in a natal chart, the individual may benefit initially with Vipassana meditation. This creates the space for awareness to release the pressure of Uranus' impulsiveness. As one becomes skillful in spiritual activity, Uranus can play a stronger role bestowing liberal and spontaneous qualities to the area where it falls in the natal chart.

Uranus in the First House

Uranus in the first house stimulates the personality to be spontaneous and independent. That high sense of originality and impulsiveness can make these people appear to be nonconformists. A lesser manifestation of this is to be liberally minded when meeting others. It is a good placement for someone who is a comedian or public speaker. They express what others might fear to talk about.

An unbalanced attitude could create great obstacles to communication. The ideas are presented in a confused and disorganized manner. The problem comes when attempting to do things too fast or without foresight. Impulsive actions and speech are right on the surface with no deeper buffer to slow them down.

If these individuals have a heart of loving compassion, they need have no fear of the results of their actions, as the motivation is kindhearted. Generally, this influence might make them difficult to understand. Individuality is strong and needs space for self-expression.

Uranus in the Second House

Uranus in the second house generates a free spirit related to the material plane. Little attachment is felt to material objects. Spontaneous generosity is possible. If these people are not aware of Uranus' influence, then material goods appear to come and go haphazardly. They may feel that possessions are totally unreliable. This is due partially to an attitude that lacks mindfulness. It does not have enough awareness to be responsible.

Individuals with a positive and self-confident attitude may view property and possessions with little attachment. They may give and receive possessions easily. A liberated view observes the physical world. This view generates from an experience of the transitory nature of the world. Material possessions are not reliable. Artistically, this placement can produce unique images and expression. There may be an interest in uncommon and rare religious items if there is an inclination toward spirituality.

Uranus in the Third House

Uranus in the third house generates a liberal interpretation of education. The general effect is to make these individuals self-motivated when they study. They might find that they cram for exams rather than study in a disciplined manner. They may desire to be their own master and study and understand things in a unique way.

The quality of genius is sometimes evident with this placement. The downside of the influence is a chaotic presentation of information. The genius lies in spontaneous realizations and the ability to comprehend difficult subjects. The mind can think outside the box.

Uranus in the Fourth House

Uranus in the fourth house could create a chaotic home life. This means that the individual's experience of the birth-family environment was unsettled or that he or she was the chaotic member of the family. There is a restlessness that requires a lot of freedom.

People with a negative attitude may constantly cause discomfort to those around them. If they attempt to conform to social norms by settling down and becoming commonplace, then there may be a great deal of stress. This placement requires a more liberal interpretation of what creates a home. Even if these people do have a long-established home, they may travel regularly. Another aspect is to have a chaotic and messy home. This can be taken to the mental-emotional level. There might be little awareness of one's roots or bonding with one's heritage or family. Uranus likes freedom and defies tradition.

A wiser attitude could be one that does not worry about setting up strong roots in any one place. This aspect is beneficial for those seeking spiritual freedom, as they may feel little connection to anything around them. This may require a great deal of self-confidence, as society routinely applies pressure to make most people conform to social norms.

Uranus in the Fifth House

Uranus in the fifth house can stimulate creative energies that are impulsive and often scattered. Generally, with this place-ment planned parenthood is not part of this person's experi-ence. The conception of a child is a spontaneous event. This also applies to other creative ventures. If these people are artists, they may need to wait for the spirit of creativity to enter them to produce artwork. Creative expression happens when least expected.

The unskillful attitude might have difficulty completing tasks. The ability to follow through can be weak unless other planets are favorably positioned. This is because Uranus gets inspired for short periods of time only.

The wise spiritual individual is spontaneous in action and could become an excellent artist. Therapeutic work with others is another excellent possibility. This placement generates a lib-eral, creative approach to viewing other people's problems.

Uranus in the Sixth House

Uranus in the sixth house might give the individual a liberal view of employment. Employment may consist of short-term contracts. The individual has many skills to offer an employer. Self-employment or contracted work is a better choice with this placement. If the job is too restrictive and controlled, Uranus might tend to rebel.

Those with an unskillful attitude with Uranus in the sixth house could build up grudges and anger because life never seems to be consistent. This is caused partially by having the wrong attitude about employment. Freelance employment and flexible work situations are better choices.

A wise attitude can generate great freedom regarding work when coupled with social skill. Awareness of positive motivational forces and a kindhearted sensitivity toward others help generate that attitude. Occupations that offer freedom of time or little supervision are best. Strong creativity motivates employment with this placement, but that requires a liberal employer or self-employment. Risks that are a challenge can be attractive and need to be balanced with sound judgment.

Uranus in the Seventh House

Uranus in the seventh house may find a liberal expression in friendship. Social constraints might feel burdensome. People with this placement often have exotic friends because their unconventionality makes them attractive. This can be interesting, but can also cause heartbreak and confusion due to their friends' eccentric behavior.

An unskillful attitude may cause other people unhappiness because of unpredictable activity. These people might seem unreliable because of Uranus' stimulation. They could also feel that others are unreliable as a compensating factor to the restlessness they experience in friendships.

Individuals with a balanced attitude have great potential to intervene in other people's lives because of a liberated perspective. The key here is being skillful. Uranus bestows the ability to cut abruptly through deluded behavior in friends.

Uranus in the Eighth House

Uranus in the eighth house might stimulate emotional spontaneity with others. A lively nature or spirit abides within these people. They have the ability to be a catalyst with others.

An unskillful attitude may create obstacles by being too rude or abrupt. Spontaneity in action or speech creates many regrets in hindsight.

This placement may generate sudden flashes of insight into what others are doing or saying. Uranus is free of a conventional approach to life and therefore sees things in a unique manner. These individuals, when they relate to others, may generate a great deal of stimulation. This is a good aspect for a comedian because of the witty nature of Uranus.

Uranus in the Ninth House

People with Uranus in the ninth house may need to be careful about joining large congregations or organized religions. Their interpretation of religion might be far too liberated to agree with a conservative religious presentation. This does not mean that they should not attend public teachings or be members of a spiritual group. They have a naturally open and liberal attitude, so when someone expresses a conservative opinion, they might find it overly constrictive and narrow-minded.

This aspect is found in independent thinkers and is useful in rejuvenating a stale philosophical tradition. New inspiration and insight spontaneously manifest.

Uranus in the Tenth House

People with Uranus in the tenth house may never conform to social norms. Their personal vision of what they want to become is unconventional. This placement can stimulate incredibly interesting life choices. Conservative friends never understand the eccentricity of these people.

The negative manifestation is a restless nature that never settles down. People with Uranus in this house might consider integrating this understanding strongly into their lives. This applies especially when dealing with parents or friends who emphasize stability as the source of success. It may be better to just appreciate that their eccentric inclinations are the norm. That removes the guilt or stress that could develop. Spiritually inclined individuals have an excellent opportunity to gain liberation in this life. They may feel liberated from conventional goals and see the potential of spiritual attainment.

Uranus in the Eleventh House

Uranus in the eleventh house bestows freedom from socially restrictive norms. Society offers unlimited opportunity for such people. They have an innovative view of what is possible in society.

An unskillful attitude might create a social misfit. Anger and disruptive social activity come easily with the wrong attitude. This manifests as a lack of ability to harmonize socially with the masses. Social anarchy could be the most extreme aspect of this placement.

A skillful presentation of Uranus in the eleventh house indicates the freedom to move in society. This placement has the potential to stimulate society out of its normal lethargy. People who like to act on stage and be unconventional might have Uranus in the eleventh house strongly aspected. This is a good aspect for a social activist.

Uranus in the Twelfth House

Uranus in the twelfth house stimulates a spontaneous inner life. Spontaneous desires and actions arise from no observable cause. There may be an inner sense of potential freedom that these people cannot quite grasp. Individuals with an extroverted attitude may be easily agitated and have trouble calming their mind. Ideas and impulses constantly motivate them to act.

Once a more contemplative attitude is established, these people can have wonderful satori-like experiences. Meditative experiences may be difficult initially with Uranus in the twelfth house because of the impulsive nature it manifests. If these individuals are not able to settle their wandering mind, they experience constant agitation and short bursts of anger when unhappy. Self-discipline is necessary with this influence. The benefit of discipline is the control and wisdom it exerts on Uranus' tendency to be liberal and impulsive.

Neptune in the Houses

Neptune is a sensitive planet. It is related to images and visionary experiences. A certain level of introspection and meditation are necessary to develop Neptune's qualities. There is a strong possibility of daydreaming and wasting time without the discipline of meditation practice. The sensitivity and imaginativeness of Neptune benefit from the discipline offered with Zen or Vipassana meditation techniques.

There are three planets related to sensitivity: the Moon, Neptune, and Pluto. The Moon is emotional sensitivity in the immediate environment. It relates to compassion and empathy. Pluto's sensitivity relates to the body's response to situations. It is often referred to as a gut feeling. This sensitivity can extend to a natural awareness of the energy or power in a geographical location. Neptune's sensitivity manifests through images and intuition. There is a need in all three of these capacities to develop detachment. If there is no detachment, then the sensitivity stimulates people unconsciously. They become victims of their sensitivity. Detachment gives them the opportunity to understand or see what is transpiring. It allows strong feelings and realizations to pass through without disrupting equilibrium. Good psychics have an inner core of peacefulness, or they run the risk of emotional confusion.

Neptune in the First House

Neptune in the first house stimulates the personality to appear vague and easygoing. These individuals could realize great sensitivity and utilize the appearance of being vague to review and reflect on things. They are like a barometer for what is happening around them in the early years of life. Children have few filters to block the emotional and mental energy of others. They simply respond to stimulation. Maturity brings stronger personal definition and perspective. Neptune can exercise this sensitivity to understand others and situations on deep levels.

People with an unbalanced attitude may have the tendency to be scattered and unrealistic. The imagination works overtime and brings no clarity to action. Speech may be affected and conversations meander with no clear thread.

Individuals with a skillful and positive attitude find Neptune similar to an antenna aimed at the world. They immediately pick up mental images of what is happening. This type of sensitivity requires differentiating personal thoughts and desires from those of other people in order to be effective.

Neptune in the Second House

People with Neptune in the second house tend to place less importance on physical acquisition. These people may develop a strong material base but spiritual or philosophical considerations may be more important. The imagination plays a strong role with material considerations. The physical side of life is expanded with vision and idealism. Neptune in this house can bestow the ability to understand the spiritual side of ritual and religious objects.

Individuals with an unbalanced attitude with this placement may be scattered and make bad decisions when dealing with money and property. They may not even care about the maintenance of their possessions and wealth. This is a good placement if one is a cloistered recluse with no concerns about livelihood.

A balanced approach to life often includes spiritual considerations. This placement of Neptune is excellent for dealing with religious objects. There can be an appreciation for the meaning found in rituals and symbols. If there is sharpened awareness, these people can have gifted perception. Few details slip by, and they can easily intuit if anything is out of balance.

This placement can bestow sensitivity toward physical locations, and these people might be able to sense the beneficial or harmful emanations from temples and buildings. Neptune placed here also indicates artistic capacity. The imaginativeness of this planet helps these individuals see things from new perspectives.

Neptune in the Third House

Neptune in the third house brings sensitivity to learning situations. This applies to the quality of the teacher and, to some extent, to the subject matter. Neptune is like an antenna aimed at the instructor. If the instructor is not inspired when teaching, then this placement could cause the student to daydream. This is because the instructor did not creatively catch the imagination of the student. If the instructor is inspired when teaching, the sensitivity of Neptune responds proportionately. The negative side of Neptune's influence is a lack of inspiration and focus when studying.

This placement can indicate a strong interest in imaginative educational subjects. If the subject is physical or basic in its content, then the imagination and intuition are not engaged, but if there are possibilities and options available with the content, the inspiration is stronger. People with this placement might look carefully for a quality teacher. They benefit if the instructor's enthusiasm and realization are present.

Neptune in the Fourth House

Neptune in the fourth house might demonstrate little interest for the material side of home and family. These individuals may feel deeply connected to their family spiritually, but may not find it necessary to sustain frequent physical contact.

Individuals with an unskillful attitude might be inclined to never settle down. They lack roots and connections to people and places. The vagueness of Neptune influences them to wander, looking for better situations elsewhere.

Those with a more balanced and skillful attitude create a greater vision about family and home. They can have a high sensitivity toward family members and may even intuitively know or dream of things that are happening to those people. There is an inclination toward spiritual values. They draw on the spiritual background of the family. Imaginative and spiritual family members can be an inspiration to people with this placement.

Open-mindedness and spiritual roots are easily experienced. There may be a strong connection to the lineage of any faith that validates past lives and personal development. People with Neptune in the fourth house have the ability to sense past lives and incorporate the expanded perspective of multiple lifetimes.

Neptune in the Fifth House

People with Neptune in the fifth house have wonderful imaginative creativity. The imagination and intuition work well with any project that holds their interest. This aspect could make parents with this placement feel relaxed with their children. They are sensitive toward them and may have premonitions or dreams about what their offspring experience. They are drawn to the vision of being a parent more than to the daily grind of child care. This aspect can indicate few or no offspring.

An unbalanced attitude can make these individuals dreamers and impractical in any project. They lack focus and are easily distracted by too many ideas. Those with a more balanced attitude may see the possibilities, but they maintain a clear focus. These individuals can execute activities, including child rearing, with greater focus when planets such as Mars and Saturn make a favorable aspect to the fifth-house Neptune.

This placement is excellent in spiritual interests, as the ability to imagine the possibilities of spiritual growth is increased. Neptune in the fifth house is useful for therapists and counselors.

Neptune in the Sixth House

Neptune in the sixth house can be more spiritually minded with work and employment. The sixth house mixed with Neptune's influence does not easily deal with little details but rather holds the larger vision of what is possible. This can be helpful if the person is a planner for a company.

People with an unskillful attitude may be vague about what kind of employment appears interesting. They drift from job to job, always uncertain about what is correct for them. Any time Neptune exerts too much influence in a house, it creates doubt and uncertainty.

When a balanced and practical attitude is fostered, the intuition can be an asset in employment. These individuals may be able to accomplish tasks with a sense of magic in their work. The imagination assists them, bestowing a larger view and a sense of vision to the work. This placement is excellent for healers, therapists, and counselors, as this sensitivity lets them deal intuitively with people.

Neptune in the Seventh House

Neptune in the seventh house is like an antenna aimed directly at friends and associates. The sensitivity responds to what the spouse or friends express. The negative manifestation of Neptune in the seventh house is vague and unrealistic expectations of friends. These people may ignore obvious signs of a problem and offer impractical advice. Unaware individuals can be easily influenced if the sensitivity is not controlled by mindfulness.

Individuals with a balanced attitude may demonstrate the ability to have foresight with others. They look at friends through the lens of spiritual connections. They may intuitively know things about people they have just met, and if they develop their intuition through meditation, they can gain deep insight into others. Their dreams and visions can contain revealing information.

Neptune in the Eighth House

Neptune in the eighth house may have excellent psychic ability. This does not have to manifest as being mystical but simply as a high level of insight. The eighth house has an image of the chemistry between two people. This placement brings intuition to relationships.

Individuals with an unbalanced attitude could have difficulty understanding and relating to others. They constantly lose a sense of boundaries between themselves and others. Initially this may surface as an ability to finish another person's sentence, but the undercurrent is a lack of differentiation. If these individuals do not clearly define their personal boundaries, they can be easily influenced.

People with a more balanced attitude also have all the sensitivity just described. These people could improve by developing the ability to empty their minds of personal expectations and wishes. They can then better perceive what is going on clairvoyantly. If personal projections are not relaxed, then this placement can tend to make a person superstitious. There is an inclination to be overly imaginative. The ability to be a good clairvoyant depends on the ability to remove a biased and judgmental attitude.

Neptune in the Ninth House

People with Neptune in the ninth house have natural spiritual interests based more on intuition than facts. Neptune can tend to seek the spiritual side of religion, not caring for the more mundane rules or dogma. The common effect of this placement is to have an open-minded approach to life and issues. The imposition of specific rules and regulations is against the theme of spiritual growth for this placement of Neptune.

An unskillful attitude may tend to be vague and impractical philosophically. The desire to go with the flow may manifest. A charismatic presentation of philosophy could overly sway these people if they are not careful. The influence makes them non-specific and idealistic.

A balanced and wise attitude may see the validity of other spiritual traditions. Their view is open-minded. This aspect requires a high-quality teacher to increase the depth of personal realization. This is because these people intuitively respond to the presence of a realized teacher. Empathetic realizations arise from that contact. There is a need to develop the personal capacity to hold and integrate those shared experiences. The teacher could become the object of fascination rather than a catalyst for growth if this is not developed. The issue of personal boundaries is important due to the sensitivity of Neptune.

Neptune in the Tenth House

Neptune in the tenth house stimulates idealism. These people may become spiritually minded about goals. They do not care about material considerations; rather the ideal is more important.

People with an impractical attitude could lack a sense of direction. There is no motivation for personal growth. These people lose perspective and wander from one goal to another. This is due in part to a lack of clarity and individuation. Neptune can have visions, but the issue is how to apply or disregard those visions that count.

Individuals with a balanced attitude definitely have an expansive vision of life. They tend to work for goals that are broad in perspective. The need for material attainment is not great, although they can do well materially. Material success tends to validate their vision. This placement moves them toward spiritual or idealistic goals.

Neptune in the Eleventh House

Neptune in the eleventh house brings forth strong social awareness. The antenna of sensitivity is aimed at society. This can be both a blessing and a curse. People with an unbalanced attitude may feel fear and superstition about large events. Their sensitivity is aimed toward large groups and a feeling of being inundated can ensue. If their general attitude about life is negative, then they may mistrust the government and society.

People with a balanced approach to life have the ability to quickly appreciate what goes on within any group or organization. They have an antenna aimed at the world and can be a barometer registering society's pulse. This placement is excellent for teachers and people who work with large audiences. They can quickly respond to the temperament of the crowd and adjust their teaching content. Fashion designers and advertisers benefit from Neptune in this house.

Neptune in the Twelfth House

Neptune in the twelfth house may give the inner life an expanded imaginativeness. When these people meditate, they intuit expansively about life and people. Their inner life has a wellspring of intuition.

People with an unbalanced attitude can be overwhelmed by daydreams, superstition, and suspicion. Their imagination is unconsciously active and they might tend to exaggerate situations to inappropriate proportions. This happens principally because of not going within to investigate and consciously express the images and intuition.

Individuals with a balanced attitude can develop the ability to visualize and work with complex ideas. This is enhanced if a downtime activity like meditation is used to cultivate inner awareness. The dream life, meditation, and relaxation time are all full of speculative and imaginative ideas. The study of Tantra or archetypal psychology might be useful. These studies demonstrate the power and symbolism of inner vision and imagery.

Pluto in the Houses

Pluto affects the deep instinctual side of life. This can manifest on a variety of levels, starting with the physical body and continuing up to the emotional and spiritual levels. Pluto can physically affect the metabolism, hormonal secretions, function of the organs, and the movement of the energy in the nerve channels. This is not independent of the emotional response to these stimulations, so this expands to include mood and temperament. Intellectually, this manifests as sincerity of thought. The body and mind in balance manifests as harmony and sincerity between speech and thought. This has spiritual implications. The expression of deep spiritual feeling is exhibited when the body and mind harmonize. Naturally, when individuals are not in harmony with their body and mind, they exhibit illness, physical disorders, moodiness, despondency, and depression, all of which are part of Pluto's domain.

Pluto in the First House

Pluto in the first house manifests as strong sincerity. Pluto is not an intellectual planet; it works on a gut level toward events. This creates the initial appearance of being quiet and reserved. Once these people feel comfortable with a situation, they can show stronger feelings about anything that is important to them.

Individuals with an unbalanced attitude might have tendencies toward moodiness and dark thoughts in stressful situations. Their deeper feelings are directly on the surface for others to see. Normally these people have trouble hiding their feelings when depressed. This also becomes a problem with the expression of feeling, as the depth of emotion is too great to fathom quickly.

People with a positive attitude together with Pluto in the first house have an excellent ability to read situations. Their gut feeling might tell them about a situation. They can be authentic and sincere in response to the needs of others. The sense of affinity to others will be natural if these individuals develop empathetic feelings such as love and compassion. Their spiritual faith will be obvious for others to perceive.

Pluto in the Second House

Pluto in the second house relates to the material world with deep feelings. A Buddhist point of view on this placement stresses awareness about the personal environment one creates. If the principal place of residence is in a bad neighborhood or a depressing area, depression or moodiness could result. This placement means that the body responds to the place of residence and even to the furnishings and decor. Choosing a house with sunny exposures and fresh air is advisable. Avoiding dark colors in clothing and in the place of residence could be important considerations. Food that produces a heavy sensation in the body may not be beneficial. It is advisable to be aware of the response the body generates to the living environment.

Pluto establishes attachment to people and objects of long-term familiarity. Attachment does not have to be negative if one responds in a positive manner. Attachment is a problem when it clings to old situations. If miserliness and craving are familiar to their consciousness, then Pluto in the second house influences these individuals to be moody and despondent when situations do not progress well. The maintenance of a positive attitude is important. This could be cultivated with meditations that develop both detachment and devotion.

Pluto in the Third House

Pluto in the third house relates to a sincere response to education. Pluto is a nonintellectual planet, so this placement can cause these individuals to relate to personal growth via their feelings. They may become depressed or moody if they are unhappy with a particular subject of study.

The best educational choices may be those that deal with life issues. These people should ask themselves questions such as "Does this subject speak to me?" "Do I resonate with this material?" Math or economics might not be their first choice, whereas sports and healthcare may be natural areas of interest. The placement of other planets in aspect to Pluto could alter this effect and bring forth the sincere side of Pluto. This placement can also stimulate a sincere relationship between teacher and student.

Pluto in the Fourth House

People with Pluto in the fourth house might easily develop an attachment to family and home. This does not necessarily mean positive relationships, but it does indicate the potential for deep roots for home and family. They might feel more at home in a familiar place. Arrival at a new location may cause anxiety and the wish to seek a home base quickly.

This placement can produce emotions of sincerity and reliability. Deep faith arises in spirituality. Pluto in the fourth house seeks a deeper connection with spiritual values. The deeper feeling may include a nonconceptual sense of past lives and the need for heartfelt spiritual values.

Pluto in the Fifth House

Pluto in the fifth house may respond on a deep level to personal interests. There is a powerful dedication to beliefs. Child rearing generates a deep emotional response. A negative environment and attachment can stimulate a moody and despondent response. Extreme manifestations of attachment are illness and negative fixation.

A positive environment stimulates faith and goodwill to be diligent. Strong love and nurturing aspects exist with this placement. If children are suffering, these individuals will feel the distress to their very core. Caregiving and holistic forms of healing are good career choices. Not only is the mind dedicated to healing, even the body responds on a deep level to assist the healing of both oneself and others.

Pluto in the Sixth House

People with Pluto in the sixth house must have a work environment that suits their emotional temperament. A job that does not agree with personal preference generates depression and despondency. A negative attitude can translate into health difficulties when undertaking work on long-term projects. This despondency can translate into physical illness, especially if Pluto has any square aspects to it. It is wise to carefully choose employment where it is easy to maintain a positive perspective about the job and work environment.

Individuals with a balanced and healthy attitude work well in any caregiving employment. Relationships develop with others in a natural manner. If the work involves any physical healing, such as massage or energy work, the power of Pluto's placement brings positive benefits. Spiritual practices dealing with healing, such as the Medicine Buddha and White Tara in Buddhist Tantra, are beneficial to undertake for those with Pluto in the sixth house. These meditation practices focus and perfect the healing energy of Pluto.

Pluto in the Seventh House

Pluto in the seventh house stimulates long-term and sincere friendships. Pluto placed here brings forth a physical response to friends and translates that into attachment. Essentially, the mood and deep feelings are stimulated by relationship.

An unskillful attitude definitely fosters attachment, moodiness, and depression. Control and separation anxieties arise from not recognizing the negative aspects of attachment. There is almost a physical dependency created if the instinctual side of life is followed without any self-reflection.

Individuals with a balanced emotional attitude express deep sincerity in relationship. Family and friendships are important throughout their entire life. It is almost inevitable that attachments form with this placement. The question lies in how codependent the situation becomes. The best expression of this placement is heartfelt support without expectations.

Pluto in the Eighth House

Pluto in the eighth house can build relationships through empathy and dedication. This is a strong aspect for Pluto as it relates to the chemistry between people. Pluto here looks for rapport and increased emotional connections. This is a good aspect for people who give support to others.

An unbalanced attitude may cause difficulty in relationships. Personal emotional needs are strong and demanding. Moodiness may affect the relationship if one has no emotional balance. The desire for a sincere response lies at the root of the feelings.

A healthy attitude adds emotional wisdom to the chemistry of relationships. Pluto stimulates a deeper understanding and empathy toward others. This gains a clear expression because the attachment Pluto often feels is managed with the wisdom of both personal impermanence and the nature of reality. Those meditations are strongly promoted in Buddhist literature to equalize sensations of attachment and clinging. The ability to heal and influence others is strong with this placement. Meditations with the Medicine Buddha and White Tara are useful to learn and practice.

Pluto in the Ninth House

Pluto in the ninth house inspires deep faith. The nonintellectual influence of Pluto may mean that spiritual practice works at a gut level. The correct spiritual mentor for these people can be realized merely by being in the teacher's presence. The choice of spiritual practice may be based on a sense of affinity to the practice. Deep faith and dedication to practice are indicated with this placement.

An unhealthy attitude may generate blind faith. The cause for blind faith is based on attachment to the feelings related to the teacher or spiritual exercises. Gaining an intellectual understanding about spiritual practice helps lighten up the intense emotions that Pluto can stimulate. A positive aspect of Pluto in the ninth house is a deep underlying dedication. It merely requires a reflective intellectual mind to balance the faith.

Pluto in the Tenth House

Pluto in the tenth house nurtures life choices that resonate on the deeper ground of connectedness. If these people resonate with what they do, there is little that can stop their dedication to that goal. If they make unskillful life choices, then depression and despondency can result. Essentially, these people need to see or feel the connection to their choice.

Individuals with Pluto in the tenth house mixed with a positive and skillful attitude have strong determination. If a life choice is in harmony with deep feelings, few things can deter them from their goal. Humanitarian objectives or a spiritually meaningful lifestyle may be important components of success.

Pluto in the Eleventh House

People with Pluto in the eleventh house have a physical response to society. Pluto is nonintellectual and in this house is a rather subtle influence. This placement gives them a sense or gut feeling about places and crowds. This can be useful to determine or judge what is going on, but the feeling is so basic that it may not mean much. This aspect could influence these individuals to be devoted to a group or club out of attachment to a feeling of camaraderie. Similarly, depression and despondency can result with isolation from those people even if the attachment is only based on a superficial identification. An unskillful attitude could develop into blind faith in groups or associations that are not beneficial.

A positive attitude could stimulate emotional reliability. These people establish a heartfelt association with anyone who has similar interests. Work in healthcare environments is a good choice due to this sincerity.

Pluto in the Twelfth House

Pluto in the twelfth house fosters a deep, quiet inner nature. This aspect is not overtly obvious as Pluto is nonintellectual. These people have access to a deep abiding faith or emotional depth. An unskillful person who is busy and distracted externally may experience uncontrolled moodiness. There is a need to find inner connections via some activity like meditation in order to avoid mood-related disorders. The negative aspect of this placement for spiritual practitioners is a loss of soul, but this only happens because of not looking within for the soul.

Pluto exists in this position very quietly until the person does something that is contrary to his or her nature. If that negative activity is repetitively performed, Pluto stimulates illness, depression, and despondency.

A balanced attitude harmonizes the inner feelings and faith by resting periodically and reflecting on life and its meaning. This gives strength to the inner life. Regular meditation is beneficial for people with Pluto in the twelfth house.

Eleven

Aspects of the Moon and Sun

The aspects discussed are the conjunction between two planets and the angles of 60, 90, 120, and 180 degrees. In astrology, these are called the *sextile, square, trine,* and *opposition,* respectively. The two angles of 60 and 120 degrees are considered harmonious and beneficial. This influence harmonizes with the physical and emotional environment of the native. An angle of 90 degrees is stressful, but can be viewed from two perspectives. A positive environment, where one experiences happiness and joy, reduces the potential stress of a square aspect. The effect of the square aspect is different in a stressful setting. The challenge of a stressful physical and emotional environment is increased with this 90-degree aspect. There is not only a challenge, but astrologically there is added strain.

A 180-degree angle has a mixed effect. An opposition is like a pendulum swinging back and forth. The planet's polarity creates a dynamic tension. If a good attitude is expressed daily, then an opposition causes few if any problems. The positive attitude protects the individual from the extremes of the opposition. If a balance between the opposite poles is not found, one side or the other gains emphasis. This creates imbalance and the possibility of extreme responses.

The Moon in Aspect to the Sun

Conjunction

Sensitivity and the sense of self are conjunct. This aspect indicates that the individual was born on a New Moon day. Emotions and the sense of self combine. Emotions are experienced in a more intense manner. Compassion and empathy mix with the sense of self. Responsive and empathetic emotions develop in positive environments, but in negative settings there may be an overreaction.

The New Moon day is auspicious in the Buddhist calendar. On this day, the monks and nuns do the bimonthly confession service. Asian countries consider the astrology of children born on this day to have auspicious influences.

Square

Sensitivity and the sense of self are stressfully aspected at 90 degrees. These individuals may be sensitive and thin-skinned about emotional issues. Compassion may overwhelm them. They have trouble expressing compassion, as it feels too strong. To protect themselves, they may appear uncaring. There could be issues with the mother and other women, plus stress with compassionate people. The Moon's receptivity is reflected in these contacts. These individuals tend to respond too strongly when interacting emotionally with others.

The positive component of this aspect is strong compassion. It is not possible for these people to be apathetic about sensitive issues. Their emotional response time is quick and direct. Two factors can bring forth positive qualities: a happy environment and a constructive self-awareness. Tara, a female Buddha, or Avalokiteshvara, the Buddha of love and compassion, are beneficial practices to release some of this emotional tension.

Opposition

Sensitivity and the sense of self are in opposition. An opposition is like a pendulum swinging back and forth. You have to look at the two planets to get a sense of the dynamics that influence the individual. This placement stimulates sensitivity and compassion. The person is emotionally responsive.

A problem could occur with the inability to establish boundaries between oneself and others. Emotional sensitivity might cause strong compassion to well up, but the person could lack the ability to control the feeling. Similarly, a selfish concern could develop that focuses on one's feelings to the exclusion of others. Both these positions indicate a need for balance.

To be aware of one's personal needs and yet remain sensitive to others is the balance. Tara, a female Tantric Buddha, could empower this person's life. Her posture demonstrates the ability to control strong emotions. It is a Full Moon day, an auspicious day in the Buddhist calendar. On this day, the monks and nuns do the bimonthly confession service.

Sextile and Trine

The sensitivity and the sense of self are well aspected. This indicates harmony between emotions and the sense of self. The expression of compassionate empathy arrives in a smooth manner without conflict. If a situation invokes tears, these people cry; if the situation calls for joy, they laugh. The emotional sensitivity blesses the sense of self. One may easily know the emotional temperament of others.

The Moon in Aspect to Mercury

Conjunction

Sensitivity and intellect are in union. One tends to think about emotional material. Verbal expression includes a natural quality of emotion. A positive environment produces pleasant speech. An instructor can deliver compassionate and moving

discourses. Stressful settings may enhance emotional disharmony. One's feelings interfere with communication skills. This
aspect mixes compassion and the intellect.

Square

Sensitivity and the intellect are stressfully aspected. Thoughts
have a strong emotional dynamic. A good environment stimulates passionate speech. Others may easily detect the emotions
of this person. Stressful situations can invoke disharmonious
feelings that interfere with constructive communications skills.
The mind feels distress with emotionally sensitive issues. Meditations such as Vipassana and Zen are excellent with this aspect as they allow space between feelings and verbal expression.

Opposition

Sensitivity and the intellect are polarized. One side is sensitive
and compassionate and the other is intellectual. The two extremes may manifest as feelings with no intelligence or words
with no feeling. Often the situation dictates which side gains
the greatest expression. Dialogue brings forth the intellect;
emotion the sensitivity. The opposition presents the opportunity to learn to balance personal feelings and intellectual content. Maturity helps one learn how to unify the heart and mind
constructively. The perfect balance is strong empathetic communication. The worst expression of this aspect is emotional
outbursts with little communication skill.

Sextile and Trine

Sensitivity and the intellect harmonize. Words are well balanced with emotional impact. Sensitivity guides the mind to
respond easily to other people's emotions. This aspect is beneficial for teachers and instructors as compassion pervades their
instruction.

The Moon in Aspect to Venus

Conjunction

Sensitivity and sensuality are mixed. The feeling nature of this individual is strong. To feel compassion is to love another. Compassion gains all the colorfulness of the senses such as form, shape, color, harmonies, and the rest. Negative situations agitate the mind with emotion. There may be trouble understanding the situation intellectually. Emotional confusion is avoided, provided the attitude is composed and organized. Meditations in the Vipassana and Zen style help remove the overreactive influence of this conjunction.

Beneficially, this aspect is excellent for Tara and Avalokiteshvara meditations. These deities manifest love and compassion, which bring forth the best aspects of the Moon and Venus. The individual is often attractive when these two planets are conjoined.

Square

Sensitivity and sensuality stress one another. Sensitivity and affection respond strongly to any emotional issue. This can make relationships a lively event, but can be problematic when trying to deal rationally with another. The sensitivity makes the sensual side of this person vulnerable and brings forth a higher level of emotional interaction. Meditations such as Vipassana and Zen are beneficial in controlling this aspect because of the detachment these meditations cultivate.

Love and compassion are strong forces in a positive setting. These people respond quickly to the shifting patterns of a love affair. They feel and empathize for the other person. The ability to manifest the positive aspects of this angle depends on being centered and detached. Affection is powerful and requires a clear mind to manage it.

Opposition

Sensitivity and sensuality sit in opposition. One side is sensitive and compassionate while the other has feelings of sensual stimulation. These two are feeling-based planets and therefore do not cause a polarity. The empathy and love felt for others is expressive. This could produce stress when this influence does not disengage. Satisfaction in a relationship can be a complicated matter. This aspect brings forth love and compassion, but for an unbalanced individual it creates confusing attachments.

Any meditation practice from the Amitabha family of deities such as Avalokiteshvara and Tara are excellent. These practices focus on skillful compassion. The individual possibly could balance this influence with a Vipassana, Zen, or Manjushri practice. All three of these meditation practices cause detachment, which gives a better capacity to deal with strong feelings. These meditation styles avoid "idiot" compassion, which only makes situations more complicated. Idiot compassion is considered an emotional response that does not benefit the people involved. It appears as an expression of personal feeling without an appreciation for the recipient's needs.

Sextile and Trine

Sensitivity and sensuality run smoothly together. This means that loving affection is mixed with emotional sensitivity. A good example to demonstrate this is the exact opposite. If emotional sensitivity and affection are not balanced, then demands for love are made. The person is blind to what the other may feel, whereas a person expressing the beneficial influence easily recognizes the needs of everyone. Harmony and sensitivity exist between love and compassion.

The Moon in Aspect to Mars

Conjunction

Sensitivity and willpower directly mix. Empathy and compassion do not wait to express themselves. The softer side of the

Moon tends to be lost with the dynamic energy of Mars. The individual responds quickly to anything related to emotion. Negative settings invoke emotions that are hot and intense. Feelings are inflamed and expressed strongly. In a positive environment, there is a forthright presentation of feelings. The emotional life is dynamic and uninhibited.

Square

Sensitivity and willpower stress one another. These individuals respond quickly to any emotional issue. They may appear rash and impulsive because of strong feelings. The emotional life is expressive in a positive setting, making them fun to be around. Stressful situations stimulate a defensive response. They are overly sensitive about harmful and aggressive behavior. Quietude meditations are beneficial to control this aspect due to the space these meditations cultivate between emotional stimulation and response.

Opposition

Sensitivity and willpower are polarized. Sensitivity and compassion move in opposite directions from willpower and capacity. This could motivate these individuals to react when feeling empathy. They understand the emotional experience of another, but decide to act in a rash or impulsive manner. An unbalanced presentation of this polarity could make these people agitated and busy. They might feel compassionate toward another, but give too much. The expressive and active side of Mars needs to slow down the response to emotional stimulation. The balanced expression of this aspect is the bodhisattva Vajrapani, who represents power, ability, and capacity balanced with a compassionate attitude. Any opposition has the potential for balance. The key is self-awareness.

Sextile and Trine

Sensitivity and willpower are well aspected. The will to act sensitively harmonizes with the emotions. This is a beneficial aspect for a bodhisattva, as it is an *engaged compassion*. This is a term used in Mahayana Buddhism that means the individual acts on his or her compassionate feelings. The harmonious aspects between these two planets are not pushy or overbearing. To feel compassion is to act on it. There is an empowerment of empathy.

The Moon in Aspect to Jupiter

Conjunction

Sensitivity and expansion are one entity. These people tend to have a happy nature. Their emotions are expanded and they feel little need to be unhappy or despondent about anything. They express their happiness and joy enthusiastically. These people often have many female friends. The negative side of this aspect is overexcitement and a lack of good judgment. There is a need to limit the amount of euphoria and optimism that constantly arises.

Square

Sensitivity and expansion are in stressful aspect. These individuals have to be careful about emotional intoxication. They can be naturally happy and joyful in a positive setting. There is a need to recognize a harmful situation before it develops. People with this aspect tend to ignore any signs that something could be wrong. Stressful situations generate a lively response. The principal problem is getting too excited.

Opposition

Sensitivity and expansion stretch apart. One side is sensitive and compassionate and the other is enthusiastic. These planets harmonize easily. The enthusiasm of Jupiter excites the sensitivity of the Moon and vice versa. This aspect could make the person easily excitable and stimulated. The unbalanced response suggests too much optimism. There is a tendency to be overly friendly and try to do too much. These people can be difficult to bear if they are always emotionally energized. There may be a lack of sensitivity toward others. The balanced approach indicates a happy person who is full of goodwill. The general response to difficult situations is to just move on and not dwell on the pain. It is hard for these people to remain depressed for any length of time.

Sextile and Trine

Sensitivity and expansion help one another. This means that goodwill and emotional sensitivity function spontaneously together. Jupiter brings forth goodwill and enthusiasm and, with the Moon beneficially positioned, a natural friendliness. Altruism, bodhicitta, and an inclination toward the Mahayana attitude, working for the benefit of all, can be present with this aspect.

The Moon in Aspect to Saturn

Conjunction

Sensitivity and a conservative nature mix. A realistic emotional life is the central focus. These individuals may appear cool and detached. They may even seem to lack compassion, but this is simply because their compassion responds slowly. They want to see what is happening before they respond.

The negative side of this aspect is to be cold and detached, appearing distant from feelings. Excellent wisdom develops in the later phases of life and the individual can be a wise and thoughtful soul. Deep understanding and compassion are the strongest expressions of this conjunction. Saturn's component needs to be reflective and observant and the Moon requires empathetic feelings. These two facets polish the diamond of deep heartfelt wisdom.

Square

Sensitivity is stressed by conservative observations. These individuals may feel uncomfortable with situations that involve emotion. They might appear cold and detached, but on a deep level they desire security. There can be problems with women, especially the mother, and with people who express compassion. People with this aspect may feel that compassionate people are not realistic and care too much.

Individuals who express the positive side of this aspect are analytical and deal with difficult situations skillfully. The positive side develops with regular meditation. These techniques include Vipassana, Zen, and quietude meditation. Although there may be a sense of emotional insecurity, with regular meditation these individuals can cultivate excellent empathy for others.

This aspect has both introverted and extroverted expressions. The section on Saturn in chapter 7 describes how this may manifest. An image for Saturn in square aspect to any planet is like a ball and shackle: Saturn slows down the expression of the planet in aspect. The positive expression of this is deep contemplation of the aspected planet. Contemplative meditations conjoined with a positive or compassionate attitude bring forth the best qualities of Saturn.

Opposition

Sensitivity and the desire to control are polarized. Sensitivity and compassion sit opposite a conservative, judgmental nature. Saturn weighs and judges everything, and in this case it is the emotions. Feelings are subjected to the harsh light of self-criticism. An unbalanced attitude may be at either end of the spectrum: emotional with little control, or overly controlled with little sensitivity. The balanced position between these two points is wise compassion: the ability to judge a situation on its merit and yet still have empathy for suffering. This aspect can bring forth profound wisdom in the later years of life. This is because Saturn gains insight with experience and age.

Sextile and Trine

Sensitivity and judgment benefit one another. This means that the sensitivity and the ability to appraise situations work well together. The emotional feelings of these people have a steady nature. These individuals do not overreact to excitement or depression. That does not mean that they will never experience depression, just that they tend to be practical about suffering and don't indulge in it. This aspect generates wise, mature compassion. People with this aspect are often good listeners, and friends seek out their counsel.

The Moon in Aspect to Uranus

Conjunction

Sensitivity and revolution are conjunct. A lively, expressive nature dominates the emotional life. Friends may find these people too stimulating as constant companions. These individuals respond quickly and emotionally to everything. The unfavorable manifestation of this influence is emotionally fickle relationships. These people might seem chaotic when in sensitive situations. They can feel raw and easily upset if they have low self-esteem. Confident individuals can be wonderfully expressive. The positive side bestows an independent emotional nature and feelings that are liberal and free. Women with this aspect may benefit from Tantric practice, especially the wrathful female deities. Uranus and the Moon conjunct can stimulate women to new levels of freedom and independence.

Square

Sensitivity and revolution are in stressful aspect. There can be great difficulty in controlling emotional responsiveness. These people are lively in positive environments, appearing quite liberated from social norms. There are strong highs and lows with this aspect. Sudden feelings and energy motivate these people. Stressful situations might cause a rash response. There is no filter to slow down the emotions as they arise. Emotional issues may feel chaotic, and in a man's chart there may be fear of women. People with this placement can also attract eccentric women.

Opposition

Sensitivity and revolution bounce off one another. One side is sensitive compassion and the other is revolution and chaos. This may stimulate rapid emotional swings. The sensitivity moves rapidly. The positive expression of this influence is freedom for emotional expression, but when it is unbalanced without wisdom, it may appear chaotic. Quietude meditation is an excellent asset, as it allows the full experience of the emotion without necessarily responding unskillfully. Women have a high potential to attain enlightenment because of Uranus' liberal spirit.

Sextile and Trine

Sensitivity and revolution support one another. This creates a free and easygoing emotional expression. Uranus generates a great deal of freedom in whatever area of the chart it is placed. This aspect blesses the emotions with liberty and self-expression. Individuals with this may not understand other people's emotional hesitation. This aspect is beneficial for extroverted individuals, as they can cut through difficult emotional situations. The practice of wrathful female deities such as Vajravahari, Vajrayogini, and Maha Kali are beneficial.

The Moon in Aspect to Neptune

Conjunction

Sensitivity and the spiritual pole mix together. These individuals have a highly sensitive nature. The appearance of emotional vagueness, being a space cadet, can predominate. This is because the feelings are imaginative and lose focus on the immediate situation. The dream life may be full, and psychic empathy may be strong with others.

The Moon, Neptune, and Pluto are all related to sensitivity. The Moon for emotional content, Neptune for images and intuition, and Pluto for the body's sensitivity. Two of these three are conjunct and the third planet, Pluto, is there for everyone from 1945 until 1985. Pluto and Neptune were sextile during those years. The three levels of sensitivity—gut intuition, emotional intuition, and mental intuition—work together. Therefore, this person's empathetic nature and imagination are strong. Such a powerful mixture can develop spiritual wisdom to a profound level.

Square

Sensitivity and the spiritual pole are in stressful aspect. These individuals may misunderstand or exaggerate emotional content. Neptune is like the lens of a camera. It suggests that emotional and empathetic responses are unrealistic or unfocused. This aspect may indicate psychic development, but the expression of this sensitivity may be inappropriate. These people may mystify others by how they talk or respond to situations. The occult influence is too strong.

All aspects in astrology are only influences. It is not difficult to control the negative implications of a Moon-Neptune square. Meditations that focus on quietude such as Vipassana and Zen are beneficial to diminish the heightened sensitivity.

Opposition

Sensitivity and the spiritual pole stimulate one another. The swing is between sensitivity and imaginative intuition. These two planets are similar to each other and beneficially mix emotion and intuition. They complement spiritual insights.

Any intuitive person has to cultivate a peaceful inner state to best take advantage of this sensitivity. If personal biases and judgment are disengaged, it helps clairvoyance manifest in the open field of consciousness. There can be the ability to differentiate personal feelings from the emotional content of others.

Sextile and Trine

Sensitivity and the spiritual pole are in harmony. These two planets assist in the ability to gauge another person's emotional state of being. The enhancement of this capacity comes from meditation and could bring forth the best aspects of this influence. If meditation is done regularly, the potential for intuitive work is high. The Tantric deity Tara, a female Buddha, can increase this spiritual development.

The Moon in Aspect to Pluto

Conjunction

Sensitivity and the instinctual pole mix as one. Strong feelings flow with compassion. The body and heart respond with depth and sincerity. If these individuals develop an unbalanced attitude, then the negative side of this aspect is moodiness. It is hard to separate feelings of compassion from attachment. These individuals may identify deeply with family and friends.

A positive attitude stimulates faith. Faith is deeply felt but could suffer from blind devotion. A practice of Manjushri, the Buddha of wisdom, or a Vipassana style of meditation could be beneficial. These meditations bring forth wisdom and help reduce excessive attachment to friends. These people could be effective healers if interested in that form of work.

Square

Sensitivity and the instinctual pole stress one another. Deep feelings manifest in almost all situations. Depression or mood disorders can dominate with strong emotional situations. People with this aspect might carefully consider what physical and emotional environment they create. If the physical environment is dark and cold, they will be easily depressed. Limited exposure to emotional issues might be another consideration if feasible. There is a tendency to be overly sincere. The positive effect is insight into deep emotions. The development of a heightened awareness with meditation may manifest spontaneous empathetic communication.

Opposition

Sensitivity and the instinctual pole are polar opposites. The pendulum moves between sensitive compassion and deep feelings. This aspect may indicate that the individual has the capacity to feel strongly about important issues. Mood swings are common when relationships become complicated. Essentially, the emotional sensitivity is attached to deep physical feelings. These two planets are similar in their nature and only vary in the depth of the feeling. Strong faith and attachment express themselves regularly in this placement.

The bond with a spiritual mentor may last a lifetime with this placement. Emotional neediness could develop without detachment. The feelings are strong and deep, irrespective of what object, positive or negative, is the focus.

Sextile and Trine

Sensitivity and the instinctual pole are in harmony. This aspect manifests faith and sincerity. It would be difficult to be emotionally deceptive because the deceit could appear as physical disharmony and unhappiness. Friends and family enjoy these people's company because of their ability to empathize. If regular meditation is developed, they can instinctively know when others are unhappy. This aspect is good for healers and social workers.

The Sun in Aspect to Mercury

Conjunction

The sense of self and the intellect are together. This conjunction gives these individuals an intellectual capacity. Their basic sense of self and the ability to think are synonymous. They are inquisitive and any interest brings forth the wish to know more about the subject. This aspect could make a person overly intellectual and question everything, but the beneficial aspect is to be intelligent and communicative. The practice of Manjushri, the Buddha of wisdom, could complement this individual.

Note: The Sun and Mercury are never more than 28 degrees apart, so the conjunction is the only major aspect that can occur in a natal chart.

The Sun in Aspect to Venus

Conjunction

The sense of self and sensuality mix. Here the sense doors and the self work closely together. These individuals are sensually interactive with the world around them. The ability to express love and affection comes easily. Pleasurable feelings are experienced with the world. The negative side of this aspect is a demand for stimulation and affection. It is based on a selfish attitude. Some people could be self-indulgent. The hunger for satisfaction is strong.

If these individuals have a positive and kindhearted attitude, then they are fun loving and share everything. The positive influence can be perfected with altruistic meditation. This aspect tends to make the recipient physically attractive.

Note: The Sun and Venus are never more than 48 degrees apart, so the conjunction is the only major aspect that can occur in a natal chart.

The Sun in Aspect to Mars

Conjunction

The sense of self and willpower are together. This aspect makes these people powerful. They may act immediately on a motivation. Mars and the Sun are both fire planets, so the activity level of these people is high. A positive setting encourages the achievement of great goals. The negative side could be aggressive activity. These individuals might recognize that they are "doers" and know that they need projects. The practice of quietude meditations and love tone down the aggressive side of this conjunction.

Square

The sense of self and willpower stress one another. This manifests as a strong assertiveness. It can be a beneficial influence if these people deal successfully with their anger. A positive situation stimulates the desire to get tasks done. Negative settings tend to encourage rash and opinionated activity. These people push their energy at others. This type of aspect can make someone a workaholic, always feeling driven to do new things. Quietude meditations and a focus on compassionate interactions are the best remedies for the aggression of Mars.

Opposition

The sense of self and willpower are opposed. These two are similar in nature and element, both being fire planets. Mars enjoys doing things, and with this aspect there are strong personal dynamics at play. Negative situations may quickly generate frustration, but in positive environments people with this influence can accomplish great tasks. The practice of wrathful deities in the Vajrayana would be beneficial. Those practices give an outlet for the powerful energy. This meditation style could remove interferences for both themselves and others. To control the strong feelings of Mars, quietude meditations are recommended initially. As these individuals strengthen personal willpower, they could transfer practice to the Vajrayana.

Sextile and Trine

The sense of self and willpower are in harmony. Someone having these aspects could accomplish tasks easily with dynamic enthusiasm. These planets inspire capacity. Willpower inspires self-confidence.

The Sun in Aspect to Jupiter

Conjunction

The sense of self and expansion mix. This aspect makes these individuals enthusiastic about life. The sense of opportunity and abundance are mixed with the sense of self. If people with this aspect become too busy, they lose focus and may not be properly centered. The busyness comes because they see too many opportunities. On the positive side, these people see a golden future, and the expansive nature of Jupiter makes them full of life.

Square

The sense of self and expansion stress one another. Excitement is part of this aspect. Positive settings encourage a busy and enthusiastic nature. These people tend to exhaust themselves with too many tasks. They see the positive side of what needs to be done and they overwork.

The negative manifestation of this influence is someone who is always physically and emotionally agitated. A meditation that solves this problem is quietude practice.

This aspect indicates that the *chi* (Tibetan: *lung*) element is strong and easily agitated. Chi, or energy, follows the mind. A calm and peaceful approach to life quiets the agitation.

Opposition

The sense of self and expansion are in opposition. The pendulum swings between the self and expanded optimism. This aspect makes these individuals excitable and busy. The negative expression of this influence is too much optimism, which creates just as many problems as too little optimism. Problems are not clearly seen and bad judgment creates difficult situations. People with a positive balance of this opposition see the bright side of things. Altruism and generosity are easily expressed. Breathing meditation calms the excitement. These people tend to be happy.

Sextile and Trine

The sense of self and expansion are well aspected. Goodwill is the predominate attitude. If these people meet with obstacles, they look for solutions quickly. Flexibility of attitude is part of Jupiter's beneficial influence. Wherever Jupiter falls in the natal chart indicates where enthusiasm is the greatest.

The Sun in Aspect to Saturn

Conjunction

The sense of self and being conservative are combined. This aspect influences these individuals to be practical in all situations. There is a strong wish to avoid being vulnerable. This can be an indicator of why a person is conservative. These individuals want life to be under control. Their ability to judge and weigh situations is good, but if taken to the extreme they could have a judgmental and demeaning attitude.

The beneficial influence of this aspect makes these people wise. The wisdom of Saturn shines forth as they age and makes them a storehouse of wise words. Tantric deities like Guhyasamaja and Manjushri are good to practice. These Buddhist deities embody the composure that this aspect manifests.

Square

The sense of self and a conservative attitude stress one another. These people could suffer from low self-esteem, frustration, and inhibition. There are introverted and extroverted expressions of this aspect. The introverts look down on themselves and are pessimistic. The judgmental side of Saturn is focused on the self in a negative manner. The extroverts often seek to control others. These individuals may hate being uncomfortable or vulnerable. The extroverts express their unhappiness. They may attempt to control others through criticism. The underlying feeling is the same in both cases: insecurity. It is the expression of this feeling that differs.

Meditations that focus on the flow of reality are useful. These include Mahamudra and Tzok Chen in Buddhist practice. The practice of Zen perhaps should be avoided. The Zen style emphasizes a strict and militant approach to sitting. People with this aspect may overidentify with that discipline and become uncaring. Compassion is important with a Saturn square. Compassion helps moisten the feelings and opposes insecurity.

A Sun-Saturn square can produce incredible wisdom. These people are thoughtful because of the gradual manner in which Saturn lets things unfold. The wisdom side of this aspect is nurtured with the right attitude of patience and insight.

Opposition

The sense of self and a conservative influence are in opposition. There is both wisdom and frustration with this placement. The negative influence could cripple individual expression. These individuals might weigh and judge situations too strongly and hesitate. The need to control actions can interfere with the development of an inner sense of security.

On the positive side, these people hold the ability to reflect deeply on life. This influence may produce individuals who are a solid source of wisdom and support. Meditation practice could come very naturally to them. Buddhist practices like Manjushri and high Tantric deities like Guhyasamaja are excellent with this placement. If the balance between the two extremes is found, a wise, dignified nature manifests.

Sextile and Trine

The sense of self and being practical support one another. This produces a realistic approach to life. A sense of pragmatism is central with this aspect. The wisdom of Saturn tends to go slowly into activities and accomplishes them professionally. A mature attitude generates a wise and stable presentation. These aspects benefit these people throughout their lives.

The Sun in Aspect to Uranus

Conjunction

The sense of self and revolution mix together. This can make these individuals appear very liberal. There is little chance of them being conformists. This aspect makes them independent and spontaneous. They see themselves as unique.

The negative side of this aspect is eccentric and odd activity. These people appear chaotic. The beneficial side is liberty. They may feel free of social dictates and norms. They might accomplish unbelievable feats in this life. If these people lack self-esteem, they may feel like social misfits and look down on themselves. This is the product of having a bad self-image. People who demonstrate alternative approaches to life are important in society. They reveal the shortcomings that society may unconsciously hold. Meditation may be difficult initially because of impulsive physical energy.

Square

The sense of self and revolution are in stressful aspect. This normally translates into being an individualist. This aspect might give these individuals a wonderful opportunity to seek self-expression. The ability to be free from social expectations is present. The negative expression of this influence is to be a complete eccentric. These individuals have a tendency to express themselves in an unpredictable way.

If these people lack self-esteem, they may fear the unexpected. This is the introverted effect of this aspect. The extroverted expression is to be a nonconformist. A positive attitude with this aspect can produce people who have an expressive and stimulating personality. They might initiate action and activity fearlessly.

Opposition

The sense of self and revolution are opposed. This influence can make these individuals appear chaotic in stressful situations. They may tend to be independent and free thinkers. The possibility of liberation is high. This influence encourages self-expression. The negative influence could make some people feel disassociated from society. The world may seem unpredictable and fearsome to them.

Sextile and Trine

The sense of self and revolution are in harmony. These individuals may have an easygoing spontaneity. This aspect is excellent for not getting stuck in a rut. It urges a spontaneous sense of freedom. These people are quick-witted and lively.

Altruistically minded people may find this placement a great asset when working with difficult sentient beings. No matter how difficult the situation may appear, they remain flexible.

The Sun in Aspect to Neptune

Conjunction

The sense of self and the spiritual pole are together. These individuals are sensitive and imaginative. This imaginativeness is one with their core nature. The negative influence produces people who are dreamers, but this is a label placed on them by a materialistic society. Buddhists view this aspect as a cause for a spiritual life. India sees such individuals as mystics and wandering mendicants. This influence stimulates the idealism of monks and nuns.

The negative expression of this aspect is to be out of touch with reality. These people perceive too many options and get lost in speculation. Another distraction is to become overwhelmed by visualizations. A final issue is personal boundaries. This aspect makes a person sensitive and therefore easily influenced by others. These individuals must differentiate between their own intentions and the intentions of other people. This can be accomplished with meditation styles that cultivate detachment and clarity.

Square

The sense of self and the spiritual pole are in stressful aspect. Neptune is like a lens on a camera; it brings things into focus. Neptune makes everything appear out of focus when stress is felt. These individuals are prone to misunderstandings and superstition. Their imagination has a strong impact on their sense of self. They have inappropriate ideas about things.

Artists and spiritual practitioners find this aspect beneficial. They are wonderfully imaginative, and their meditations are profound. Neptune's influence is expansive, and explaining the visions or experience may be complicated. This aspect gives these individuals the ability to have profound dreams and altered perceptions of reality. They may seem out of touch with the regular world but that is because our culture does not support mystics. The only qualities required to make this aspect beneficial are detachment and clarity of perspective.

Opposition

The sense of self and the spiritual pole are opposed. This aspect might make these people highly sensitive and easily influenced if they have not defined their boundaries. There is a need to be able to differentiate their personal feelings from those of others. They are capable of profound perceptions once clarity of mind is realized. This aspect is like an antenna aimed directly at the area where Neptune falls in the natal chart.

The unbalanced aspect is for these individuals to be either out of touch with their personal reality or egotistical and superstitious. The positive side is to be clairvoyant and have a rich dream life and expanded sense of consciousness.

Sextile and Trine

The sense of self and the spiritual pole are in harmony. This creates a nice blend of intuition and imagination. The aspect bestows spiritual integration. Neptune placed in this aspect automatically includes Pluto in a positive aspect for everyone born between 1945 and 1985. Imaginative intuition and gut feelings are in harmony. Imagination and foresight are spontaneous. Regular meditation develops spiritual awareness quickly.

The Sun in Aspect to Pluto

Conjunction

The sense of self and the instinctual pole are together. This aspect generates a sincere expression of faith. Deep feelings are synonymous with the core nature. The negative influence might make a person focus on mundane issues. This happens because Pluto relates to the body.

The body and the sense of self are deeply interconnected, so alcohol and drugs can have a dramatic effect. It is advisable to avoid alcohol. The body is astrologically prone to depression, and alcohol stimulates depression.

The beneficial aspect is an excellent capacity to recognize sacred objects and places. The intuitive aspect of Pluto is through the body and gut feelings. Individuals who have spiritual interests can enjoy locations that have a long history of spiritual activity.

People with this aspect are encouraged to become conscious of their physical environment. They are easily influenced by locations and need mindful awareness to avoid constructing a negative environment.

Square

The sense of self and the instinctual pole are in stressful aspect. Pluto affects mood, temperament, and deep feelings. This aspect stimulates tension between the sense of self and deep feelings. Negative situations can produce moodiness and despondency. People with this aspect can be more vulnerable to negative environments and can manifest a dark and withdrawn appearance. The negative influence is especially compounded if the person has a pessimistic attitude. Pluto can generate attachment to even negative situations. The bad judgment makes the process of healing and release more complicated.

A positive environment will enhance a deep connection to others. This makes these people empathetic, but in a manner that easily leads to attachment. Their body responds in a deep physical manner. Alcohol and drugs should definitely be avoided in this case. The environment physically and emotionally has a stronger influence. They might try to pick an environment that is sunny and be with people who are upbeat and positive.

Opposition

The sense of self and the instinctual pole are opposed. This aspect may cause craving and attachment. The unbalanced expression of this influence swings between moody self-awareness to self-centered attachment.

The balanced aspect might manifest as people with a strong commitment to others and a clear set of personal boundaries. These boundaries are defined by where the faith of the individual is found. Deep faith and the ability to inspire others emotionally could also be beneficial aspects of this opposition. The balanced aspect contains wise feelings of compassion rather than idiot compassion. The term *idiot compassion* is a Buddhist expression for feelings that lack skillful delivery. The person expresses the emotional content of his or her wish to be helpful without forethought or reflective wisdom. This type of emotional response can actually complicate a relationship.

Sextile and Trine

The sense of self and the instinctual pole complement one another. These individuals are sincere and in harmony with their feelings. These two planets work together to generate a sense of emotional integration.

Everyone born between 1945 and 1985 has Pluto sextile Neptune. This aspect indicates that the instincts and intuition support one another with feelings of luck and synchronicity. Heartfelt emotions can arise naturally for these people. Even if they are involved in negative activity, they can show a level of sincerity, like being an honest crook. Daily meditation integrates the emotional life smoothly. Dreams and intuition will come to them effortlessly.

Twelve
Aspects of the Inner Planets

Mercury's effect is enhanced with contemplative meditation. These meditations allow the mind to work with ideas in a quiet and peaceful environment. All meditations are not categorized as quietude techniques. Buddhism accepts several types of meditation, including contemplation, single-pointed quietude, and deity practices. All these techniques aim to benefit and hone the mind to a higher perfection. Deity practices like Manjushri and Saraswati, the two Buddhas related to wisdom and the arts, are excellent practices to develop. They enhance the wisdom of the mind together with the performing arts, music, writing, and poetry. Mercury stimulates the intellect; these practices polish the mind to shine with intelligence and grace.

Mercury in Aspect to Venus

Conjunction

The intellect and sensuality are synonymous. These individuals think with graphic examples, motif, and analogy. The sensual world and intellectual processes naturally include one another.

Affectionate, pleasing speech delivered in an expressive, sensual manner comes with this placement. The ideas are expressed in poetic terms. Artistic ability includes both the mind and the hands. Saraswati and Manjushri, the Tantric deities related to the arts and wisdom, are especially beneficial to practice.

Sextile

The trine aspect is not possible for these two planets; just the sextile. Intellect and sensuality work together well. The grace of Venus assists the intellectual expression of Mercury. The sensual world and one's thoughts naturally include each other. These individuals can present ideas affectionately. They can speak in a manner that moves other people's emotions. The golden speech of Manjushri, the Buddha of wisdom, comes from this aspect. Saraswati and Manjushri are excellent deities to practice. Saraswati is the goddess of the performing arts and writing. Daily practice of her meditation or a periodic retreat can enhance any artistic expression. Daily practice of Manjushri can increase writing and communication skills.

Note: Mercury and Venus are never more than 76 degrees apart, so the conjunction and the sextile are the only major aspects that can occur in a natal chart.

Mercury in Aspect to Mars

Conjunction

The intellectual functions of investigation are mixed with willpower and determination. The intellect is strengthened by the determination to act. These individuals are to turn their mind to any subject with discipline and order. Mars generally gives a person a sense of capacity, and in this aspect the mind is motivated. The negative manifestation of this conjunction is forceful, uncompromising ideas. These individuals may quickly raise their voice when they think no one is listening. The power of debate, direct clear speech, and investigation are all improved. Teaching, instructing, and supervisory positions are all suitable occupations for people with this aspect.

Square

The intellect and willpower are in stressful aspect. This combination makes the speech powerful, and in a positive, happy environment there is a direct and forthright manner of communication. Thoughts are expressed in a vigorous and enthusiastic manner. A negative, stressful situation can make the speech and thoughts angry and defensive. The general influence makes the intellect strong, and this can affect the blood pressure. Mars generates *chi* (Tibetan: *lung*) energy in the body, so in a stressful situation, anger agitates the body. Quietude meditation techniques are excellent for people with this aspect. Zen meditation may not be a suitable technique because of its strong emphasis on discipline. That style might increase power and authority in an inappropriate manner.

Opposition

The intellect and willpower are polarized. This square can make a person a powerful intellectual. The negative influence manifests as overbearingly aggressive explanations. Ideas are experienced intensely in the mind. The positive effect helps the mind process information with determination. The desire to act on ideas manifests quickly.

Sextile and Trine

The intellect and willpower are well aspected. The intellect is mixed with willpower and determination. The intellectual functions have a good delivery. These individuals are able to use discipline to master anything. The power of debate, direct clear speech, and investigation are all improved. Employment that uses the mind and communication skills is an excellent choice.

Mercury in Aspect to Jupiter

Conjunction

The intellect and expansion are mixed. This aspect stimulates flexibility of thought. Jupiter is vibrant and enthusiastic wherever it is placed in a chart. With this aspect, Mercury's inquisitive and intellectual qualities express versatility. Everything is seen in positive terms. An altruistic attitude is also part of this influence. There is a generosity of thought, so ease of speech is facilitated.

Square

The intellect and expansion are in stressful aspect. The mind becomes excitable. These individuals may suffer from the inability to remain quiet for any length of time. Thoughts are strong, enthusiastic, and joyful with this aspect. Stressful situations or a busy job environment may exhaust these individuals. They try to do too much. The mind is extremely versatile but easily overstimulated. The beneficial expression of this aspect is to be flexible and quick-witted. Manjushri practice can be beneficial as it organizes the thoughts.

Opposition

The intellect and expansion are opposed. This polarity stimulates enthusiasm when thinking about projects. The two sides of the opposition inspire one another. One side thinks about the project and the other side gets excited. Being overzealous could be the negative influence. A generally optimistic attitude is the positive influence. Versatility of thought and insightful new ideas are natural qualities. Employment that involves the mind and communication is a good choice.

Sextile and Trine

The intellect and expansion are beneficially aspected. Thoughts are flexible and inspired. Jupiter's vibrancy is supportive to Mercury. A sense of positive buoyancy pervades life. These individuals are good-natured and have a generous intellectual nature.

Mercury in Aspect to Saturn

Conjunction

The intellect and structure are synonymous. Mercury is inquisitive and likes to understand everything. Saturn is a practical and pragmatic influence. These two create a rational appraisal of the world. The astute intellectual faculties of the mind are increased with practical application. The depth of wisdom develops as one reflects on life. If these individuals practice spiritually throughout their lives, profound and practical benefits are realized with this conjunction.

The negative influence is to be stubborn and resist change. When surprised or unsettled, people with this conjunction tend to retreat to a close-minded position. Conservative thought patterns predominate. There is a capacity to debate if time is given for preparation.

This aspect is beneficial for teachers, instructors, and people who work in areas where authority is important. Meditational deities such as Manjushri and Vajrapani work well with both these planets. Exposure to a wide range of teachings would also be beneficial, provided it is done in a gradual, structured manner. The practice of guru yoga could increase inspiration and blessings. Association with a qualified teacher generates self-confidence.

Square

The intellect and a conservative structure stress one another. Mercury's intellectual inquisitiveness is constrained by the fear and insecurity Saturn can generate. Saturn's influence expresses itself either in an introverted or extroverted manner. The introverts may be quiet and withdrawn. This relates particularly to communication ability. They may have trouble talking about how they feel, etc., until a secure feeling arises. The mind anchors itself around its thought processes. The anchor is either an inferiority complex or a negative, critical attitude. The extroverts can express stubborn, close-minded opinions. They are more expressive, but this is tied to a need to control situations. Their fear is expressive of their vulnerability.

The positive manifestation of this aspect can be astute observations. The mind is wise but might become pessimistic easily. Meditations on love and compassion are excellent antidotes to this judgmental and biased influence. Self-esteem and skillful interactions with authority figures are areas to develop.

Opposition

The intellect and conservative views are in opposition. This opposition can stimulate a critical and judgmental attitude. If there is personal pain or unresolved feelings, this influence can create sarcastic negativity about everything. The individual is judgmental and opinionated.

A positive attitude inspires the ability to weigh and judge things according to their merits. The difference between the positive and negative influence is the attitude. The careful cultivation of a positive attitude brings forth profound, disciplined thought.

Sextile and Trine

The intellect and a conservative perspective are well aspected. This aspect is similar to the conjunction between Mercury and Saturn, except that the influence is softened. The power of disciplined thought and the ability to structure ideas benefit one another. The need to be right or in control is not present. Any employment that requires supervisory skill is a good choice.

Mercury in Aspect to Uranus

Conjunction

The intellect and revolution are mixed. Mercury's intellectual influence is made brilliant with this aspect. Uranus is witty and spontaneous. Spiritual individuals may find that Uranus can bestow sudden revelations to intellectual understanding. Brilliant ideas arise spontaneously. This beneficial influence can create people who are genuises. Liberal and independent ideas are generated.

There is a negative effect from this conjunction. If little discipline is applied to study, then the mind can be disorganized. The need to control the impulsive side of Uranus is important in order to bring forth the positive aspects. The practice of quietude meditation techniques is a particularly good choice. They harness the spontaneity of Uranus.

Square

The intellect and revolutionary ideas stress one another. The intellect is in revolution. Positive situations produce brilliant and refreshing conversations. Ideas are flexible and quickly expressed. The negative aspects manifest in stressful or insecure situations when the more chaotic side of Uranus is present. These people may share thoughts that are not coherent and logical. Their thoughts are expressed as a torrent of information. Rash, inappropriate things are said.

This aspect is excellent for appreciating the craziness of samsara. Life is unpredictable. If these people are self-confident, then they are unconventional. When they feel vulnerable, this square generates nervous feelings. They appear jumpy and agitated.

The use of meditation techniques that stress discipline and quietude is the best way to control the chaotic nature of Uranus.

Opposition

The intellect and revolution are opposed. One side of the pendulum swings toward intellectual inquiry and the other toward revolution. This polarity stimulates brilliant discussions. Care must be taken to avoid degenerating into a confused, chaotic presentation of information. The negative effects are scattered thoughts and difficulty with meditation.

The positive influence produces versatile thoughts. There is spontaneous enthusiasm with new ideas. A study of Buddhist dialectics, the skillful use of words in spiritual practice, benefits people with this aspect tremendously. This utilizes the quickness of the mind in a beneficial manner.

Sextile and Trine

The intellect can benefit from the spontaneity of Uranus. Quick-witted and funny dialogue is part of these harmonious aspects. All the individuality and energy of Uranus flows into the intellectual capacity. Review the information regarding the other aspects between Mercury and Uranus to get a broader perspective.

Mercury in Aspect to Neptune

Conjunction

The intellect and the spiritual pole mix. The intelligent, inquisitive influence of Mercury is aided by the imagination and intuition. The mind becomes imaginative. If these individuals meditate regularly, they have no trouble doing visualization practices. Neptune is like an antenna, and the conjunction makes the mind gain intuitive understanding. Dreams can be prophetic and knowledge of other people's thoughts is possible. There is a necessity to differentiate between personal thoughts and the thoughts of other people. It may be a subtle effect, but if this capacity is not developed, one becomes easily confused and influenced. Practices with Manjushri, the Buddha of wisdom, help clarify the profundity of images and ideas that Neptune may generate in this conjunction.

Square

The intellect and the spiritual pole stress one another. The intellect, which influences inquisitiveness and ideas, is spiritual in perspective. The square can make communication difficult. The conversation expands in many directions. There is a broad, imaginative point of view. The worst expression of this influence is scattered, intellectual babbling.

The negative influence particularly affects the intellect with anxiety and fear. The imagination distorts the situation. Neptune is like a camera lens, and in this case it is out of focus.

The beneficial influence produces profound insights into spiritual matters. A deep understanding of psychic experience is possible. These individuals may have visions. Eastern cultures offer more acceptance of this type of activity. The West calls these people dreamers. Their ability to see things from different points of view is extraordinary. Meditations of calm abiding and quietude are good to eliminate the lack of focus that this aspect can stimulate.

Opposition

The intellect and the spiritual pole are in opposition. One extreme is intellectual inquiry and the other is expansion. The opposition can stimulate profound spiritual thought. The imagination works powerfully on the intellect. Meditative discipline is necessary to control the imaginative side of Neptune. The negative influence causes vague, scattered thoughts with little practical value. The positive influence is the ability to see the larger picture. Vast and profound subjects are understood intuitively. Meditation that emphasizes visualization and ritual benefits those with this polarity.

Sextile and Trine

The harmonious aspects of Neptune to Mercury are similar to the conjunction. The influence is not as strong, but the imaginative and intuitive effects are there.

Mercury in Aspect to Pluto

Conjunction

The intellect and the instinctual pole mix together. Deep physical feeling is mixed with the thoughts and intellect of the individual. This manifests as sincerity and faith as components of intellectual inquiry. The base side of humanity and life can appear vividly with Pluto mixed so directly with Mercury. If no effort is made to develop a spiritual perspective, banal and mundane thoughts may predominate. A good attitude stimulates empathy and caring. These individuals might not express their feelings openly, but if they do, it can be an extraordinarily heartfelt expression.

Square

The intellect and the instinctual pole stress one another. A square between these planets means that moods and deep feelings stress the mind. The effect often manifests as a quiet and shy individual. These people have the ability to see the dark and instinctual side of life. It is not easy for them to open up and talk about hurtful experiences. This depth can be beneficial in understanding suffering and feeling empathy. Empathy turns into depression if some element of detachment is not available. These individuals do not rebound from emotional wounds quickly. It might take them several years to recover from emotionally stressful events such as a death or the break-up of a relationship. Their feelings transform slowly.

Positive settings engender sincerity and faithfulness. Relationships are taken seriously. A commitment to help another person will not be forgotten for many years.

Opposition

The intellect and the instinctual pole are at opposite sides of the chart. The one side is intellectual inquiry and the other is instinct. This is a polarity between the mind and physical feelings. The belief in an ideal may be overemphasized. The body and mood affect the intellect. There is quiet and heartfelt discussion. Moodiness and dark thoughts are promoted if the attitude is negative.

A positive attitude understands people empathetically. This aspect is excellent for healers and caregivers. Meditations on altruism, love, and compassion are a positive expression of this opposition.

Sextile and Trine

The intellect and the instinctual pole are well aspected. Deep feeling is mixed with the thought patterns of the individual. This stimulates great sincerity. Faith in spiritual teaching can be strong. These individuals can understand the deeper meaning of the Tantras, and meditations dealing with the body will be easily realized. Some natives may need to be careful not to emphasize the base side of humanity. A good attitude ensures that empathy and caring will be strong. These people will not be overly expressive of what they feel, but they do understand themselves in a much deeper manner than most.

Venus in Aspect to Mars

Conjunction

Sensuality and willpower mix together. Determination is added to the pursuit of pleasure. Vibrant displays of passion are possible, both emotionally and artistically. The sexual feelings are strong and healthy.

The negative aspect of this conjunction is indulgence and lust. These responses are a product of selfishness. That can be changed if a compassionate sensitivity toward others is increased. This aspect does not support an austere style of spiritual practice, which could lead to suppression and frustration. A more productive spiritual practice might be enlightened hedonism. That is defined as sharing pleasure with others. It is considered more positive because it is not self-indulgent. The desire to give and receive pleasure comes from this aspect. The practice of Tantra is an excellent choice. The placement of Venus is important to determine where fulfillment and satisfaction can be found. Mars facilitates that attainment, and thus they benefit each other.

Square

Sensuality and willpower are stressfully aspected. The sensuality of Venus relates to the sense objects to find pleasure and satisfaction from that interplay. Willpower adds stress to the process and urges the pursuit of pleasure. Stressful occasions can manifest as indulgence and selfishness. There could be a lack of proportion and understanding of when to stop the search for pleasure. Sexually these individuals are enthusiastic, but again they could extend their desire beyond appropriate levels. The sensual and pleasurable side of life is stressed by strong desire.

Positive environments enhance joy and affectionate interplay. These people can be fun to be around. This aspect could be used beneficially when it is coupled with an altruistic attitude. It then expresses love and relatedness without a deluded, self-centered grasping. Spiritual teachers say it is easier to use attachment to benefit others than aversion. If this aspect is present, it might be useful to develop an attitude of sharing and compassion to ensure that the positive components manifest.

Opposition

Sensuality and willpower are in opposition. This aspect stimulates strong affection and sexuality. The two planets bring forth a vigorous sensual interplay with the world. The will to do things stimulates sensual activity, or conversely any attractive object generates the desire to interact with it. A negative influence of this aspect is indulgence in sensual pleasures. The positive influence is to have active affection. This positive influence stimulates the wish for others to be happy. Generosity is easily felt with this aspect.

Sextile and Trine

The sextile and trine aspects are similar to the conjunction, but the urge to be sensual is not as strong. The tendency is to have a healthy expression of sensuality and love. When the willpower motivates action, Venus' grace is present.

Venus in Aspect to Jupiter

Conjunction

Sensuality and expansion mix together. The expansion and enthusiasm of Jupiter increases the sensual activity that Venus influences. The sense doors are alive and awake. There is a love for vivid experiences. The general expression of love and affection is easy. A conjunction is a strong aspect and there is a need to be aware of sensual extravagance. This aspect takes sensuality beyond a general appreciation to an expanded enjoyment of it.

When conjunct, these planets make the spiritual practice of altruism natural. Artistic expression and the enjoyment of beauty are increased. Generosity, both physical and emotional, is part of this expression.

Square

Sensuality and expansion are in stressful aspect. The optimism and enthusiasm of Jupiter affects the sensual realm and can create agitation and dissatisfaction. There is excitement on a sensual level. This aspect is pleasant for relationships. The positive effect is to be fun loving. The negative influence may be bothersome because of the need for constant stimulation. The negative effects are more apparent if one tries to meditate. The mind does not settle quickly. Buddha said that humans are in the realm of desire. He based this statement on the activity of the five sense doors and the distraction that these create. This astrological aspect heightens that distraction.

People with this aspect can easily benefit others out of goodwill and affection. There is enthusiasm to help others. Overwork and excessive stimulation are obstacles to working comfortably with compassion. Exhaustion inhibits productive activity.

Opposition

Sensuality and expansion are in opposition. The sense doors— eyes, ears, nose, tongue, and body—are stimulated by expansion, optimism, and enthusiasm. There is a swing between exciting possibilities and pleasure. The opposition of Jupiter and Venus enhances sensual data. These individuals could be motivated to do many tasks. The inspiration relates to affection and warmth. Their desire to appreciate beauty is heightened, but their desire to have fun may create a problem. People with this aspect are playful and may not limit themselves to only a little fun. A sense of proportion and balance can prevent overstimulation.

Sextile and Trine

All the beauty and grace of Venus unites with these two as- pects. The goodwill and generosity of Jupiter abound. Even in difficult situations there is the option to be graceful. The emo- tional temperament is affectionate. The attitude of these indi- viduals plays a key role in how this aspect might manifest. People with a negative attitude cannot use this influence as successfully as those with a positive attitude. Positive feelings are in harmony with the expansive love astrologically present here.

Venus in Aspect to Saturn

Conjunction

Sensuality and conservative feelings combine. Saturn tends to structure things in its desire to have security and reliability. Venus' affection and love are made practical. Relationships tend to be durable and long term. A short relationship may not be comfortable. There is a preference for structure in the relationship, and the partner has to be reliable. The negative manifestation of this influence might be to cling too tightly to a relationship. These emotional responses come from a negative attitude and insecurity. If the negative attitude is strong, there are many problems with expectations of the partner or friends.

Positive expression of this aspect means that artistic capacity may be lost somewhat because of the realism that Saturn demands of the sensual world. Long-term artistic projects and beautiful art pieces are appreciated. A balanced attitude fosters wise love. Expectations about love and relationships are reasonable. There is a gradual growth into a relationship, and once the warmth is established, it can last a lifetime.

Square

Sensuality and conservative structure are stressfully aspected. This aspect manifests in two ways. Introverted individuals may feel insecure about expressing love and affection. This can extend to any pleasurable activity. They are uncomfortable with sensuality and pull back from the activity. Relationships tend to develop slowly. Once established, these individuals may experience strong grasping because of fear of loss. These people can even stop expressing affection because they fear vulnerability.

The extroverts have a more demanding expression. They may flirt and be quite showy with others. If they look deeper into their motivation, it can reveal a sense of insecurity pervading all actions. This insecurity stimulates them to flirt to generate the feeling that they are loved. Once a relationship is established, people with this aspect can demand stability from the partner. Expectations are high and the extrovert expresses displeasure avidly. Both introverts and extroverts respond to the basic feeling of insecurity.

It is important for people with a Venus-Saturn square to differentiate between feelings of warmth and a sense of insecurity. The two do not need to be mixed. The confusion lies in projecting personal insecurity onto another. If personal feelings can be limited to the individual arena, there is a better capacity to avoid confusion. The positive side of this aspect is to be practical and pragmatic about love and relationships. There can be great wisdom with any aspect to Saturn. The wisdom needs a reflective capacity as the foundation on which to build a wise, thoughtful nature.

Opposition

Sensuality and the desire for control are in opposition. The pendulum swings between sensual rapport and conservatism. This aspect affects the expression of attachment. The general motive in a relationship issue is fear and judgment. The need for security in a love relationship is strong. The worst effect of this square is to be controlling or manipulative due to fear. Both cases have fear as the motivator.

The positive manifestation is reliable stability in relationships due to a realistic attitude about love and attachment. Saturn can bestow great wisdom, and here Saturn bestows deep wisdom to the heart. This wisdom learns to balance the feelings of personal security and the right of the loved one to self-expression.

Sextile and Trine

Saturn and Venus in these harmonious aspects produce a sense of stability in life and love. The wisdom of Saturn benefits the affection of Venus. A practical wisdom pervades sensual activity.

Venus in Aspect to Uranus

Conjunction

Sensuality and revolution mix. Uranus tends to inspire spontaneity wherever it is placed in the natal chart. This aspect generates an incredibly strong sense of free expression in areas where love is felt. Love for one individual tends to spread and be expressed to everyone. The feelings of love tend to explode outwardly into the world. This aspect can produce playful and artistic qualities. The art may be nontraditional but will have individual charm. Spontaneous love toward others and short-term affairs could be a common occurrence.

There can be the feeling that love is unreliable and attraction is felt for all the wrong people. These people may feel like they are victims of chaotic relationships. Problems result if they are not extroverted enough to deal with Uranus' spontaneous stimulation. If these individuals are self-confident and kindhearted, they can express their love liberally. Tantra works well with this conjunction. The Anutara Yoga Tantras of Heruka Chakrasambhara and Vajrayogini are excellent practices. These deities deal with the transformation of lust and desire into a spiritual path to enlightenment.

Square

Sensuality and revolution stress one another. Relationships become chaotic. The need for freedom in love and affection is strong. These people may fall in love suddenly and then end the affair just as quickly. A prolonged relationship seems unsatisfying. Independence and unpredictable spontaneity might negatively affect relationships. Another negative aspect of this square is the possibility of feeling like they are the victim of bad relationships. These people may attract interesting but unreliable people. They try their best in relationships, but things develop unpredictably.

Artists and people in theater find this aspect stimulating. Their sensuality is free-spirited. The artists can produce exceptionally interesting art forms through whatever medium they choose. The actors are exciting to be around. Friends and associates become exhausted after several days of interaction with such individuals.

The beneficial effect of this aspect harmonizes with the practice of Tantra provided an altruistic attitude is in place. The altruism hinders hurtful action. The individual is free-spirited.

Opposition

Sensuality and revolution are polarized. People with a Venus-Uranus opposition are lively and fun to be around. Unexpected demonstrations of love and playfulness are common. The negative influence is to be too independent in relationships. The worst influence is to fall in love rashly and experience chaos when working out the details. The opposition could make these people nervous about love affairs if they are insecure.

Sextile and Trine

The positive manifestation of this influence is a liberated heart. The sensual doors are inspired with a sense of freedom. A balance between freedom and love stimulates playfulness and joy. This aspect is particularly beneficial to Tantric practice as the transcendental components of love and lovemaking can be obvious when mixing Uranus with an enlightened Tantric attitude.

Venus in Aspect to Neptune

Conjunction

Sensuality and the spiritual pole are together. This aspect brings forth the true romantic. The imaginative and intuitive aspects of Neptune influence the sensual realms. Love is a spiritual and nonphysical experience. This produces pleasure in the anticipation and atmosphere of a love affair. The actual physical act of lovemaking may not interest these individuals as much as a beautiful candlelit dinner.

The negative expression of this influence is to daydream about a relationship rather than establish one. This aspect can make these people shy and vague, and unable to manifest or articulate their feelings.

The other side of this influence is the spiritual dimensions of love. Love transcends to the ultimate level of reality. Meditation can produce a profound experience of being at one with the universe. The imagination works well with affection and pleasure.

Neptune also lets these people intuitively know that others are attracted to them. The only problem with this aspect is the lack of physical ground for Venus to stand on. There is a need for pragmatic reflection to settle the cosmic spaciousness of Neptune.

Square

Sensuality and the spiritual pole stress one another. The sensitivity of Neptune is like the lens of a camera that enlarges whatever it has in focus. The lens can be out of focus with the square angle. The perceptions can be false and illusory. Expectations in relationships may never be met. People with this aspect might be romantic but possibly impractical in manifesting authentic love. The worst manifestation of this influence is to ignore the lover or feel suspicious of his or her actions. Sensitivity and imagination stress one another.

A positive and grounded attitude inspires spiritual affection. The individual could be a lover of the universe. Altruistic feelings and devotion to a spiritual mentor can be strong. The main cause of the positive influence is a realistic attitude that keeps the imagination in check.

Opposition

Sensuality and the spiritual pole are opposite one another. Imagination and sensuality are at opposite ends of the pendulum. The swing moves between a broad perspective and form, sound, smell, taste, and touch. This is a good aspect for artists and spiritual people. The imagination and intuition work together to increase physical sensitivity.

The negative aspect causes these individuals to have difficulty expressing love. Under Neptune's influence, they daydream too much and do not tell their partner the details of how they feel. The other side of the spectrum is idealized love with no practical application. The feelings of love are mixed with the hope of finding the ultimate soul mate. These people tend to be impractical.

The positive influence comes from a balanced attitude. Spiritual practices can open the heart and reveal the nature of love. The main issue is a balanced and realistic attitude.

Sextile and Trine

Sensitivity and affection work together. Venus benefits with spiritual insight. A graceful and refined approach can express through the imagination. Artists, writers, and poets gain deep access to beauty and express this in their work. Spiritual individuals can sense the emotional temperament of friends. All the imagination and intuition of Neptune harmonizes with the sensual affection of Venus.

Venus in Aspect to Pluto

Conjunction

Sensuality and the instinctual pole are one. Pluto gravitates toward the body's response to situations. The affection and love of Venus mix with Pluto and the body. Falling in love is a physical event. Love is experienced at a biological or cellular level. To love and to feel a strong attraction and attachment are synonymous. Pluto's influence can generate strong attachments in long-term associations other people. A balance for this is regular meditation on impermanence. The main problem is that attachment and craving are strong. If the attitude is unrealistic, the problems escalate. Generally, love and affection are deep, sincere, and long lasting.

Body intuition is part of Pluto's influence. It can assist the ability to heal others. Buddhist meditations with White Tara, the Medicine Buddha, and Amitayus are good practices to increase the healing ability.

Square

Sensuality and the instinctual pole are stressed. Deep physical feelings generated by Pluto move toward attachment and clinging. Care is necessary with substances that give pleasure such as drugs and alcohol. There is a tendency to become physically addicted easily.

Strong relationships form as the individuals get to know one another. If the relationship fails, this square creates suffering attachments. Attachment is felt as a physical sensation in the body. These people could be sexually demanding if they are insensitive. Depression and melancholy are common with a separation or loss of a loved one.

People with this aspect can give tremendous support to others in positive environments. Dedication and love are deep. The sincerity may be overstated, but it accurately matches their level of dedication and feeling.

Opposition

Sensuality and the instinctual pole are opposite one another. This opposition can stimulate a strong love with deep physical feelings. The pendulum can swing from the body's need for love and a committed relationship to the other extreme of experiencing powerful, magnetic attractions to beautiful objects and people.

The negative manifestation of this influence is attachment and little peace of mind. The sexual response is strong. This is because the body and the sense doors bounce off one another. To fall in love is to feel it on a physical level. Buddhism recommends meditations reflecting on personal impermanence to diminish the negative effects of Pluto's attachment.

Under the positive influence of this opposition, these people make their friends feel warm and sincerely loved. Deep faith in the Dharma and a strong connection to the teacher are part of Pluto's effect.

Sextile and Trine

The remaining harmonious aspects are similar but weaker in expression than the conjunction and opposition. Review those sections and look at the more beneficial components of the influence. Essentially, love and faith are sincere.

Mars in Aspect to Jupiter

Conjunction

Willpower and expansion are mixed together. The determination and capacity of Mars is complemented by Jupiter's sense of enthusiasm and optimism. Abundant energy manifests in all activities. The more possibilities are seen in a project, the more powerful is the attempt to do the work. This aspect could make the person a workaholic. There is a great tendency to be enthusiastic about everything.

Engaged Buddhists could utilize these planets well. Their vision is to help others, and this conjunction inspires goodwill and generosity. Meditations that clarify good intention are helpful to ensure a positive direction. Meditations to enhance peacefulness and release stress are important to avoid becoming a workaholic.

Square

Willpower and expansion stress one another. Mars' desire to accomplish activities is extended beyond what is practical. People with this aspect have a strong tendency to be workaholics. They are always busy. Some individuals might feel easily agitated and, although positively motivated, become exhausted quickly. This aspect creates difficulties for long, quiet sessions of meditation. These individuals may find it more beneficial to set up daily meditation sessions than to do long retreats. The desire to be active can be overstimulated with this aspect.

Opposition

Willpower and expansion are in opposition. This opposition can make these people extremely energized and enthusiastic. The swings of the pendulum are between planets of a similar nature. The willfulness of Mars and the optimism of Jupiter complement one another. The worst influence here is to rush into things rashly. The positive influence manifests as the desire to act and assist. Engaged spiritual practice is an excellent direction to choose. Finding a balance between the expenditure of energy and peacefulness is necessary.

Sextile and Trine

Willpower and expansion are well aspected. The willpower and capacity of Mars is complemented by Jupiter's enthusiasm. These individuals feel optimistic about the work they undertake. The more excited they feel about the job at hand, the more new possibilities they can see. This aspect could make a person a workaholic. As Jupiter tends to be a beneficial influence, there is a tendency to just be excited about projects. The Mahayana style of Buddhist practice, being an engaged practitioner, would be an excellent expression for these harmoniously aspected planets.

Mars in Aspect to Saturn

Conjunction

Willpower and a conservative nature combine. Mars is capable of great accomplishments. Saturn is practical and slow moving. This conjunction works to the advantage of the individual. A measured pace for work and the ability to make long-term commitments is present. The influence of Saturn, being conservative and disliking insecurity, could initially make these people slow at starting tasks. They may wish to control projects and can be disciplinarians. They might become stubborn if they feel insecure.

The positive expression of Saturn is to be steadfast and hardworking. These people become steady and reliable members of spiritual groups. They are consistent in meditation practice.

Square

Willpower and a conservative approach stress one another. Mars' desire to accomplish activities is complicated by Saturn's desire for security and control. This aspect influences these individuals to seek positions of authority to avoid stress. The problems can increase and cause greater suffering to both themselves and others if the workload is too great. People with this square desire to avoid errors, which may make it difficult for affairs to progress smoothly.

A negative environment causes Saturn to be insecure. It seeks to protect itself. Mars' desire to do things stimulates Saturn to overuse control factors. Stubborn attitudes and fear paralyze activity.

A positive environment and attitude changes most of the negative effects of this square. These individuals take their responsibilities seriously and therefore can attain great goals. It is good to undertake tasks that proceed in a slow and progressive manner. It is best to avoid the tendency to judge others. Meditations with love and compassion help diminish anxiety and frustration, which are part of a Mars-Saturn square.

Opposition

Willpower and control are polar opposites. The pendulum swings between willfulness of action and practical application. The positive manifestation of this influence is the accomplishment of activities. The practical and pragmatic approach of Saturn controls the activity of Mars.

The worst influence of this aspect is to be a control freak. The negative influence comes from insecurity around activities. A lack of personal security, self-control, and self-esteem generates the fear and anxiety that Saturn hates. A positive attitude, in contrast, creates an excellent ability to judge situations. This aspect, when matched with a compassionate attitude, makes the individual a good supervisor.

Sextile and Trine

Willpower and control benefit one another. These two aspects create a dedicated worker. The determination to accomplish tasks supports the willpower, and vice versa.

Mars in Aspect to Uranus

Conjunction

Mars and Uranus, as fire planets, are full of energy and spontaneity. The conjunction inspires optimistic activity. The negative side of this influence has the greatest impact in an environment that is competitive and uncompassionate. Love and compassion are the best opponents to this aggressive influence. Meditation is an excellent way to control this fiery energy. Active physical forms of meditation like tai chi and yoga are also beneficial to practice on a daily basis.

This conjunction produces the self-starter. These people work best on their own and can move quickly to accomplish tasks. If working with others is necessary, then finding those of a similar nature is the best option. These people are able to work well into the night when others are exhausted. This is why it is beneficial to be independent and self-motivated.

It may take some time for meditation practice to slow the impulsive enthusiasm of this aspect. There is a need to develop self-control and discipline. These people could have an aggressive sexual manner. Buddhism suggests that individuals with this aspect might practice wrathful Tantric deities well. An engaged style of spiritual practice is also beneficial. People with this conjunction have powerful energy (chi) and could turn that force toward healing and energy work.

Square

Willpower and revolution are stressed. The desire to accomplish tasks is strong with Mars and the square makes action impulsive and reckless. There is a need to pause before initiating an activity. The most negative expression of this influence is sudden rage. Individuals can be jumpy and easily startled because of the pressure that Uranus exerts. They could also have an aggressive sexual manner.

A positive environment supports dynamic motivation. The willpower and sense of freedom complement one another. There is a need to slow down when excitement or pressure is felt. Quietude meditations help pacify the rash side of this square.

Opposition

Willpower and revolution are opposed. These two planets have similar energy, and the opposition generates lively interactions. This can make some people not rest until they are exhausted. The worst expression of this influence is uncontrolled anger and rash aggression.

A positive effect is incredible flexibility. There is a spontaneous capacity to deal with issues. Meditation practices that work with energy (chi) will be easily realized. Although the energy is strong, the ability to work with it requires some training. Chi gong and tai chi are excellent training techniques.

Sextile and Trine

Mars and Uranus work together well. Their elemental nature is the same: fire. The harmonious aspects merge these two planets together to create a positive expression of power. Uranus is liberal and free of constraints. Mars acts with decisiveness. These two aspects manifest a sense of free will that is fearless. Even if these individuals are not self-confident, their actions demonstrate an energetic, self-expressive nature.

Mars in Aspect to Neptune

Conjunction

Willpower and the imagination are conjunct. The capacity and determination of Mars loses some of its power with this aspect. Neptune likes to be open-minded. Actions can have an intuitive quality. The right thing is done at the correct moment. The intuitive component manifests best when there is no pressure to finish. Neptune likes a grand picture or a vista rather than the little details immediately before it. Mars likes clearly defined tasks and may feel vague and lost in this conjunction. The imagination works with ideas and possibilities. The spiritual dimensions of this conjunction are good. Consciousness is strengthened. These people have a strong ability to meditate and direct consciousness willfully. Healing is a profession they might consider provided the Moon and Pluto are well aspected.

Square

Willpower and the spiritual pole mystify one another. The desire to accomplish tasks, a Mars activity, is undermined by the imagination of Neptune. Neptune acts like the lens of a camera that is out of focus. The lens distorts the image and the willpower cannot act decisively. These individuals may waver on decisions and worry about what to do. Intuition may be distorted into superstition as the imagination becomes impulsive with Mars energy.

If the mind becomes unclear, the imagination wastes time and daydreams. Regular quietude meditation diminishes the negative effect of this square. A clear, focused mind controls and limits the distortion of Neptune.

Opposition

Willpower and the spiritual pole are opposed. This opposition undermines the initiation of activities. Neptune inspires daydreaming and fantasies, thus taking away the dynamic energy of Mars. The worst aspect of this influence is procrastination and an inability to act on inspiration.

A benefit of this aspect can be a rich imagination. If Mars has at least one complementary aspect to it from another planet, the beneficial influences apply. If there are no aspects to Mars other than this opposition, there is a necessity to avoid idle fantasy. The conscious awareness is the filter that stops mindless daydreaming.

Sextile and Trine

The intuition leads any action. Neptune brings a component of spiritual or imaginative insight to the willfulness of Mars. Sensitivity in action is a byproduct of these harmonious angles.

Mars in Aspect to Pluto

Conjunction

Willpower and the instinctual pole are conjunct. This aspect creates a powerful dynamic with any activity. This applies even more when faith is involved. Pluto, which is related to temperament and mood, mixes directly with willpower and determination. Faith in what one does translates into powerful activities. That response applies naturally when the activity warrants a heartfelt response. The stronger the belief in the activity, the stronger the determination.

This aspect could make the person fanatical. Pluto is not an intellectual planet and it tends to drive Mars into action without thought. When the activity is balanced with an open-minded attitude, then the person has the capacity to achieve great things. Meditation practices with the nerve channels and energy are experienced with little effort. Healing arts like massage therapy are a good choice of profession. Whatever profession is chosen, the blessing of drive and determination comes forth.

Square

Willpower and the instinctual pole are stressed. Mars generates enthusiastic action and Pluto inspires deep feelings. This square may create strong compulsion. A negative situation creates the potential for anger. There may be a refusal to see the hopelessness of a situation. Awareness needs to manage the aggressive desire to get jobs finished. Sexual enthusiasm is strong, but it can be overbearing and demanding on the partner.

There is a need to be careful with drugs and alcohol. The body and desire are stressed, thus craving becomes a problem. Illnesses like high blood pressure are common with this aspect. Anger can also negatively affect the body. This is according to Tibetan medicine. These people may be assertive about what they want to do; therefore, adopting the right attitude is important to ensure happiness. Compassion counterbalances the power of this square.

Opposition

Willpower and the instinctual pole are in opposition. The pendulum swings between willfulness and instinct. Pluto relates to deep physical feelings and sits opposite to willpower and determination. These two planets are complementary because they are action-oriented. Pluto adds sincerity and depth of feeling to the activity of Mars. An imbalance between willfulness and deep conviction might create an overzealous attitude. The desire can be strong, forceful, or manipulative. The individual gradually learns balance and how to manage strong personal energy. There can also be problems with deep anger. Pluto and Mars need a compassionate and patient attitude to avoid emotional intensity.

Sextile and Trine

Depth of feeling and willpower assist one another. Any activity that involves a component of faith is powerfully accomplished. Mars and Pluto help each other with determination and self-confidence.

Jupiter in Aspect to Saturn

Conjunction

Expansion and a conservative nature combine. Jupiter's joy and enthusiasm benefits Saturn's competence. Saturn dislikes quick action; it can be a perfectionist and does things slowly. Saturn slows down the energy and generosity of Jupiter. Saturn and Jupiter conjunct can make an excellent organizer. A negative manifestation of this influence is to be fussy about details. This depends on the attitude and is not directly the product of the conjunction. Jupiter tends to be uplifted and joyful, so the attitude has to create a negative framework to bring out the negative side. This individual's life is most likely well organized and successful because of this beneficial aspect.

Square

Expansion and conservative structure stress one another. The optimism of Jupiter is complicated by a desire for security. Jupiter's goodwill and generosity is dominated by Saturn's wish to control. This is because Saturn exercises more influence than Jupiter. Often this square makes people stubborn and fearful if their associates and friends move too fast. Problems revolve around being fussy and overly concerned with details.

Positive settings help people with this aspect become efficient. These individuals take their responsibilities seriously and therefore can attain great goals. Generally it is good to undertake tasks that are worked on slowly and progressively. The attitude has to be confident enough to balance the stress of control issues. Saturn's wisdom can help these individuals avoid the tendency to control others when it combines with Jupiter's expansive, holistic view of life. The beneficial influence of this square is developed with a good heart, love, and compassion.

Opposition

Expansion and control are in opposition. One side of the pendulum is optimistic and the other is pragmatic. This aspect can be skillful in all activities. The practical and pragmatic approach of Saturn balances the expansiveness and generosity of Jupiter. The worst expression of this influence is to be domineering. The negative influence comes from insecurity. The need to control things can dominate. If the person is aware of the insecurity, then this opposition becomes a great asset. There is an excellent ability to judge situations and to work efficiently. A person with this aspect when matched with a compassionate attitude makes a good supervisor.

Sextile and Trine

Jupiter and Saturn benefit each other with these two harmonious aspects. Structure is added to joyful enthusiasm. The effect is similar to a conjunction, just not as strong an influence.

Jupiter in Aspect to Uranus

Conjunction

Expansion and revolution are mixed. The enthusiasm of Jupiter increases with the spontaneity of Uranus. Jupiter, Uranus, and Mars have similar effects. All of these planets stimulate an expression of energy. The influence of a Uranus-Jupiter conjunction differs from that of a Mars-Jupiter conjunction because Jupiter becomes excitable. Care must be taken to recognize the signs of failure or a bad decision because individuals with this aspect tend to rush forward without foresight. They may confuse impulsiveness with joy or pleasure. In positive situations, people with this aspect are excellent motivators. Negative situations cause hyper and excitable activity. This conjunction generally stimulates optimism.

Square

Expansion and revolution are stressed. The optimism of Jupiter is strong with Uranus in this aspect, and that can contribute to a reckless approach. There is a need to pause before initiating action. The most negative expression of this influence is exploding energetically. One pursues a goal with no foresight. Meditation and self-awareness are excellent tools to manage this spontaneous enthusiasm.

Positive environments help people with this aspect motivate themselves and others energetically. Their optimism is complemented by the freedom that Uranus bestows. Mental exercises like counting to ten or taking three deep breaths before starting on a new venture are beneficial. There is a need to slow down when excitement or pressure is felt. Tai chi and yoga are good exercises to do regularly. These exercises help balance the physical and mental energies.

Opposition

Expansion and revolution are polar opposites. The swing of the pendulum moves between two similar planets, both of which revolve around energetic optimism. The negative manifestation of this influence is rash or impulsive action. The person gets too excited about personal interests. There is a need to control energy and action. Self-awareness and mindfulness are excellent tools to establish the balance between these two planets. Tai chi and yoga are also useful tools.

Sextile and Trine

Jupiter and Uranus harmonize with each other. The planets involved in trine and sextile aspects normally work well together. If there are any negative effects, a negative or unskillful attitude has to be the instigator. The positive expression of these two aspects is joy. The negative expression could be excitability, which is a lack of mindfulness regarding physical and emotional energy.

Jupiter in Aspect to Neptune

Conjunction

Expansion and the spiritual pole mix together. The expansive quality of Jupiter increases the intuition and imagination. This conjunction has a strong effect on Neptune. The dream life may be elaborate, and during meditations the mind could generate expansive visualizations. This aspect basically increases all the psychic, intuitive, and imaginative qualities.

A negative effect of this influence can be daydreaming, but with the discipline of a good meditation technique there can be more benefit than harm. The issue is having an imagination that is so active that the person is distracted. When stress is experienced, people with this conjunction can become superstitious. There needs to be a strong component of fear for these individuals to experience this, as Jupiter tends to have abundant goodwill. Artists who work for advertisement agencies do well with this conjunction. Their intuition is responsive and adaptable to the movements of society.

Square

Expansion and the spiritual pole are in a stressful relationship. People with this aspect tend to be imaginative in an unproductive manner. Their intuition is overactive. Stressful situations cause anxiety. The imagination becomes negative and creates fearful scenarios. The flight of imagination goes in a negative direction. Positive environments stimulate well-being and expansive openness. The ideas may appear unrealistic, but the motivation is optimistic. If regular meditation is practiced, this square stimulates a strong visualization capacity and dream life.

Opposition

Expansion and the spiritual pole are opposed. The enthusiastic quality of Jupiter expands intuition and imagination. A balance may exist with mindfulness that limits speculation and unrealistic optimism. Saturn, if well aspected to these planets, assists with practical wisdom. If Saturn is not in aspect, the control has to come from personal awareness.

Sextile and Trine

Neptune and Jupiter work together in these two aspects. The imagination is blessed with a positive enthusiasm. Versatility of perception is part of the influence. Jupiter creates positive visions with Neptune's assistance.

Jupiter in Aspect to Pluto

Conjunction

Expansion and the instinctual pole combine. The joy, enthusiasm, and optimism of Jupiter lighten up the mood and deep feelings of Pluto. This aspect gives these people a happy temperament about life. Their deep feelings are expanded and generous with Jupiter's good influence. The body may heal itself vigorously. Pluto is enhanced by positive energy. This type of conjunction can give the ability to heal others. Buddhist meditations with White Tara, the Medicine Buddha, and Amitayus are good practices if the person pursues a healing profession.

Square

Expansion and the instinctual pole are stressed. Jupiter is enthusiastic and full of goodwill, and this square does not generally stimulate moodiness or depression. It does make the body elements vigorous and could cause illness instead. The Tibetan medical point of view says that the body responds to strong emotional stimulation and excitement. This square can easily throw the energy (chi), phlegm, and bile humors out of balance. Jupiter, as an air planet, has a relationship with energy (chi). The energy illnesses gain a foothold if the body is cold or subjected to extensive fasting or diets. Quietude meditation can benefit the strong energy created by these two planets.

Opposition

Expansion and the instinctual pole are in opposition. This aspect generally indicates a happy temperament. Deep feelings are expanded and generous with Jupiter's positive influence. Jupiter in any aspect tends to uplift the expression of the particular planet. Jupiter and Pluto combined can support a more positive mood and motivation. One is open to expansive ideas and can easily translate new information into positive action. A negative component of this aspect can manifest as fervent beliefs that lack wisdom. There is less interference from intense emotions provided that the person is reflective or contemplative.

Sextile and Trine

The joy of Jupiter lightens the deep feelings of Pluto. These two aspects consistently generate happy feelings.

Saturn in Aspect to Uranus

Conjunction

Conservative structure and revolution combine. The practical and structured influence of Saturn receives a boost from Uranian spontaneity. Uranus' independent, unpredictable, and spontaneous influence integrates with Saturn's conservative nature. This conjunction brings fresh innovation to old, established modes of operation and fosters strong character. The individual has opinions and principles. There is a tendency toward self-employment or work as an independent agent. The ability to be a supervisor is strong. Meditation has a dynamic force behind it. Tantric deities that embody majesty and authority are excellent choices for meditation.

Square

Conservative structure and revolution stress one another. The personal sense of character may appear unbalanced. Negative environments stimulate Saturn to become insecure and seek protection. Uranus adds to this with an impulsive desire for independence. The individual's opinions may differ intensely from the consensus. A stubborn attitude and fear could perpetuate difficult interactions with others. There is a need for awareness to identify the feelings that underlie the negativity and release it.

A positive attitude helps change the dynamics of this square. People with this aspect can accomplish great tasks because they have personal motivation. Their character is strong and positive, which impresses others. Self-employment or a job with little supervision are the best choices. Quietude meditation can help these people understand the high level of personal expectation this aspect may generate.

Opposition

A conservative feeling opposes revolution. This aspect is similar to the harmonious ones, except that a balance needs to be found between control and spontaneity. This balance is found by realizing the power that one possesses. Saturn is a strong steady planet and Uranus is an independently minded planet. These two together or in opposition are similar in that they create a definite sense of character. A compassionate attitude helps soften the intensity that a Saturn-Uranus aspect stimulates.

Sextile and Trine

The power of self-determination manifests with these two harmonious aspects. One may feel empowered with self-confidence in the areas symbolized by the houses in which these planets reside.

Saturn in Aspect to Neptune

Conjunction

Conservative structure and the spiritual pole mix. Saturn, with a tendency toward pragmatism and security, diminishes the imaginative and intuitive qualities of Neptune. The intuition is still there, but an inner voice comments about any intuitive or imaginative subject. This counsel presents a limited version of the vision. It is important to avoid generating a close-minded attitude because if Saturn feels insecure, it shuts down spiritual input.

A positive attitude joined with this aspect is excellent for regular meditation practice. There is no wish to go beyond practical spiritual principles. A reasonable and just approach manifests. The wisdom of Saturn is increased by the perceptiveness of Neptune. This conjunction creates a resource base of wisdom when the individual reaches maturity.

Square

Conservative views and the spiritual pole are stressed. The conservative and practical nature of Saturn tones down the imaginative influence of Neptune. This aspect can manifest as a skeptical and judgmental point of view. This is because a squared Saturn tends toward a pessimistic perspective. Saturn mixed with a negative attitude stimulates a belittling and mean influence. The other expression of Saturn's influence is to be skeptical of spiritual insight, thus limiting the beneficial effects. For example, if a satori realization is experienced, there may be doubt that such an experience even happened. The mind is negatively inquisitive.

A positive environment can produce an astute investigative quality. There can be deep spiritual inquiry with this square. Saturn is a wisdom planet. This aspect can support the development of a spiritually altruistic attitude. The compassion is levelheaded.

Opposition

A conservative influence is opposite the spiritual pole. These two planets are dissimilar in that Saturn likes to be in control and Neptune is open-minded and easygoing. Saturn generally tends to be the stronger influence in an opposition. It is skeptical and judgmental. The perceptiveness of Neptune is used by Saturn to observe what takes place. The balance between these two planets can be found with meditations on love and compassion. These meditations soften the hard and calculating side of Saturn and increase the beneficial influence of Neptune.

Sextile and Trine

These two aspects reinforce and deepen the potential for Neptune's spiritual expression. Practical magic is created. Realism pervades spiritual insights. Saturn's wisdom deepens with a meditative lifestyle. Meditation also strengthens the imaginative and intuitive abilities. These are excellent aspects for therapists and psychologists. A mature individual with either of these harmonious aspects is a wonderful source of wisdom.

Saturn in Aspect to Pluto

Conjunction

Conservative structure and the instinctual pole blend together. Saturn is inclined toward a calm, collected approach to life. Pluto's realm of influence is mood and temperament, and Saturn in this conjunction stimulates emotional reliability. There is slow movement on anything that requires an emotional response. The outer appearance may seem sedate. The wisdom of Saturn inspires a calm nature.

Occasionally this aspect can cause health issues. The body may respond slowly to healing techniques. The mood and temperament shift slowly. These people have to be patient about the length of recovery that is necessary because their body's energy moves slowly. Astrology is only one component of health. If the body's DNA from the parents is free of defects, then there is little cause for astrologically stimulated illness. Health is the product of many influences, including attitude, diet, lifestyle, and the body's basic nature. People with this placement could work successfully in a healing profession. There is deep physical knowledge available to them.

Square

Conservative feelings and the instinctual pole stress one another. Saturn dislikes insecurity and tends to slow down any planet it aspects. This stressful Saturn square slows the body and mood of the individual. Negative settings can create deep depression and sadness. The body can be negatively affected and not heal quickly. Avoidance of alcohol and drugs is recommended, as the body does not rebound quickly from intoxication. This is especially true of alcohol, which is a depressant.

Care of the body and mind with a positive attitude and good-quality food is important. A more conscious awareness of mood and feelings is necessary. A lack of awareness may facilitate depression. Quietude meditation is excellent to help avoid this problem. Zen meditation could be more beneficial due to its stricter discipline.

Opposition

A conservative feeling opposes the instinctual pole. This aspect is similar to the influence of the conjunction except that the planets are opposed to each other. A need for balance is necessary. The balance is between resistance to change and the feelings of the body. Either extreme creates problems. Saturn does not open up to the deeper feelings, and Pluto never forgets a sad feeling. The balance is found in recognizing the deeper feelings but not dwelling on them. An analytical capacity is available because of Saturn's effect and is excellent for therapists. The desire to overanalyze a feeling must be avoided. These people must be aware of what is transpiring without becoming fixated on something they see. All aspects between Pluto and Saturn indicate that the emotional life moves slowly.

Sextile and Trine

Conservative structure and the instinctual pole are well aspected. Saturn influences the person to make choices that pursue a calm, collected approach to life. Pluto's realm of influence is the moods and deep feelings of the person, so Saturn in a harmonious aspect can bestow a very consistent deeper nature. There will be a tendency to move slowly regarding the emotions. These people may be identified as quiet and sedate when responding to situations. This is merely because their emotional nature moves slowly. They don't let excitement affect them on a deeper level. The wisdom of Saturn will give these individuals an excellent calm nature that will develop as they mature into midlife.

Thirteen

Aspects of the Outer Planets

The outer planets move slowly around the Sun. Uranus takes approximately eighty years to complete the cycle, and Neptune and Pluto take triple that time. This slow movement causes many people to have the same astrological signatures for these planets. Historical trends and themes can be identified by similar events experienced by generations of people who share the same aspects and signatures of the outer planets. These planets interact with the personal planets to create a unique expression within each chart.

Uranus in Aspect to Neptune

Conjunction

Revolution and the spiritual pole are conjunct. The spontaneity of Uranus stimulates the intuition and imagination beneficially. There are flash experiences and perceptions. Zen Buddhism, the school of sudden enlightenment, suits this aspect perfectly. Sudden realizations and profound insights are experienced in a moment of inspiration. Ideas, visions, and insights

appear abruptly. Regular meditation may calm down this effect, but when meditation is initially started, the experiences
can arise in a startling manner. The door to new perceptions
suddenly bursts open.

There are potential negative effects with this conjunction. A
problem lies with understanding the experience after it passes.
Strange and colorful dreams are common. Conversations can
be eccentric and outlandish. There is a need for discipline to
organize consciousness into a structured manner.

A qualified spiritual mentor can assist a person in developing this conjunction. If there is no guidance, the person's experiences may fall by the wayside. This individual has the ability
to spontaneously realize the meaning of something that has
been the source of a long-standing struggle for others.

Square

Revolution and the spiritual pole stress each other. The spontaneity of Uranus stimulates sudden experiences. The problem
is that the experiences have no categories. The square can produce unorthodox visions. The spiritual life may manifest in an
eccentric manner. Strange, indecipherable dreams are common. The negative influence manifests as an alternate perception of reality. The spiritual ideas border on the extreme. There
can be moments of fear and anxiety if situations become stressful. The stress increases imagination and the mind misinter-
prets the event.

The beneficial influences come with discipline applied to
the inner life. A good teacher and education help format the
experiences into something that can be useful. The practice
and discipline of Zen Buddhism is an excellent choice. The discipline establishes an excellent platform for satori experiences.
The essential point is that this square inspires odd visions.

Opposition

Revolution and the spiritual pole are in opposition. The spontaneity of Uranus stimulates intuition and imagination. The pendulum swings between individuality and imagination. This is a positive polarity as Uranus gives life to Neptune's intuition. Problems could come from being too imaginative and therefore unrealistic. Another negative effect is to be nervous and anxious about upcoming events. The imagination is too active.

The solution to most of these negative influences is discipline. Quietude meditations to calm the mind are useful. If there is too much excitement, this opposition can create problems. Impulsive Uranus becomes rash and there are no buffers to slow it down.

Sextile and Trine

Uranus is the more active planet when in any aspect to Neptune. The inspiration and sudden enthusiasm of Uranus assists Neptune's intuition. There is a more liberal expression of spiritual ideas with either of these harmonious aspects. Many of the beneficial points mentioned in the section on the conjunction apply.

Uranus in Aspect to Pluto

Conjunction

Revolution and the instinctual pole unite. The spontaneity of Uranus stimulates the mood and deep feelings. The body can be affected with sudden changes of temperament. This aspect can cause illness if other planets are stressfully aspected. The physical energy is easily agitated. Tibetan medicine suggests that a disorder of the energy (chi) element is possible. Diet and lifestyle can correct this problem. A diet with meat and alcohol in moderation is useful. Regular sexual activity and avoiding drafts and cold are part of the remedy. More awareness of the body is required if the lifestyle is chaotic and busy. Quietude meditations calm the negative effects of this conjunction. The power of the body can manifest with sudden experiences. Meditations that focus yogic transformation, like psychic heat, need to be practiced under the guidance of a qualified teacher.

Square

Revolution and the instinctual pole are stressfully aspected. Uranus is highly spontaneous and might cause the mood and body to change quickly. Pluto affects the body in areas including metabolism, hormonal levels, and weight. This square can adversely stimulate any of these. Because astrology is only one factor in the total picture of influences, the negative effects of this square can be balanced. Mindfulness of body and temperament is required. The other area that Pluto affects is the deeper emotional life. Stress and anger could be strong if one is not mindful of one's development. Regular meditation on empathy and compassion are the opponents to these negative emotions. The main meditative opponent to anger is love. This calms the body and feelings. Meditation with the Medicine Buddha is a useful practice to assist the body in staying healthy.

Opposition

Revolution and the instinctual pole are opposed. The spontaneity of Uranus stimulates the body. This aspect is less problematic than the square, as the pendulum is not as agitating. The mood and temperament could swing unpredictably, but not as disruptively. Uranus generally brings spontaneity and in this case the moods are energized. Extra care should be taken for the body with exercise and diet. This supports physical health. The mood swings that this aspect can stimulate depend on where the planets are placed in the natal chart. One has to be mindful of what the trigger points are for a particular mood. Meditations that calm the body and mind are best.

Sextile and Trine

Revolution and the instinctual pole are beneficially aspected. The spontaneity of Uranus stimulates the moods and deep feelings of the person. This aspect is excellent for a strong, healthy body. Uranus tends to give the body a lift and make the moods and deep feelings shift quickly. The person will feel energized on a physical level. Practices such as Vipassana and the Mahayana mind training techniques are excellent for dealing with the stimulation caused by these aspects. These individuals have an excellent ability to heal and do energy work on others. Meditation on the Medicine Buddha would be a good practice to learn if one is involved in healing modalities.

Neptune in Aspect to Pluto

Sextile and Trine

The spiritual pole and the instinctual pole are in harmony. The intuitive, imaginative energy combines with deep feelings in these harmonious aspects. A sextile aspect between Neptune and Pluto appears in the natal chart of everyone born between 1945 and 1985, beginning with the baby boomer generation. The awakening to new dimensions of consciousness and a large worldview find expression with this aspect. Those people who consciously seek spiritual integration benefit more profoundly than the general populace.

If the Moon is well aspected to these two planets, then all three integrate sensitivity. The emotional sensitivity of the Moon, the image-related sensitivity of Neptune, and the gut feelings of Pluto support one another. These three planets aspected beneficially work best in areas where intuition is a useful asset.

The support Neptune and Pluto offer applies to a lesser degree with other planets like Mercury and Venus. The literary and artistic skills benefit with a solid, gut-level intuitiveness. Love and affection have a heartfelt and sensitive quality. The active planets like the Sun, Mars, Jupiter, and Uranus in an aspect to these two are benefited with sincere intuition. The sincerity is from Pluto and the intuition is from Neptune. Saturn well aspected may develop an insightful wisdom about life. All cases of Neptune and Pluto well aspected stimulate sincere sensitivity.

Note: The movement of Neptune and Pluto is extremely slow in astrology. The primary angle between these two planets has been a sextile aspect, formed between 1945 and 1985. This aspect affected four generations of rebirths, including baby boomers and Generation X. These two planets continue to move in beneficial aspect until 2045, when they will start to form a square aspect to each other.

Astrology is an interdependent influence, and part of the impact is colored by the the nature of society at the time of a particular transit or aspect. Therefore, the square and opposition aspects between Neptune and Pluto will not be dealt with at this time. The wisdom of future astrologers will better present the impact and interpretation of these aspects.

Fourteen
Buddhist Meditations and Personal Astrology

The terms and references made in this book are unique to Buddhist practice. The Mahayana Buddhists say that all practices are steps on the path toward becoming a bodhisattva and finally an enlightened being, a Buddha. Faith traditions all present a spiritual destination. A destination is described as a resting place; it may be a stage on the way. Buddhists feel that enlightenment is a dynamic force; it is not inactive. It is complete self-realization and the full development of consciousness. They believe that consciousness expresses wisdom, unbiased love, and compassion.

The various forms of Buddhist meditation have their own special flavor and style. Traditionally, one would travel to different Buddhist countries to experience these techniques. Currently these are available throughout the world. The following presentation will introduce some of the known techniques popular today. The meditations can help an individual understand how to work skillfully with stressful astrological aspects.

Vipassana Meditation

Vipassana, strictly speaking, means "insight meditation." This refers to the use of investigative meditation to understand the nature of reality. All forms of Buddhism refer to Vipassana. Each group will practice with slight variations.

One famous style of Vipassana meditation is presently taught in the Burmese tradition of U Ba Kin. Starting in the 1970s, a wealthy Indian man, S. N. Goenka, taught this meditation. Most Western practitioners of Vipassana who traveled to India were exposed to his ten-day retreats.

I (Jhampa) did a ten-day course in 1974 with a large group of Tibetan monks. His Holiness the Fourteenth Dalai Lama invited Goenka to present a course for the young monks of the dialectic school in Dharamsala. Dialectics study philosophy, and although meditation is important, it is not formally practiced. Lia Tucker, a Western resident in Dharamsala, helped organize the ten-day retreat held in the Tibetan Library. Tibetan Buddhism is full of colorful forms, intellectual debate, and ritual. Goenka contrasts this with a simple technique free from most forms of ritual. He is strict in his interpretation of Buddhist practice. The presentation strips away intellectual elaborations and deals with direct experience. The only ritual is his deep, beautiful chanting before each section.

The style of the ten-day retreat is formal and structured. The first few days use breathing meditation to stabilize the mind. This is called *Anapanasatti.* One focuses on the sensation of the air passing through the nostrils to the exclusion of everything else. This technique develops concentration and equanimity. The Buddha prescribed breathing meditation to quiet the busy mind. It soothes the body and mind and sets a quiet stage for realizations.

On the third day, one starts slowly sweeping the body from head to toe with focused awareness. The sessions are a minimum of one hour long and one is expected not to move at all after the fifth day. Feelings and sensations develop into intense experiences. Although one is just sitting, a lot happens on a subtle level. Goenka explains not to grasp at any particular sensation, rather just scan the body with equanimity. One watches the impermanent ebb and flow of sensation; pain or pleasure. All are the same. Profound realizations come from this simple observation. This meditation couples concentration, equanimity, and the appreciation of coarse and subtle impermanence.

Various Buddhist principles are introduced as the retreat continues. The idea of impermanence is a central principle. Everything we experience is *Anicha*, the Pali word for *impermanent*. Nothing abides forever. Participants are asked to observe the flow of energy and feelings in their bodies. They observe the constant flow of thoughts and energy in the mind and body to become aware that nothing abides forever.

Together with the idea of impermanence is the understanding that the mind is under the effect of constant craving. It is either motivated by craving or aversion. It swings back and forth between craving the pleasant and avoiding the unpleasant. This is suffering. It is the suffering of expectations and projections. This particular vision of reality is based on delusion. Goenka uses the Pali word *Dukha* to represent this suffering. Everyone is familiar with their Anicha and Dukha by the fourth and fifth days of the retreat. It manifests as waves of pain, stiffness, frustration, and agitation within the impermanent body. Occasionally there are good moments when the energy flows in a blissful manner.

Vipassana is one of the best techniques to become grounded and stop the cycle of craving and aversion. I saw many friends make great personal strides with this technique in my early years in India. I was a monk in the Tibetan tradition, where the approach is slow. The Tibetan lamas put emphasis on attitude and becoming intellectually familiar with Buddhist principles. My friends who practiced the Vipassana technique were more settled and calm than I. Vipassana works much more quickly than Tibetan practice to center the individual. This is because

Vipassana strips away extraneous experience and brings one back to harmony of body and mind. A simple aware mind gains the direct experience of a world without projections.

Goenka introduces Metta meditation on the last day of the retreat. This meditation sends loving-kindness to all sentient beings. The prayer used with the meditation is "May all beings have happiness and the causes of happiness. May all beings be free from suffering and the causes of suffering." This is called the sharing of merit.

The full ten-day retreat is transforming for anyone who takes it seriously. The first days help one focus and stabilize the mind. The next six days are devoted to scanning and insight. One gains insight directly because of the repeated sessions each day. There is no escape during the ten-day period. No reading material or conversation is allowed. Participants have to sit and experience themselves. This is a powerful and humbling experience for most. Generally, people feel that they are in control. Vipassana provides an opportunity to experience oneself and judge oneself in the light of an ever-changing reality.

Personally, that retreat shocked me. I discovered how intellectual my practice was. My first reaction was to consider dropping the Tibetan practices. They were so imaginary compared to what I had just experienced. Vipassana required mindful awareness and positive intention, nothing more. How simple it all was. A few days after the retreat, I came to realize that my current Tibetan studies had their value, too. They deepened the experience of Vipassana. It is good to be grounded and without expectation, a benefit of Vipassana. But it is of equal benefit to expand awareness with study, altruism, and love, a benefit of Tibetan practice.

Years later I met some of those friends who initially chose the Vipassana route. Some of them had expanded from the Vipassana technique to other forms of Buddhist practice. They were hungry for details about attitude and the mind. The Tibetan system, in particular, has a profound presentation of the psychology of meditation. This presentation has developed over the last twenty-five centuries. Currently His Holiness the Dalai Lama and specialists from many medical and psychological disciplines meet annually in Dharamsala to discuss these techniques.

A good mix of the Tibetan Mahayana tradition and Vipassana is found in North America at the Insight Meditation Society in Barre, Massachusetts. Western founders Jack Kornfield, Sharon Salzberg, and Joseph Goldstein integrate these two traditions. The Vipassana establishes the grounding effect and the Tibetan system enhances the compassionate context. It is of interest that quite a number of these Western Buddhist practitioners, upon their return from India, attended universities and earned degrees in psychology. Jack Kornfield is a good example of this double course of study, mixing the East and the West.

Vipassana and Astrology

Vipassana is extremely useful from the astrological perspective. It is an excellent practice for everyone to do initially. Vipassana separates the muddy delusions from consciousness to solve many basic problems. The calm awareness coupled with wisdom stops the cycle of deluded craving and aversion. The mind gains peace and fulfillment.

Buddhism places great emphasis on mindful awareness as the source of an enlightened life. There are more choices available if one is aware and wise. There is a greater expression of free will. Bodhisattvas have varying levels of free will, and Buddhas have the complete expression of it. A Buddha's awareness never responds unconsciously to stimulation. Buddhists feel that kindhearted awareness and wisdom are the progressive source of all spiritual realizations.

Awareness and wisdom also grant freedom from harsh astrological influences. It is mindful awareness that chooses how to respond to any stimulation. Astrological objects are external to us, but the effect to body and mind is experienced internally. As the influences enter into consciousness, one has the opportunity to choose how to respond. One doesn't even have to know that it is an astrological effect; one merely has to be aware of one's thoughts, feelings, and emotions. Shantideva, a great Indian saint, said, "It is impossible to protect the feet from thorns by covering the world with leather. Instead cover one's soles with leather and the same has been accomplished." The mind and body with mindful awareness receive natural protection from all hindrances including astrology.

Vipassana is so extensive in its benefits that it is similar to aspirin. It helps alleviate suffering from any affliction. Vipassana benefits individuals no matter what their astrology chart indicates. The agitating and aggressive planets like Jupiter, Mars, and Uranus benefit with Vipassana because of the calming nature of meditation. This includes the planetary aspects of conjunction, square, and opposition. Vipassana slows the person down and stimulates mindful awareness. If one is mindful of the disadvantages of being in a rush, impulsive, or aggressive, such feelings are easier to manage.

Planets may stimulate the body and the mind to react. If one is unconscious of one's feelings, then the planets may have more impact. When the mind is calm and mindful, the energy, feelings, and emotions are more stable. A mindful person can be calm even among busy people. The mindfulness protects the person. The planets are no different than the people one associates with daily. Some people are stimulating in positive ways and others are disruptive and agitating. The negative effects are limited if one is aware. Just because someone is rude does not mean we must retaliate.

It is exactly the same with astrological influences. We do not see the planets, but we feel the stimulation in our body and mind. Once we recognize a particular sensation or emotion that upsets us, we have greater control. The level of control is dependent upon how skillful and proficient we are at dealing with our emotions and feelings. We do not have to know that it is a Uranus or Mars transit; we just have to recognize the emotion or feeling in order to deal with it immediately. It is conceivable that we would not even have to know our astrology chart if we had a deep level of personal awareness. It might be wise to utilize both traditions of meditation and astrology. Tibetans have been doing this for centuries.

Vipassana is just one of the techniques available to deal with pressure and stress from agitating astrological aspects. The main goal of Vipassana is detachment from impulsive behavior. Detachment gives awareness the space to have choices. It allows freedom from unskillful decisions. It brings forth the realization of liberation, nirvana. The special benefit of Vipassana is its singular focus on awareness and wisdom with no extra trappings.

The following list is in order starting with the planets most benefited by Vipassana:

1. Uranus in any square aspect.

2. Mars in any square aspect.

3. Uranus in an opposition aspect.

4. Uranus conjunct another planet, the Midheaven, Ascendant, Descendant, or Nadir.

5. Mars in an opposition aspect.

6. Mars conjunct any planet, the Midheaven, Ascendant, Descendant, or Nadir.

7. Mars and/or Uranus in the twelfth house.

8. Saturn square any planet, the Midheaven, Ascendant, Descendant, or Nadir.

9. The Sun square any planet, the Midheaven, Ascendant, Descendant, or Nadir.

10. Jupiter square any planet, the Midheaven, Ascendant, Descendant, or Nadir.

Uranus and Mars are both agitating in these positions. These planets can be disruptive, stimulating, or liberating. It depends on developing the right attitude. Uranus and Mars cause harm when one is unaware and impulsive. They bestow energy and independence when one develops a positive mindful attitude.

Uranus is wonderfully liberating. It expresses unbounded freedom when coupled with the right attitude. A well-positioned Uranus bestows the possibility of spiritual liberation. The spontaneity of Uranus is unbridled by conventional, conservative restrictions. Siddhartha completely broke from tradition when he presented Buddhism with no caste system. Uranus inspired in him a new level of liberal spiritual interpretation.

Mars is not as liberal as Uranus but it is a hard worker. This determination can turn to aggressive behavior if one is not mindful of the disadvantages of aggression and anger. Mars becomes more effective with a kindhearted attitude. One of the best opponents to the aggression and anger of Mars is loving-kindness. Mars well aspected in a chart bestows power and ability. Siddhartha had Mars in his first house, giving his personality a powerful boost of capacity and ability.

Saturn is not an active planet and therefore not stimulating like Uranus and Mars. Saturn tends to slow things down. Stressful aspects can block growth. Saturn becomes conservative and limiting, and undermines self-esteem with criticism and doubt. Mindful awareness has to be more subtle to catch the negative influence of Saturn because of its quiet influence. An aware individual has to recognize Saturn's negative, judgmental attitude in order to stop it.

Saturn's positive influence helps with meditation. Vipassana meditators will most likely have Saturn significantly positioned in their chart. Saturn loves the conservative, controlled approach that Vipassana offers. Siddhartha had Saturn conjunct his Moon, which gave him deep emotional control.

Saturn is often related to the repression of emotions. One could make the assumption that Buddha actually repressed his feelings as a celibate monk with a Moon-Saturn conjunction. His Holiness the Dalai Lama gave a good example of dealing with emotions in contrast to repressing them. A group of young Western monks and nuns received an interview with His Holiness in 1974. I had been ordained for three years at that time and was part of the group. His Holiness asked a few polite questions and then inquired about how we managed our sexual feelings. We were all too shy to respond, and His Holiness burst into laughter. He said, "Personally, I call my sexual desire to have a seat in front of me. I open a debate with desire and listen to what it has to say. We may dialogue for some time over the pros and cons of desire. I explain I am a monk and have certain objectives with my life. Desire explains its position and wishes. Sometimes I win the debate and sometimes I lose!" We all laughed uproariously. This is the Buddhist view on differentiating between repression and choice.

Jupiter is not a difficult planet in almost all astrological positions. Even with a square aspect, Jupiter is not that problematic. Jupiter's big problems are overexcitement and busyness. Mindful awareness helps control the boisterous enthusiasm of Jupiter. This limits the intoxication that Jupiter tends to inject into actions. Vipassana slows down the busyness of Jupiter enough to help the person get a job done skillfully. Jupiter's beneficial influences are goodwill, optimism, and generosity.

Aspects with the Sun, in general, often deal with egocentricity. Many selfish actions are perpetrated due to a lack of sensitivity. The lack of self-awareness can be the main fuel of egotism. Egocentric people only see the world from their own viewpoint. One has to discriminate carefully between self-expression and egocentric activity.

Ego is also an important function of personality. For example, Buddha must have had a charismatic personality to affect most of the people of Asia. This is a healthy ego without selfish overtones. The Sun's placement stimulates the area where we may show the greatest interest in life.

Vipassana's central objective is self-awareness. If people become self-aware, then they are in a good position to see the effect they have on people and situations. Self-realization is when one becomes aware of what is happening within oneself. If the attitude and actions are unskillful, it will become obvious quickly with self-awareness. No one can change another more than they can change themselves. Vipassana works effectively to facilitate personal growth.

Zen Meditation

We are most familiar with Japanese Zen Buddhism in the West. The tradition of Zen actually comes from the Chinese Chan tradition. Dogen Zengi, the originator of Japanese Zen, removed all the accumulated ritual and hierarchy of Chinese Buddhist practice. He distilled the practice down to a simple statement: "The body is Buddha, and the mind is Buddha." There are no ordained celibate priests in the Japanese traditions, but there are monasteries and monks.

Zen practitioners hold four vows of practice: "All beings one body I vow to liberate. Endless blind passions I vow to uproot. Dharma gates without number I vow to penetrate. The great way of Buddha I vow to attain." These four statements encompass the philosophy and practice of Zen Buddhism.

I experienced Zen Buddhism in Bodhgaya, India, where Buddha gained enlightenment. The Japanese built a huge temple and hotel complex there in 1970. This was to help the Japanese tourists visit Bodhgaya more comfortably. A fellow Western monk named Kevin Rigby and I stayed there. We studied Zen for three months during the winter of 1975. We were given a small maintenance room at the side of the temple as our quarters.

Shabhuya San and Tori San were the two monks who ran the temple. Tori San was from the Rinzi sect and Shabhuya San was from the Soto sect. Shabhuya San instructed Kevin and I in Soto practice on a daily basis. This tradition believes in strict meditation sessions and brief instructional sessions with the master. Tori San, from the Rinzi sect, would have used a koan in the interview. The koan breaks the desire for logic and intellectual clinging.

Shabhuya San had us sit for one hour in the morning and the evening. He taught the basics of Zen technique in the afternoon. One thing that differs between Zen and Vipassana is the focus to attain enlightenment for the benefit of all sentient beings. This is the focus of Mahayana Buddhism, which embodies the wish to benefit everyone. Although Vipassana emphasizes *Metta* (love and compassion) toward all, there is no emphasis to liberate both oneself and others. The vow of the Zen practitioner, "All beings one body I vow to liberate," means that one is interdependent and connected with everything in the universe. If enlightenment is attained, one naturally works to enlighten all others. Mahayana Buddhism literally translated means "the large or great vehicle." The practice is large because it includes everyone in the process of becoming enlightened. It is like traveling in a bus to enlightenment. Hinayana is compared to a private car for self-liberation.

Strictly speaking, this Mahayana attitude is not related to a country or style of practice. If individuals feel the interconnection between themselves and others and act on that, they become bodhisattvas and Mahayana practitioners. In contrast, if they are in a Mahayana tradition but work for their own spiritual benefit, they are practitioners of the small vehicle, the Hinayana. This spiritual vehicle will only carry themselves to liberation. The greater or lesser vehicle refers to an attitude of practice, not an outer form, style, or country.

The Zen Body

The sitting style of Zen is comprised of two thirty-minute sessions with a brief walk between these meditations. Body posture is strictly observed. This conforms to the Buddhist idea that everything in the world is perfect. One needs to drop delusions and illusions and return to the state of purity. The perfect body posture is called *Body is Buddha*. A Buddha body is free from imperfection. The instructor comes around to adjust posture and help the student attain perfection. If the student does not maintain the posture, he or she may be hit on the nape of the neck with a long stick. This practice depends on the instructor of the temple. Not all teachers do this. The hit is to reinforce the idea of strict control of the body. Being hit does not hurt, but it does startle the individual into strong mindfulness. I got hit several times in my course of study. This happened in the early morning sessions when I did not wake up.

The walking session lasts for about five minutes and is comprised of either slow or fast walking around the perimeter of the temple room. One walks with the hands held against the abdomen, spine erect, and eyes straightforward. Normal group sessions have people walk behind each other in a long line. This discipline develops mindfulness in all actions, whether sitting or walking. When the walking session is complete, participants sit for another thirty minutes.

The Zen Mind

The mind's concentration in Soto Buddhism focuses on the palms of the hands. The hands are held at the level of the navel, and one breathes like a vertical bellows. The hands are held against the abdomen in the perfect mudra of meditation. A mudra is symbolic of the state of mind. The meditative mind is calm and clear. This is the ideal of meditation. The hands are against the navel area because that is close to the hara. The hara is the central balance point of the body. Its position is the lower abdomen, halfway between the back and the front of the body. Focusing on that area grounds the individual and does not stimulate distracting emotions. *Bellows breathing* means full inhalations with the diaphragm. The student is mindful of the inhalation and exhalation as the meditation continues. This fulfills the statement "Mind is Buddha." The mind of the Buddha is free from distraction, pure with awareness and focus. This relates to the second vow: "Endless blind passions I vow to uproot."

Pure dedication to Zen practice develops strong mental focus and clarity. Instruction in the basic principles of Buddhism structures the meditational experience. Japanese students first go to a university and learn Buddhist principles. They go to a monastery to practice after those studies. Students in Western countries generally cannot follow that order, so instruction is given at the meditation hall.

Zen meditative experiences are characterized with a special terminology. If an experience is profound, which can happen with a flash of insight, it is called a *satori*. Meditators have many satori experiences as they progress on the path to enlightenment. Satori experiences indicate the mind's deeper penetration of reality. This relates to the third vow: "Dharma gates without number I vow to penetrate."

The final ideal in Zen is the fourth vow: "The great way of Buddha I vow to attain." This refers to the overall concept that enlightenment encompasses all existence. To be enlightened is to be present, focused, and liberated from all encumbering delusions. The wisdom consciousness of Zen is the experience of openness to reality. This is a consciousness realizing complete interdependence with the universe. Zen practice rejects the idea of isolation. To feel insignificant comes from the small mind. Zen strives to attain the big mind. The big mind embodies the ideas of openness, interconnectedness, and liberation. This is the great path Buddha realized and presented.

Zen and Astrology

The utilization of Zen practice to deal with stressful astrological aspects differs from using Vipassana techniques. The difference lies in the strictness of Zen practice. To some extent, it depends on the teacher, but Zen can be presented in quite a militant fashion. The strict need to sit perfectly and focus can stimulate several of the more aggressive planetary influences. The implementation of Zen may lack softness and compassion. This depends on the instructor; it is not inherent to Zen practice.

Individuals with stressful aspects, particularly those involving Mars, might be attracted to Zen meditation. This is because of the formal and disciplined manner of practice. The person must sit perfectly. One must be in control and discipline body and mind. Mars stimulates a sense of capacity and ability, so a person with a stressful Mars aspect may take Zen practice and become too serious. This may further stimulate the tendency to deal with the world in a harsh manner. Mars stressfully aspected is known to produce frustration and anger. The Zen ideology supports discipline, but can stimulate a militant attitude.

The code of discipline and ethics of the samurai warriors is a good example. If the perfect body/mind ideal becomes overemphasized, a martial attitude may be generated in relation to everything. People can be intimidating when they use the purity of Zen focus to do something. They are focused and decisive, yet they may lack love and compassion.

Saturn is another planet to take into consideration regarding Zen meditation. If Saturn is stressfully aspected, the desire to be serious can cause obstacles. Saturn may influence the person to be a perfectionist. This attitude suits Zen meditation perfectly. The perfection of body and mind becomes a call to control the body and mind. Japanese do everything with simple beauty and free of egotism. The tea ceremony is a good example. This practice instructs the individual how to act with perfect control and style. Astrologically, one could surmise that the planet Saturn and Japan have a special relationship. Whatever the case, a stressfully aspected Saturn can take the ideal of perfection and create many new problems.

People with hard aspects to either Mars or Saturn might review their interest in Zen meditation. It could exacerbate an existing astrological problem instead of solving it. The middle path is always stressed in Buddhism. The middle path lies between militant control and kindhearted compassion.

The planets that benefit from Zen practice are Mercury, Venus, Neptune, and Pluto. These planets are assisted because of the discipline and beauty of Zen. There is majesty and yet simplicity in the Zen style. This is the correct manner in which to practice Zen, with grace and composure.

Mercury is assisted by the clear-mindedness of Zen meditation. Zen will calm and discipline the wandering mind if the individual is overly intellectual. The expression "Intellectual people are all in their heads" describes this tendency. Zen's focus is on the hara at the navel and breathing like a bellows. This shifts cerebral consciousness to a different area of the body. The meditation is more direct and powerful than Vipassana. The physical focus on the abdomen grounds the meditator to be less emotional and flighty. Zen can produce increased results of depth and calmness when the focus of breath and meditation are combined. This helps remove the intellectual tension sometimes apparent with Mercury.

Venus stimulates an interest in sensual objects and beauty. Zen helps polish the beauty and qualities of Venus. It adds calm composure to attractive objects and actions. There is a great deal of grace in Zen meditation, and Venus could enjoy that perfection. Venus' negative influence is sensual indulgence, and Zen could help control that inclination. The second Zen vow, eliminating endless blind passions, identifies the mastery of indulgent passions. Passion is fine, provided there is grace and dignity. Self-indulgence and overstimulation only increase distraction and delusion.

Neptune stimulates intuition and imagination. Zen is an intuitive style of practice. The daily sessions of placing the body and mind in perfect posture establish a foundation for intuitive flashes and insight. Zen prides itself on setting the stage for sudden enlightenment. The satori experience can only come within the framework of the stable ground of focused consciousness. Zen retreats are often held in silence, which also helps eliminate intellectualism and unnecessary internal dialogue.

The imaginative side of Neptune can be an asset and a deficit in Zen practice. The positive side of Neptune is the ability to see or imagine many possibilities. Neptune can be open-minded and flexible in approaching new, interesting subjects. This positive influence helps the Zen practitioner gain progressive insight and satori experiences. The negative influence of Neptune may cause the person to be vague and doubtful. Neptune negatively aspected is like a camera lens out of focus. The distortion affects the influence of the planet in aspect. The distortion may be experienced as fear and anxiety, or the inability to focus clearly. If the person acts carelessly, the distorted focus may produce many unskillful actions.

The negative effects of Neptune find expression in the mind and emotions of the person. Those effects are related to conscious perceptions, yet they can be adjusted. Zen helps eliminate all these unproductive influences with discipline, style, and structure. One has to sit, walk, and eat with awareness and focus. There is no place to be vague and mindless in Zen meditation retreats. The silence of a retreat and the focus of awareness help train the mind away from idle daydreaming and fantasy.

Pluto is the final planet to take into consideration with Zen practice. Pluto affects the body, mood, and temperament of an individual. Pluto's influence may produce illness, although it is not the sole cause of illness. Pluto is a factor contributing to illnesses, especially if an individual has inherited physical problems. The mood and temperament of an individual are also under the influence of Pluto's aspects and transits. Zen helps in all these cases with the perfection of physical posture.

The body and spine are where the nerves and energy channels run. The energy of consciousness can flow easily and smoothly if the body is healthy. One of the effects of good Zen sitting is to purge the body and mind of bad posture. Blocked and obstructed energy will accumulate and finally produce imbalances in the internal organs; therefore, Zen sitting may help remove some of the causes for illness with just the physical posture. Good posture and discipline keep the nerves in their proper position and let the energy flow as it needs to throughout the body.

The discipline of Zen also helps the emotional life of an individual. For example, consider people who are suffering from depression. They may slump their shoulders and hang their head down. The sad and depressed feelings express themselves in poor body posture. Zen works to combat this physical effect. The energy flows smoothly if the body is consciously held in a good posture. Good posture helps prevent the sad mind from deeply influencing the body. This is the first benefit Zen offers to people suffering from depression.

Another benefit is the regular exchange of air with Zen bellows breathing. Bellows breathing helps remove sad emotions from the body. My Tibetan teachers said that when people sigh sadly, they pollute their body with sad emotional energy. The sad feeling and energy will not leave until the air is exchanged. The emotions mix with the breath and create extended negative effects on the body. Zen sitting promotes smooth, full inhalations and exhalations, thus cycling the air in the body efficiently, removing bad feelings.

Depression and New Modalities

There is interesting new research related to depression and how to alleviate it. There was a seminar at Oxford University, England, dealing with depression in the summer of 1999.[1] The researcher created three groups of 200 people each, all suffering from depression. They compared three different models of treatment for depression. Two of the treatments were based on therapy and medication, respectively. The third model was Vipassana meditation.

The three groups were observed in therapy for one year. The results showed approximately a 45 percent success rate with the groups treated with therapy and medication. The Vipassana group showed a success rate of 75 percent. Many of the psychologists at the conference contested the results and said that there must have been some falsification of the data. To help prove the validity of the tests, the researcher agreed to a second set of trials to be held in England, the United States, and Canada.

The results of those trials are not compiled yet, but there is strong evidence that meditation helps people deal with depression. Both Zen and Vipassana are similar in their styles of meditation. They focus on breathing and awareness. The clinical research provides a good example that meditation can effectively assist physical and mental health. In astrology, Pluto appears to play a significant role with the body and emotions. It would seem reasonable that meditation may diminish the negative effects of Pluto's influence. The present research appears to validate the role that meditation can play in promoting good mental and physical health.

Tantra

Mahayana Buddhism is the basis for the practice of Tantra. Tantric teachings contain profound techniques for transforming daily experience. Tibet holds most of the Tantric lineages of Buddhist practice that exist in the world. This came about due to historical factors. Buddhism was destroyed in India due to invading armies and war in the eleventh century. The good fortune was the arrival of the Tibetans. Tibet started to have a strong interest in Buddhist tenants. The full spectrum of Mahayana and Tantric Buddhist texts were translated into Tibetan from Sanskrit at that time. Tibet became the sole holder of many of these rare and precious lineages. These teachings were isolated from most of the civilized world for the next ten centuries. The invasion of Tibet in 1959 by the Chinese Communist army released these teachings back into the world.

Tantra is the practice of deity yoga. There are two levels of transformation undertaken in practice. The first level purifies the perception of the body and physical world as mundane and impure. The second level works with the nerve channels and mental energy. Tantric practitioners transform themselves completely with these two techniques.

The mind is the creator of each individual's experience. The world is a reflection of one's perception of it. We only see what we know and understand. Tantra recreates a more skillful vision and experience. If you think the world is impure, that is what you will experience. If you think the world is pure, then the world is pure. This is not an impractical, idealistic attitude; it is an attempt to see the potential latent in everything.

As human beings, we have the ability to change our experience of reality with knowledge. For example, at one time we believed the world was flat and the earth was the center of the solar system. Now we know differently, thus our experience of reality was transformed.

Tantra works with the three wisdom principles of impermanence, interdependence, and voidness. We can transform because we are impermanent, because positive causes create enlightening effects, and because we are empty of any inherently fixed nature. These three principles are the basis of Tantric attitude. Love and compassion are the expressions of that Tantric attitude.

Tantra and Astrology

There are many deities that could work well with astrology. This is because the object of Tantra is to transform the mind.

Tantric practitioners deal skillfully with whatever happens around them, in a holistic and inclusive manner. Awareness and wisdom establish this perspective. The deities are archetypes that symbolize these principles. Meditation focused on a deity can balance the body and mind. The balance can eliminate negative astrological influences. These techniques have been practiced for thousands of years.

A few of the deities that might be strongly considered for use with astrology are Green Tara, White Tara, Avalokiteshvara, Vajrapani, Amitayus, and the Medicine Buddha. Green Tara helps the individual deal with interferences to fulfillment, especially those involving the Moon, women, and feelings. White Tara and Amitayus help cure illness and life-energy interferences. Avalokiteshvara helps generate love and compassion, which is useful when dealing with anger and aggression. The Medicine Buddha helps heal health-related interferences. Each of these deities requires a qualified teacher, receiving initiation and instruction and doing a short retreat or daily practice. Most of the practices can be taught over one weekend.

Of all the deities mentioned, Vajrapani is particularly related to removing astrological interferences. The actual name for Vajrapani in Tibetan is *Jungpo Trulkor*, "the subduer of the demons and planets." He protects the individual from harm that can arise from beneath the earth, on the earth, or in the sky. The planets are an influence from the sky above. Not all influences in astrology are harmful, but there are some problems to health and happiness that have an astrological source.

Tibetan doctors generally are the ones who decide whether there are astrological interferences involved. Doctors in Tibet are trained to be aware of many sources of illness. They have a holistic approach to treating patients. The source of an illness for them is principally related to attitude, diet, and body type. Regarding attitude, they advise a patient to have a peaceful and calm approach to life. Anger or strong attachment affects the body adversely and promotes imbalance and illness. An individual's attitude is an important factor when dealing with delusions that distort the world and affect the body. An attitude that supports delusion creates causes for illness.

Next, a Tibetan doctor looks at one's diet. Diet should suit the season. In the winter one should eat heavier foods, and in the summer light foods. This helps the body deal with the temperatures of the seasons. The body responds to each season differently. The wrong diet for a season will negatively affect the body and health.

The physical shape and size of an individual is the final thing the doctor observes. The body may indicate a higher potential for certain health imbalances. A Tibetan doctor knows a great deal about a patient by observing attitude, diet, and body type. Tibetan doctors then use the pulse to discover exactly what imbalance is affecting the patient. All these help the doctor prescribe the correct path to recovery. It may involve herbal medicine or it might just require a change of diet and attitude.

The doctor may consult astrology if a patient does not recover from an illness. Stressful astrological aspects can indicate that interferences to health may be experienced. This is remedied by relying on various deities. The client may be required to do a retreat of the deity or just daily practice. If the body is weak, the patient is told to practice the Medicine Buddha meditations. This includes both visualization and mantra recitation. The person is told to practice White Tara or Amitayus if the life force appears weak. Finally, if all those areas are secure, then the meditation of Vajrapani would be suggested.

This particular aspect of Vajrapani, "Controller of Spirits," has three components: Vajrapani, Hyagriva, and Gauda. These three protect the individual from spirits under the earth, on the earth, and in space above. The spirits of space include the planets and other astrological bodies. The main figure is Vajrapani, standing upright with the right leg extended and holding a noose and vajra. These implements represent binding interferences and a fearless, indestructible mind. Within his flaming hair is the head of a horse, Hyagriva, and in the air directly above them both is Gauda, king of the birds.

The meditator visualizes the three-aspect vision of Vajrapani in the space in front of him or her. This visualization is done in conjunction with the recitation of a mantra and absorbing light. The use of visualization, a mantra, and light all affect consciousness. If consciousness awakens and transforms, protection is generated for the individual.

This meditation generally requires an initiation from a qualified teacher. Occasionally, the doctor will perform the initiation. More often, a Tibetan lama is recommended to the patient. The lama gives the initiation and meditation instruction. Depending on the circumstances, the patient may have to do a retreat. The retreat continues until the correct sign arises indicating that the interference is removed. Normally this is a dream, but it can be a vision of the deity saying that the person is protected. Once the sign is received, the individual is only required to do a short meditation session each day.

Tantra and astrology can also be used to assist the process of generating spiritual realizations. Auspicious dates are used to increase the positive effects of spiritual action. The Buddhist calendar is based on the lunar cycles, and holy days are placed automatically on the New and Full Moon days. This is a natural benefit of being a Buddhist. Meditators can use their knowledge of supportive astrological transits to augment spiritual experience. Depending on the effect desired, various planetary aspects are sought. These may help develop the pacification of an obstacle or the increase of energy and merit. Considering the Buddhist view of reality as one of interdependence, it seems natural that astrology would be an essential component of spiritual practice.

The Future of Buddhist Astrology

The future of the integration of astrology and Buddhist practice looks very interesting. It is possible that Western astrologers will give these teachings and initiations. To be able to bestow initiation requires receiving it first from a qualified teacher and doing a retreat. In Tibet, ordained monks and nuns were not the only sources of teachings and initiations. There were many lay practitioners who were qualified instructors of meditation at all times in the history of Buddhism. In the years to come, it would be appropriate for these teachings to be transferred to Western instructors. Just as Tibet received the teachings and initiations from Indian masters in the tenth century, we are now receiving them in the twentieth century. The sacred teachings of the Tantra are again being transmitted to a new country and cultural environment.

This concludes a brief overview of the use of meditation with astrology. Each of the techniques has its special area of proficiency. Vipassana is excellent as a basis for any meditation. It requires no dogma, not even being a Buddhist. The principal tool is self-awareness and natural wisdom. Zen is more grounded in Mahayana tenets, but also does not require the person to be a Buddhist. Anyone interested in meditation can attend a Vipassana or Zen meditation session without fear of undesired commitments.

Buddhist Tantra, strictly speaking, requires that one become a Buddhist. If an individual is interested in Tantra, it is useful to study some of the tenets of practice. Deity practice relies on knowledge of the deity and meditation instruction. It is possible to not be a Buddhist and do these meditation practices. The benefits would still be realized, but the effects and depth of practice may not be as transformative. The more knowledgeable practitioners are, the more they benefit themselves.

Buddhism is not an evangelical religion and would never push itself on others. Many of the ideals of Buddhist practice are completely compatible with other religious beliefs. The ideals of love and compassion are universal to any religion. The wisdom teachings of Buddhism are also completely compatible with all other faith traditions. The only difference in view would be around the concept of a creator entity. Buddhists hold that existence has no single source; it has abided forever without beginning or end. Reality is the interplay of infinite causes and circumstances, and is completely open to change and transformation.

His Holiness the Dalai Lama says that all religions should respect one another. Religions are like food, each with its own unique flavor and spice. Individuals will respond to a particular tradition better than to others. It is natural to respond in that manner. There is no need to feel that one food is to be eaten by everyone. That makes things boring. If we rejoice in the uniqueness of each tradition we benefit from the diversity.

The intention of this book is to introduce the principles of Buddhism to those interested in astrology. I think that there should be more written about this subject. Eastern thought has made many inroads into Western thought. Psychology, especially the cognitive approach, has shifted to a more Eastern perspective. There is an ongoing dialogue between physicists and Buddhist philosophers around the ideas of quantum mechanics and the theory of relativity. Medicine now recognizes acupuncture and the role herbs can play in healing. Now is the time for astrology to benefit from Eastern thought and see if there are realizations to be discovered.

1. See Zindel V. Segal, J. Mark G. Williams, and John D. Teasdale, foreword by Jon Kabat-Zinn, *Mindfulness-Based Cognitive Therapy for Depression: A New Approach to Preventing Relapse* (New York: Guilford Press, 2002).

Fifteen
Meditation

Meditation is a process to deepen positive personal experience. It helps an individual's existence to be grounded on principles that promote health and well-being. Western culture is busy with capitalistic ambitions. This culture constantly communicates a message that one is not healthy enough, attractive enough, thin enough, or driving the right car. Western socioeconomic culture prides itself on making everyone dissatisfied. It is the shortsighted side of society. That can change individually with a shift of emphasis. A distracted mind is not the source of peace, compassion, or wisdom.

Meditation is an internal development to promote a peaceful and wise attitude. It balances the extroversion of Western society. Meditation can overcome the opponents of inner growth.

The following meditation technique is universal and does not contradict any individual religious beliefs. All Asian religions have a component of meditation. It is a common denominator when one seeks the personal integration of serenity, wisdom, and compassion.

Posture

The first step is the correct physical posture. The body should be placed in a position that alleviates the need to move for the period of meditation. It is not necessary to sit cross-legged to meditate. It can adequately be done seated in a chair. The important points are an erect spine, hands on the lap, the head bent slightly forward, and the mouth closed. The eyes can be either shut or half open, gazing at a spot about six feet in front of the seat. The breath is not controlled; it is left to follow its natural rhythm. The seating posture is immaterial; the points mentioned are the important guidelines.

Focus

The best description of meditation is attentive awareness to the object of focus. The focal point is the sensations of the breath passing through the nostrils. If one is attentive to that object, it is the doorway to good meditation.

Awareness of the sensations of the breath relaxes the body and mind. The posture allows the breathing process to be deep and natural. This facilitates full chest breathing. Stress and anxiety often cause people to breathe from the upper portion of the chest. The body is then further stressed by not getting enough oxygen. Clean, fresh air enhances physical well-being. Meditation in a well-ventilated room is beneficial. Full, natural inhalations are an integral part of the meditation process.

Mental energy runs throughout the nerve channels of the body. If the body is agitated, then the energy is turbulent and the mind cannot settle down. Good posture and natural breathing relax the nerves and energy. The meditator, with continued attentive awareness, then enters the next phase of stabilization: working with the constant flow of thoughts.

First Signs

The first sign of good meditation is to become aware of how many thoughts pass through the mind. Many people feel upset when they see how constantly they intellectualize their lives. They assume this is not meditation. Actually, this is the first stage. Meditation is not an external phenomena, it is an internal spacious awareness. It allows one to be aware of what transpires within. If attentive focus on the breath is sustained, then distracting thoughts can subside.

The attentive awareness relaxes as time passes. There is an excellent technique to hasten this process. It is useful to check how one views the meditation experience. The mind is dualistic in perspective. The subjective observer views the sensations of the breath. If one is strongly dualistic, the positive effects of meditation are diminished. This distracting dualism can be avoided.

When the meditation session starts, the body and mind fall away from the agitation of the day. One then briefly turns one's attention to the subjective observer. A minimal effort is necessary to check and relax the observer. This ensures that the meditation can progress effectively. The goal is to settle down physically, emotionally, and mentally. If there are strong expectations on the part of the meditator, this becomes a distraction similar to agitated thoughts.

Progress

Meditation is a process. As one becomes familiar with the technique of attentive awareness toward sensation, there arises a deepening of consciousness. One is better able to observe thoughts arise and pass. There are various stimuli that cause thoughts to arise.

Stimulation may come from sounds, sensations, memories, or even astrological influences. The meditator does not worry about what stimulates the thought. The person observes the arousal, the abiding, and the passing of the stimulation. If the mind peacefully observes without speculation, then detachment and equanimity grow. Should the passing thought be too stimulating, one must learn to let go of the distraction. It is not a process of fighting distraction, but rather of letting go of the captivating nature of a thought or sensation. Even if many thoughts arise, the objective is to just observe and be aware. If the agitation starts to strongly scatter the awareness, then the meditator returns to the sensations of breath. Once detachment and equanimity are again established, then the awareness can flow smoothly.

This style of meditation benefits conscious awareness. The more aware people are of their motivation, the more they have a handle on their lives. They can direct themselves in a positive direction. Free will is defined as the ability to have choices. The more choices, the greater the expression of free will. This meditation facilitates that ability.

The meditation described here is for people who practice astrology. Astrological influences that are beneficial are not the issue. It is the negative and agitating planetary influences that everyone wants to deal with effectively. Who wishes to suffer needlessly? A particular natal aspect or transit to the natal chart can cause negative repercussions. No one wants to be haphazardly affected. Self-awareness is one of the best ways to remain conscious and see the positive potential of any event.

It is not possible to control everything that transpires, but it is possible, to some extent, to control oneself. The need to control is actually not an issue of being anal-retentive; it is a question of motive and choice. If people are not aware, then everything can affect them. They may feel insecure and react negatively. Their motives are unclear.

Personal awareness allows more options. A clear-minded motivation eliminates distractions. It deals effectively and positively with life's issues. The motive can even extend beyond personal maintenance to the desire to be of benefit. Just as one is the recipient of influences, one can also be the creator of positive effects.

All of the positive objectives an individual has about life deserve fertile ground in which to grow. Meditation can be one of the useful additives to the mixing pot of existence. Its goal is to cultivate self-awareness on a deeper level. This facilitates strong positive roots and growth. The meditation explained here is a simple method. It can be practiced easily without a teacher. It is useful to seek a qualified instructor if one develops an interest in meditation. A good mentor can enhance meditation practice and assist one's spiritual growth.

Sixteen
Biographical Sketch of Jhampa

Our life is what we make of it, no matter what the events. I have had an interesting life, and some of those events and people are now lost to history, particularly the old lamas who grew up and were educated in Tibet. I hope that by sharing these stories you may feel inspired to pursue your own spiritual goals. I never planned on becoming a Buddhist monk, but it happened. Some of you perhaps will spread the wings of your imagination and do something similar after reading this story.

Part of this journey is the astrological influence that helped stimulate me and weave a fuller picture of my journey. I was born on September 23, 1950, at 1:34 P.M. in Duncan, British Columbia, Canada. I am a baby boomer and the son of a dairy farmer, yet I ended up in India as a Buddhist monk.

My personal images as a youth never included the desire to become a monk. I didn't have any particular spiritual aspirations during those years. I did enjoy reading science fiction and was transported by Tolkien's *The Lord of the Rings*. At age thirteen I was confirmed as an Anglican at my mother's insistence, but found that the Christian classes did not speak to me at all. The music and social activities of the 1960s were my spiritual awakening, although this included no direct spiritual aspects. During these years Pluto and Uranus transited my natal Mercury, Venus, and Saturn, intense times for one going through puberty and early adulthood.

My mother helped with my move from home at eighteen. I quickly got a job, bought a new car, and became independent. This put me ahead of all my friends as they still lived at home. My apartment became a central location for everyone to visit, as there were no parents to restrict our activities. It was a time of experimentation and fun.

When my nineteenth birthday passed, life began to feel hollow and dissatisfying. I became more and more unhappy. At this point, Pluto was transiting my natal ninth-house Saturn and Uranus was transiting my natal ninth-house Sun. Life seemed so meaningless; an understatement with transits through the ninth house. Fortunately, my family had always been world travelers. I decided to go to Europe to discover new inspiration, a typical ninth-house activity! England was the first stop with the Isle of White Rock concert of 1970. That was where Jimi Hendrix performed for the last time. I continued this journey to continental Europe and the southern coast of Spain. After some time I was again unhappy and started to look even further abroad.

When I returned to London, I purchased two books. One was John Blofeld's translation of the I Ching, *The Book of Change*, and the second was *Concentration and Meditation* by Christmas Humphreys. My idea was to go to the Middle East to live in the desert and meditate. The idealistic vision was to live on dates and drink water from an oasis. The details were vague, but the idea seemed like a step in the right direction. Meditation was going to fix my problems. I found a truck with an empty seat going to Afghanistan. My departure from London and Western civilization was on September 20, 1970. During most of this time a transit of Neptune applied to my natal twelfth-house Mars while Uranus conjoined the Midheaven.

My Introduction to Buddhism

I arrived from Afghanistan at the Indian border at 6:00 P.M. on November 12, 1970. It was personally a special event. I can distinctly recall powerful feelings as I drew closer and closer to the Pakistan-Indian border. It was like returning home to my mother. Possibly this is why people refer to India as Mother India. I felt an even stronger sense of peace and harmony once over the border. India was wonderful. The locals openly exhibited warmth and many of them could speak English. There was also a distinct air of spirituality among the people. A Sikh man beside me on the train explained that he was on a pilgrimage to Delhi. He planned to attend the Full Moon celebrations and birthday of Guru Nanak, the founder of the Sikh faith, the following day. I traveled directly to Delhi and spent two weeks enjoying new sights and sounds.

I had the opportunity, during this time, to attend a huge spiritual service with Guru Charan Singh, the leader of Sat Mat. This group has a large following in the Sikh tradition. The religious conference had over 15,000 people seated cross-legged in a large field that was covered with a massive canvas. It was my first experience of a religious event that involved thousands of people, a common occurrence in India. The organizers even served lunch of curried vegetables and chapatti to everyone attending. I was truly uplifted by the whole event and even managed to see Charan Singh for a brief private interview. He was pleasant to me, but I felt no special connection to him.

My search for spirituality continued. I left Delhi on December 23. Some of my friends were living in Goa and I wanted to celebrate Christmas with them. There I met an American woman who said we should visit a Tibetan refugee camp in Karnataka State. I had no knowledge about the Tibetans, but she said His Holiness the Dalai Lama was giving the Kalachakra initiation, which sounded interesting. Although we arrived at the correct refugee camp, we missed the initiation by two weeks. This trip did set me on the path to Bodhgaya, though, as my friend explained that I could meet many Buddhist teachers there.

Bodhgaya is a very sacred site for Hindus, Moslems, and Buddhists. Many of their saints received realizations in this area. Buddhists revere it as Lord Buddha's place of enlightenment. I arrived shortly after the New Year and was told that the Gandhi Ashram was a good place to stay. There were other Westerners there and a Zen monk was giving Buddhist teachings. This seemed perfect, so I registered at the ashram and started to learn to meditate.

The main focus of Buddhist teachings is to become self-aware. This entails looking at the world in a more realistic manner. Zen Buddhism expresses this view clearly. The purity and simplicity of their technique is powerful, so with the guidance and blessings of Zengo, the Japanese monk, I discovered my spirituality. During the first few days, I stayed continually in this environment and was full of exuberance. I even decided to become a monk.

On the third day at the ashram, a friend said that a Tibetan lama was giving a lecture at the main temple. We were all welcome to attend the meeting at the main Enlightenment Stupa. The actual room was called Nagarjuna's cave, a small stone temple at the north side of the 150-foot tall main stupa. I sat down and promptly placed my feet up against the edge of the low altar. It was a small, uncomfortable space and there were too many of us.

Lama Yeshe arrived and took a seat at the doorway. The room was so full that he could not get to the front. He just sat at the doorway with a lovely smile and blissful presence. Lama quickly informed me that it was disrespectful to point feet at an altar and that I should sit cross-legged. I lacked awareness to appreciate sacred spaces.

Lama Yeshe gave the lecture in an unbelievable manner. He spoke very poor English, but communicated something far beyond words. He was both deep and insightful as he spoke and he also laughed uproariously at his own jokes. I was so moved by his talk, which was actually about basic spiritual concepts, that it helped me decide to change gurus and follow him. He was so alive and had a very infectious laughter. I felt that if I were to become a monk, it would have to be one like Lama Yeshe.

Monks have shaved heads, so I went to the village and had my hair cut off. The barber shaved everything but the tuft of hair on my crown. My hair was quite long, so I had the remaining hair braided into a pigtail and then went searching for Lama Yeshe. He was staying in the upper assembly room of the Tibetan temple. When I found him, he was sitting with a young monk at the end of the room. I did a Zen prostration and asked him to be my teacher. As this happened, the young monk burst into laughter. I thought he was being rude as I was serious at that moment. Lama smiled and accepted my request. Later I realized that the young monk was Lama Zopa Rinpoche and that they had been discussing me just prior to my arrival. I left for Kopan Monastery in Nepal shortly after that with Lama Yeshe and a small group of Western devotees.

A Russian princess named Zena had established Kopan Monastery. Kopan was on a small hill on the north side of the valley. It had been the home of the king's astrologer in olden times. Zena had purchased it especially for Western people to learn Buddhism. It was here that I attended the very first meditation course of Lama Zopa Rinpoche, Lama Yeshe's star pupil. I formally became a Buddhist after that course.

I discovered that Zena had invited Zengo, the Zen monk, to teach immediately after Lama Zopa's course. This was wonderful as I could compare two varieties of Buddhist practice. The Zen style tends to be simple and clear compared to the great variety of methods in Tibetan Buddhism. Although I preferred Tibetan practice for that reason, I actually ended up spending two more months under the daily guidance of Zengo.

Zengo arranged for the use of a small, abandoned nunnery on the side of Shivapuri, a mountain overlooking the Kathmandu valley. This was a two-hour walk up the mountain above Kopan. The monastery had a small temple for meditation and in front there were two rows of two-storied huts on each side of the courtyard. It was picturesque, high up on the mountain, and facing south over the valley. It was like Shangri-La.

There was one event at Kopan that was insightful and yet inappropriate. This happened before the move to the nunnery. Several women from the United States befriended Zengo. These women were staying at Kopan and asked Zengo to go for a morning walk up Shivapuri. Everyone was to have breakfast together and then start the walk. What they didn't tell Zengo was that they had mixed his porridge with peyote buttons. I did not actually accompany them, but heard the full story that afternoon.

The group left after breakfast on a small trail that wound up the shoulder of the mountain. They stopped mid-morning to rest under some huge, round boulders. The weather was hot and they all started to feel the effects of the peyote. Zengo was not talking and as they sat there, he quietly disappeared. When they realized that he was not in sight, they started looking around. Suddenly, above them on top of the huge boulder, they saw Zengo, his arms stretched above his head, shouting, "I have the power!"

The poor fellow thought it was a satori experience of phenomenal proportion. They had to help him climb off the boulder and explain that it was the effect of a drug. Later that evening, when we had our regular sit with Zengo, he was composed and quiet. The next day he confessed that it had been a powerful experience but did not last. He preferred meditation as there was more control and he had no interest in taking drugs again.

I continued to receive weekly instruction from Lama Yeshe during this time. Lama lived a very humble life at Kopan. He had a small room in the old building, and that particular room had a leaky roof. His prayers and Buddhist texts were all stacked neatly into the fireplace of the room. It was the only dry area during the monsoon season. Lama gave me a couple of hour's instruction once a week. He also made arrangements for me to meet his teacher in India that summer. I had asked him repeatedly for ordination, and he said I would take a novice ordination from his spiritual senior, Geshe Rabten. These events transpired as Pluto started its first transit to my natal Sun. The ordination date of July 4, 1971, was set.

June arrived, and I had to leave Nepal because my visa had expired. The easiest direction to go was south and into Bihar State. I went to the yoga ashram of Swami Satyananda with a fellow American traveler. The swami was busy establishing an international organization, the World Yoga Fellowship, so I was taught yoga by several of his students. I spent three weeks in the ashram.

I left the plains of India and traveled to Dharamsala in the northwestern province of Himachel Pradesh as monsoon rains began. There I reunited with Lama Yeshe and his female student, Sister Max. She was a black nun who had been with Lama for several years. I was all prepared to take novice monastic vows from Geshe Rabten, Lama's teacher.

The ordination inadvertently became a humorous event. Geshe Rabten was a meditating monk and lived outside the monastery on the side of the mountain. He was the main teacher for several monks who were also in retreat. A total of five monks are required to perform an ordination. Three meditators came and met Lama Yeshe at Geshe Rabten's hut on the morning of July 4. Lama was the translator as no one else spoke English. I was dressed in maroon robes with a shaved head. The room was incredibly small and dark, with a dirt floor. I entered, made three prostrations, and knelt before Geshe Rabten. Geshe Rabten looked serious and the four monks along the wall to my right were all somber and quiet. It was a meaningful moment.

Lama Yeshe sat close to me and guided the ceremony. I had to repeat a multiple-line prayer three times after Geshe Rabten to receive this ordination. Lama explained all this to me, and then I started to repeat whatever Geshe Rabten said. Lama interrupted me to correct my pronunciation on the first repetition. I tried my best, but Tibetan is a tonal language and difficult to distinguish. When the second repetition was completed, Lama started to grin, but did not interrupt me. As the third recitation progressed, Lama could not control himself and started to laugh. Geshe Rabten carried on as if nothing were wrong, but by the time I finished the last line of the ritual, all four monks were almost rolling on the ground with laughter. Lama was crying tears as he tried to control himself. Finally even Geshe Rabten lost it and started to laugh.

I had no idea what the monks were all laughing about. I just knelt there looking at Geshe Rabten, thinking this must be a secret part of the ceremony. Maybe I was getting a profound initiation from them? When Lama Yeshe calmed down, he explained what had happened. My pronunciation was so poor that I was saying, "I go for Refuge to the Buddha, I go for refuge to yogurt, I go for refuge to the spiritual community." The refuge in yogurt was too funny for Lama, who had a good sense of humor anyway. What made it worse was that he had to laugh discreetly, as Geshe Rabten, his own teacher, was right in front of him. The monks were nice to me after that and said I had made a big impact on Geshe Rabten.

At this point, I was totally broke, so Lama Yeshe's student Sister Max gave me the funds to purchase my first robes. She also paid for my accommodations in Dharamsala for four months. Sister Max's kindness helped keep me in India to continue my studies with the lamas.

I was Lama Yeshe's first male Westerner to receive ordination and one of the very few at that time to be in the Tibetan order of Buddhism. Lama Yeshe had also arranged an audience with His Holiness the Fourteenth Dalai Lama. Originally, Lama Yeshe was to accompany me, but at the last moment he had to leave for Nepal on unexpected business. I had to meet His Holiness on my own. I was only twenty years old then and rather naïve. There were so few Westerners in India at that time studying Buddhism. I decided to pick a line from an English translation of the Lankavatara Sutra and ask for His Holiness' commentary.

The line read: "Everything is a reflection of the mind." The subject material was on the ultimate nature of reality. I was ushered into the audience chamber, made three prostrations, and sat down with His Holiness and Tenzin Geyche, the translator. I politely asked what the sentence meant. His Holiness paused for a long time and then asked me, "Do you know when you are going to die?" I went into shock. Did His Holiness know I was going to die soon? It was a very uncomfortable moment for me. His Holiness then smiled and said I would have to study for a few more years before I could understand that sentence. He then asked me several pleasant questions and the interview was over.

I was fortunate that my arrival in Dharamsala coincided with His Holiness opening the Tibetan Library, which was built to facilitate teachings for Western students of Buddhism. The instruction was to be given by a qualified *Geshe*, a title given to someone who had mastered the full extent of the Mahayana Buddha Dharma. Geshe Ngawang Dhargaye was the teacher. The classes were six days a week: five days of teachings and one day of prayer and meditation. Each day had two hours of lecture and the rest of the time was for study and meditation. I moved close to the library to attend these classes. I was an oddity within the Tibetan monastic community. There were only three Western monks in Dharamsala at the time and two of them were in His Holiness' monastery. Lama Yeshe wanted me to be independent, so I was allowed to live on my own and study the best I could.

The fall is a pleasant time in Dharamsala. The weather becomes dry and clear. I had just turned twenty-one and life was interesting. Uranus was now transiting my natal Neptune in the tenth house. I managed to stay under the guidance of

Geshe Dhargaye for four months and then decided to return to Nepal to be with Lama Yeshe. I missed his love and laughter. This was an error. I was informed upon my arrival in Nepal that Lama Zopa Rinpoche and Lama Yeshe were going to Dharamsala to attend special teachings from His Holiness. I missed receiving teachings from all of my teachers.

Both lamas returned from India and we made plans to travel to Mount Everest in February of 1972. Lama Zopa had a small monastery there. This was exciting, as I strongly desired to practice meditation. My teachers had stressed that one needed to study prior to meditating, but I wanted to gain greater depth in the teachings I had already received. Lama Yeshe was always telling me to meditate. He would say, "The words of a scholar are like sawdust; they have no flavor. The words of a yogi are like chocolate; even the smallest piece tastes wonderful."

First Retreat

Lama Zopa's small monastery was called Lauduo Gompa and was situated at an attitude of 14,000 feet. It was beautifully placed on the northern side of a valley that ran east to west. It was a three-day walk from Mount Everest base camp or one day from Namche Bazaar. When we all arrived there, Lama Zopa arranged for me to stay in a small hut that his uncle had used for retreat. This coincided with a Saturn transit to my Descendant. The hut was very isolated and placed in a gorge that ran south into the larger valley and was one mile west and 1,000 feet higher than the monastery.

The peaks of the mountains that created the Thame valley were 20,000-feet high. There were glaciers and snow-peaked mountains all around. My hut was placed at the base of a 100-foot cliff that was one side of the gorge. No rain or wind could reach the hut because of this. The room was about eight-by-six feet and only had a mud fireplace and a meditation box in it.

Tibetan practitioners both meditate and sleep seated in one of these boxes. They are made of wood planks about three-feet square, with a low front and sides and a tall back to lean against. I attempted to sleep and meditate in this box, but it was impossible. I gave up and found an unused door at the monastery and carried it up to the hut. I leaned it flat against a wall over the fire pit during the daytime and folded it down at night for sleep. I think that Westerners will always have trouble trying to duplicate the seated style of sleeping that is particular to Buddhist asceticism.

The back wall of the hut was the vertical wall of the cliff. My meditation box was placed against that wall facing west, and if I leaned forward I could look out through a tiny, eighteen-inch window to a 20,000-foot peak across the valley, which was gloriously white with a huge glacier. This sight was especially inspiring early in the morning as the first sunlight reached it from the east. Pigeons would sometimes fly into the gorge in the morning, their flapping wings making great echoing sounds in the narrow area of the gorge. The wedge-shaped gorge had cliff sides that rose up about 100 feet above the flat floor. Huge boulders were scattered throughout the area and the gorge seemed to pour them out into the larger valley.

My first serious attempt at retreat was at a perfect site. I only had to walk five minutes to get my water from a small creek, and wood could be gathered from juniper trees that grew everywhere. I decided, being young and idealistic, that I needed to discipline my desirous and wandering mind. I made a vow to not speak and only eat what I minimally needed for 100 days.

I had the good fortune to have some support during this retreat. A Sherpa lady came once every two weeks and gave me bags of real Tibetan stampa (roasted barley flour) and yak butter. I had no money to repay this kindness, so I rationed myself strictly. I used to take a small mug and fill it with stampa. I then took the water from my eight offering bowls and boiled it in an old pan. I added one tablespoon of yak butter to the boiling water and mixed it together with the stampa. This is all I ate each morning for 100 days. I had one cup of hot milk made from Swiss milk powder in the afternoon. The Swiss milk powder was part of a nutritional health program offered to mountain people of Nepal. The monastery supplied me with it.

My daylight hours were spent sitting and meditating on the basic teachings of the Buddha. This included exercises to build my visualization power. To accomplish this, I suspended a picture of Buddha from the ceiling on strings about three feet in front of my face. I then closed the small window with wooden shutters and lit a small candle that sat below and in front of me. This was screened so I could not see it directly. This made the picture of Buddha Vajradhara appear to float in the space. I spent many hours focusing on this picture and closing my eyes, trying to generate the image. After 100 days, I had not been overly successful, but I had fun working at it. I then returned to Thame monastery. I can remember an Italian friend visiting at that time expressing her shock at my emaciated state. I was six feet tall and weighed about 110 pounds. Although I must have looked skinny, I was happy.

Lama Yeshe visited the monastery at this time. He was organizing a trip to India, so I requested for him to arrange my full ordination as a monk. He said I had to return to India and meet a special lama for the full ordination. We left the mountain monastery and returned to Kathmandu. I was one of the few people who managed to spend private time with Lama Yeshe in those early years. Later he became very successful and was not easy to visit. It was a great privilege to walk along the mountain trails of Nepal with Lama telling stories.

Walking with Lama was special. Here I was following a jovial Tibetan monk in burgundy robes through the high mountain valleys of the Solo Kumbo. The sky was clear and sunny as we wove our way along paths that were thousands of years old. I can still see in my mind's eye the rich green of spring on the land. Lama had a heart problem, so we moved slowly. He was diagnosed that year as only having six months to live. The story deserves a few comments.

Just before the trip to Lauduo Gompa, Lama had gone into Kathmandu to see some doctors at the American hospital. He returned with a very subdued look. He was living in the back room of the Kopan building at that point. I brought some tea for him from the kitchen and he said that the doctors who looked at his heart were in shock. They said his heart was twice the size of normal and very overworked. The damaged heart was due to scarlet fever. The doctors were so concerned that they treated Lama like an invalid as he got off the table. He withdrew for two days at Kopan to think about this health problem. He had dreams to fulfill and this was a huge setback. Finally he must have come to a strong resolution because on the third day he dropped all the sadness and started to laugh again. He said, "Well, if I am to die so soon, I might as well enjoy myself before it happens! Why be sad?" He lived a very full and active life for another twelve years, establishing the Federation for the Preservation of the Mahayana Tradition, a worldwide Buddhist organization.

Back in the Solo Kumbo valley, Lama rested every hour as we walked. He would tell me everything was fine and the walk and altitude were not a problem. He never used his illness as an excuse to not be active. When we rested, he told stories of his family in Tibet. He had seven or eight siblings; I was never that sure of the number. One funny thing was the way he referred to his brothers and sisters. He would say, "This one is same mother different father, that one is same father different mother." It was very confusing. The story goes like this: The original mother and father had three children. That mother died and the father remarried. That woman was Lama's mother, and she also had several children. Then the father died and Lama's mother remarried and had several more children. It was a large extended family.

We arrived in Kathmandu on the Full Moon day of September 23, 1972, which was my twenty-second birthday. I still marvel at the beauty of that moment. There I was standing in Buddhist monk's robes on the crest of Kopan Hill as the Full Moon rose in the east. This was a life I could never have dreamt of in Canada.

A point of interest about Kopan Hill is that the Nepalese king's astrologer used it in earlier times for nighttime consultation. He would lie there on his back and watch the movements of the night sky and look for special signs. The last portion of the hill is a perfect cone and the top has been leveled off flat. There seems to be a subtle aspect of interconnectedness to everything, as I am now a Buddhist astrologer.

Lama Yeshe gave me some good advice at this point. I had asked him how I could best preserve my experiences of the last few months in retreat. Lama responded that to remember the experiences was the important thing. They could remain fresh and inspiring by the power of memory. This later becomes the wisdom of past experience, a powerful tool to help make decisions. This is part of the wisdom used when dealing with astrological influences. Although I wanted a highly profound answer from him, I see now that there are no easy tricks to gaining realization.

Dharamsala

Leaving Kathmandu, Lama Yeshe and I traveled to Delhi and north to Dharamsala. It was the fall of 1972 and the weather was beautiful. There was added excitement on this trip, as Lama was to purchase property in Dharamsala. Lama wanted to establish a meditation center there. We spent a week there living in a hotel as Lama bargained over the price of a property he wanted. When the offer was finally accepted, we moved into Naroji Koti. This was a large house built in a similar fashion to those that were built when the British Raj was in power. Lama renamed it the Tushita Retreat Center.

Lama placed me in charge of the retreat center. It had been exciting to buy the house, and Lama was scheduled to return to Nepal. Lama told me to prepare to meet the senior tutor for His Holiness the Dalai Lama. I was unfamiliar with the important teachers and their positions in my spiritual tradition. I had only met His Holiness and the teachers related to Lama Yeshe. So on a sunny afternoon in October, Lama took me for an audience with Kyabje Ling Rinpoche.

Ling Rinpoche lived in a similar koti to Tushita Retreat Center. It was on the same ridge as Tushita and overlooked the village of Dharamsala, the Kangra Valley, and the palace of His Holiness. The southern exposure allowed the sun to shine boldly all day, so flowers grew in abundance all over the mountain. The area is the first range of the Himalayas. The first peaks just behind Dharamsala are 16,000-feet tall and the mountain range runs east to west. This sets the scene to arrive at Chopra House, the residence of Ling Rinpoche.

One feature of Chopra House was the incredible marigolds blossoming all around it. These were the largest golden marigolds I had ever seen, and they flanked the house on two sides. This gave the house a beautiful sense of being completely in another realm.

Kungo La, the manager of Ling Rinpoche, greeted Lama Yeshe and me at the house. He escorted us to a waiting room, and then after some other guests left, we were taken into the audience room. Ling Rinpoche was seated at one end of the room and Lama and I took lower seats to his left. Lama acted in a very humble manner during this interview. Since I understood no Tibetan, I just sat beside him and tried to look comfortable. The interview carried on for about an hour, and then Lama informed me that Ling Rinpoche had accepted my request for full ordination. I was also accepted to attend a special set of Tantric initiations that winter. All this was to transpire in Bodhgaya, on the central plains of India.

At that time, I was given permission to visit Ling Rinpoche whenever I wanted. That was a great privilege as Ling Rinpoche, at age sixty-eight, was in semiretirement. He was still periodically active teaching at monasteries, but he maintained his seclusion by offering only certain people freedom to visit him regularly. As the years passed, Ling Rinpoche became my chief mentor for Tantric instruction.

It was the first week of October, so one English disciple of Lama Yeshe and I stayed at Tushita. It was our job to clean the house. I also returned to study at the Tibetan Library with Geshe Dhargaye. When December arrived, I left Dharamsala for Bodhgaya to receive full ordination and Tantric teachings.

These became eventful times for me. I attended the Tantric initiation of Vajrabhairava and the ten-day teaching on Lama Chopa, a discourse about guru devotion, in Bodhgaya. This was more of a blessing than a teaching as the whole event was in Tibetan. I understood only a little Tibetan at that time. The teachings were carried out in the large assembly hall of the Tibetan monastery in Bodhgaya. There were about 600 monks in attendance and the teachings went from lunchtime until 5:30 P.M. This required sitting for two-and-a-half-hour stretches without being able to stand up or stretch. At 3:30 Ling Rinpoche would casually mention that it was time for a pee-pee break and everyone would dash outside to the adjacent field to empty their bladders. We were allowed only ten minutes for this and then returned to our seats until 6:00 P.M.

At the completion of the teachings, the ordination date was set. This took place on January 27, 1973, at 2:00 P.M. I became a fully ordained Buddhist monk. Having completed all these events, I returned to Dharamsala with Peter Kedge, an English engineer. He was to become the new manager of Tushita Retreat Center.

Second Retreat

Since Peter Kedge was the new manager of Tushita, I took the opportunity to enter a meditation retreat again. I started the preliminary practices. These involve doing four different retreats of 100,000 repetitions of mantra or prayer. They are 100,000 prostrations, 100,000 Vajrasattva mantras, 100,000 mandala offerings, and 100,000 Guru mantras. I accomplished three of these practices over the next nine months. I undertook an ascetic approach to this with a vow of silence. I also locked myself into a small room in one of the outer buildings on the property. The staff would drop off my three meals daily by the door, so I had no interruptions.

The first retreat was the 100,000 prostrations. Full-length body prostrations are considered the correct purification for physical negativities committed in the past. When I was young I had killed many fish and birds. At the time I was completely unconscious of the pain I had caused and considered fish and animals merely insentient. They had no feelings, so it seemed okay to kill them. I now regretted all the pain I had inflicted on these little creatures. I was told that prostrations were a good practice to purify negative physical karma. It took three months to complete the full 100,000 prostrations.

When finished, I began the recitation of Vajrasattva's 100-syllable mantra. This practice is done to purify mental defilements and takes approximately three months to complete. The retreat is not as physically demanding as prostrations. One sits for four two-hour sessions a day and utilizes visualization, concentration, and mantras. The practice is effective on a subtle level and uses strong archetypal images. The resultant effect is intended to bring a positive shift of attitude.

The next practice is the guru mantra recitations. The practice works to establish a better bond with one's spiritual mentors. It is either a five-line prayer to the teachers of the lineage or the recitation of one's personal guru's Sanskrit name. It is done in conjunction with a visualization of lights being absorbed into the body. The resultant effect is a better ability to integrate the teachings. One is more receptive to the inspiration of the teacher and teachings. I finished this in six weeks, bringing to a close my silent period of retreat.

I started to study with Geshe Ngawang Dhargaye at the Tibetan Library again in September of 1973. I now seriously studied Buddhist philosophy, and my Tibetan language skills began to improve. I carried on with study, teachings, and initiations for the next two years. I met many of the Western people who had been drawn to Dharamsala and Tibetan Buddhism. This included some of the more famous Western teachers and authors such as Glenn Mullin, Alan Wallace, the famous nun Tenzin Palmo, and Robert Thurman. I also met my future wife, although at that time I was a monk, and we became friends.

As time passed I slowly became ill. I had been too intent on my studies and had not taken care of my body. I weighed about 120 pounds and was suffering physically from malnutrition. These events transpired during the latter part of 1975 and coincided with a Pluto transit to my Midheaven and a Neptune transit to my Ascendant.

It is not uncommon for people to misunderstand spiritual practice and abuse their bodies. I fell into this category. My body was physical and I was trying to be spiritual. This had actually started in the fall of 1974. I was skinny and easily startled. Geshe Rabten became concerned and told me to live in his house for the winter. He was going to southern India for the winter. His house was just behind Ling Rinpoche's residence and therefore appealed greatly to me. Geshe Rabten arranged for me to live with his monk attendant, Pemba. This was a good opportunity to both improve my language and live with a fine practitioner. Pemba was a well-qualified teacher but was a humble man. He had decided to serve Geshe Rabten instead of teach. Pemba did offer to tutor me during this time, though.

Pemba's tutoring was not quite what I had expected. He did help me with my Tibetan language skills. He spoke no English, so it was a perfect opportunity for me to experience Tibetan immersion. Pemba was solid as the earth itself and lived a simple life of the Zen proverb "Chop wood, carry water." He put me in the corner of the kitchen on a bench bed and told me to take refuge in Buddha for the rest of the winter. I did well over 100,000 prayers of refuge during this time, and in between these meditation sessions Pemba told me stories of his life in Tibet.

I spent many cold, snowy nights drinking hot Tibetan butter tea and listening to him. He was a subtle and effective teacher. Pemba was a quiet practitioner, living totally what he felt spiritually. He quietly emanated the belief that negativity was totally nonproductive. He would say, "If a person is negative toward others, why mention it?" Being unhappy about the person only creates more negativity. If you can do something about it, then do so. If one cannot do anything to resolve the situation, then accept it quietly. He lived this to the letter and I never knew him to get angry or be pessimistic. He was just a quiet, lovable man. That was his offering to the universe.

When the winter was over, I tried again to study intensively, but my body could not take it. I became nervous and unhappy, and finally one of my teachers told me to return to Canada to recover my health. I was suffering from acute malnutrition and was experiencing nervous exhaustion. I took my teacher's advice and flew back to Vancouver in June of 1975. I stayed there for only two months. I disliked the exposure to Western values at that point in my life. I had received an inheritance the year earlier from my grandmother, so I was able to return to India in September a bit fatter and happier. I did a month-long retreat of my guru's mantra upon my return and relaxed back into the slower Indian way of life.

I went to Bodhgaya to visit Ling Rinpoche in December of 1975. He helped me decide to go to Australia for a year and help at Lama Yeshe's new center. It was called Chenrizig Institute and was situated in Queensland, a pleasant, semitropical state of Australia. Initially, there was a nun named Yeshe Khadro and myself at the center. Shortly after, Geshe Lodan and his translator Zasep Tulku arrived to start teaching. I attended the teachings and helped manage the center. I spent a total of eighteen months in Australia.

It was during this time that I worked on some old habit patterns. One never escapes from the past, and I had to deal with my past at some time. The Western environment allowed old feelings to surface, but the dharma center's setting was useful. It allowed me a fresh view of old emotional material that needed to be resolved. The outcome was the realization that spiritual practice was of great importance to me, so in 1977 I returned to India. Pluto started to transit my natal Neptune at that time.

Ling Rinpoche was happy to see me again. He was on pilgrimage in central India, and I met him at the deer park of Sarnath. I was invited to live with his household as they traveled. Ling Rinpoche gave many teachings on this trip. He was now seventy-six years old and I was twenty-seven. He always impressed me with his brilliance of mind. He was in his seventies and never showed any forgetfulness or lack of clarity when giving teachings. This included both reading from a text and repeating from memory interesting quotes and stories. His teaching sessions lasted on average five hours a day, seven days a week. Sometimes he used to take Sundays off and jokingly say that it was out of respect for the Christians. He continued this style of teaching until 1983 and only stopped just before his passing on Christmas Day of that year. It seems appropriate that he died on Christmas Day, as he seemed to like marking the Christian holidays.

Preparations for the Great Retreat

I asked Ling Rinpoche for permission to do a great retreat of Vajrabhairava during my stay in Bodhgaya. This takes about three years to complete. It also requires doing nine preliminary practices prior to the actual great retreat, so it really requires a total of five years to complete properly. Rinpoche gave me permission to start and we set a schedule for the teachings and practices. I had already done the 100,000 prostrations, but Rinpoche wanted me to be successful, so he encouraged me to do them again. Bodhgaya is considered the holiest Buddhist site in the world and any practices done there are considered to be of the highest merit. I started my prostrations again, but only completed 50,000 by the time I left Bodhgaya in February.

That seemed sufficient and I concluded the prostrations with prayers of dedication for the success of my retreat.

I took up residence at Tushita in Dharamsala and used a small retreat hut they offered to me. It was Lama Yeshe's A-frame cabin. I stayed there for two years. This time I did not take a vow of silence. I attended some teachings by Geshe Dhargaye at the library and worked on my preliminary practices the rest of the time. On most days I was in seclusion; only three days per week did I walk to the library to see Geshe Dhargaye. Ling Rinpoche also gave me private initiations and instruction on Tantric practice. When 1980 came, I had received the full commentaries twice for Vajrabhairava, once from Ling Rinpoche, and once from Geshe Dhargaye. I had also completed 100,000 mandala offerings, Vajrasattva mantras, Vajra Daka fire ritual mantras, Guru mantras, Samaya Vajra's mantra, refuge prayers, and finally had printed 100,000 pictures of Je Tsongkhapa.

This last practice, in case you are curious, required printing the image of a Buddha with a large hand stamp on paper. One prints the image while reciting a prayer to the Buddhas and bodhisattvas. A large stack of paper was amassed when the 100,000 images were made. Lama Yeshe later placed these in a stupa at Tushita. Some people may consider this amount of practice prior to even entering a strict retreat to be too much work. My teacher stressed that a good retreat requires much preparation. This includes not only physical preparation but also mental purification. There is much interference to doing a long retreat, so the purification practices remove them. It also sets the practitioner up for speedier realizations as he or she is well prepared by the preliminaries.

It was 1979 when I started studying astrology. My astrology instructor, Michael, lived only a few minutes from Tushita, so I went weekly and received a few hours of instruction. This lasted for a whole year. At first I thought that studying astrology might be a waste of time. I was in a semi-strict retreat and preparing for the great retreat. What motivated me to study were two things. One was Michael's interpretation of my chart. I was so surprised to have someone decipher my life and the events so easily. The second event was a dream. While I debated the pros and cons of studying astrology, I dreamt of looking at the sky and hearing a long and rumbling roar of thunder. It was so loud and powerful that it woke me up. Since astrology had to do with the sky, I took this to mean that studying astrology opened one up to powerful events. Thunder is considered the noise that dragons make when they roar, and dragons are considered powerful and special beings. I approached Michael for classes the next morning. Saturn was transiting my natal Mercury, Venus, and Saturn. It was a great time to seriously review life and its meaning.

Great Retreat

September of 1980 was the start of the great retreat. I planned it to coincide with a Saturn conjunction with my natal Sun. I felt that the power of dedication with this transit would be auspicious. Saturn continued to transit my Midheaven and natal Neptune in the tenth house for the next year.

A great retreat is actually a series of retreats. The initial retreat is focused on one Tantric deity and includes not only detailed visualization and prayer but also the recitation of over 10 million mantras. It takes about two years to complete and should be done in a strictly secluded place.

I decided to leave Tushita and arrange for a meditation hut higher on the side of the mountain. The hut I wanted was about 7,000 feet up and well away from everyone except local shepherds. There were a few other Tibetan meditators in the area, all involved in retreats similar to my own. All the huts were spread out over a small shoulder of the mountain.

The retreat started with a vow of silence. I was not sure how well I could manage two years of silence, so I made a commitment for six months. The only contact I would have was with a young Tibetan monk who would come up every two weeks to deliver my food. I was lucky to have that service offered to me. The boy's father was also in retreat on the mountain, so the son agreed to carry my food when he visited his father. The walk up from the town took just under two hours.

I managed fairly well for the first few months of retreat, being deeply involved in doing my meditations and mantras. The first session would start at about 2:30 or 3:00 A.M. and continue until dawn. I normally dozed off briefly at 5:30 A.M. and then at 6:00 I got up and cooked breakfast. To make the cooking time shorter during retreat, I organized a system. I cut the vegetables as the porridge cooked. When the porridge was done, I placed a big piece of wood in the fire and put the vegetables on to cook. I placed a pressure cooker with soybeans beside the pot of vegetables. I ate my breakfast and then started my meditations by 7:30. The vegetables and soybeans cooked until the wood was gone. I went for a walk at mid-morning, checked the vegetables, and then did another session before lunch. Each session was two hours in duration.

Lunch involved making a few pan breads as the vegetables reheated. I put the soybeans together with the vegetables, added a spoonful of miso to flavor it, and ate this with two breads. I put a little extra food aside for an evening snack, and that was all the cooking I had to do for the day. This was the routine for the next three years. Although some people may find my diet unbearable, I loved it and found the simplicity enjoyable. I did on occasion have a piece of bread with lots of peanut butter and a sweet tea in the afternoon, but outside of that I had few luxuries.

I established this routine during the first four months. This brought me to a transit of Uranus to natal Mars in the twelfth house. That was an interesting transit and some astrologers might consider it very disruptive. Uranus has such chaotic energy and Mars in the twelfth house indicates powerful unconscious urges. Personally, I found this time energizing. The sessions required lots of energy and the deity was wrathful, surrounded by flames of enthusiasm. I am not certain, but I assume that the agitation basically turned into meditative inspiration. When the sixth month arrived, shortly after the snow had melted, I had my first visitor. It was Michael, my astrology teacher. He dropped in unexpectedly to see how I was doing. It was nice to see someone and I decided to talk to him. A vow of silence seemed ridiculous since I was isolated anyway. It was during this conversation that I experienced being nervous and noncommunicative. The isolation was taking its toll on me. I wanted to come out of this retreat as a relaxed and comfortable individual, not nervous and oversensitive. I felt it might be necessary to maintain some form of communication to accomplish that goal. I decided to drop the vow of silence, and every six weeks I went for an afternoon walk to visit someone.

These periodic walks were not easy, as the retreat had some restrictions. The retreat required a distinct boundary, and going outside that area voided the retreat. This area went from just below Tushita and Ling Rinpoche's residence to anywhere up the mountain. I could only visit people within these perimeters. I did not want to be too lax and so decided to choose one friend within the boundary with whom to have tea every sixth week. My astrology teacher, Michael, now lived about one mile west of my retreat hut in a place called Dharmkot Hill. I decided that he would be a good person to visit. Six weeks later I casually walked over after lunch and dropped in on Michael and his wife, Anne. They were delighted to see me, so every six weeks I took a holiday for three hours to have a tea party. I knew that this was not strictly within the retreat guidelines, but I felt that it was an investment in my sanity. The retreat continued like this for the next two years.

Aside from these social visits, I also saw Ling Rinpoche periodically. This was acceptable to retreat rules and very beneficial for me. Ling Rinpoche normally saw people for a five-to-ten-minute interview. When I came to visit, he allowed me to stay for almost two hours. This was very blissful. Ling Rinpoche was considered an enlightened being and his special tutelary deity was Vajrabhairava. It was like being able to sit and chat with one's meditation deity. I soon learned not to talk about my spiritual practice with my teacher. In fact, I had to learn to talk about anything but the retreat. Periodically I was allowed to tell him about my dreams or experiences, but generally we only talked about the weather and simple things. It was a profound teaching, reinforcing the simple proverb "Chop wood, carry water" as the right way to live one's life.

The fall of 1982 arrived as I finished the first section of the retreat. I had completed the proper number of mantras and done my sessions according to the outlines. I invited four Tantric college monks to the hut, and they helped me perform a fire ritual to conclude the retreat. They set up a special earth platform for the fire and drew a mandala on it. The mandala lines created the sacred space where the deities were to be invoked. Firewood was placed on the mandala image, and special ingredients were collected for feeding into the fire. The ritual took the whole day, and upon completion I had finished perfectly the first part of a great retreat.

The retreat could now be completed in six months according to the meditation outline. I decided to continue to work at my meditation. Two-and-a-half years did not seem sufficient to produce a deep transformation. Although there was a shift in attitude, it was not a heartfelt experience. I chose to move further up the mountain and arranged to switch meditation huts with a monk who lived one hour above my current hut. This monk normally lived in his hut only during the summer because in the winter the mountain became impassable. The monk's main problem was a lack of money for the food to weather the winter months. This was not a problem for me and we agreed to switch huts. My present hut did not become inaccessible because of winter snow.

In October of 1982, I moved to his hut and organized myself. It was much smaller than my previous hut. The original hut was about eight-by-ten feet, whereas this was barely six-by-seven feet. It was cozy and the view of the Kangra Valley was breathtaking from 8,000 feet. I was totally cut off from everyone here and no noise came from below. It was like living in another dimension. I stored away my food and started the second phase of retreat.

The winter descended quickly and it was inspiring when the first snows came. The tranquility was magnificent. Only once did I become nervous being so isolated. It happened when two Himalayan black bears started to fight below my cave. They were looking for a sleeping place. It sounded like two 600-pound dogs roaring at each other, and I was in close range. After that brief scare, I spent the next five months closed off from the world.

There is one funny story to tell about this time. One day in the middle of December, I was sitting on my favorite rock enjoying the winter sun and looking out over the valley. Suddenly to my right I heard someone calling out. It was a couple of mountain climbers trekking through the snow. This was an unbelievable feat as the snow was waist-deep by then. Their story was interesting. They had gone for a walk up the mountain paths and as they got higher they could see smoke in the distance. They were intrigued that someone would live so isolated in the mountains. I think they thought it might be a Tibetan monk. To add to the surprise, we were all Canadians. I gave them some tea and cooked them a plate of rice and pumpkin curry. We chatted for about an hour and then they left. Later when I came back to Canada in 1984, I learned that they lived in Toronto. We had the opportunity to get together to chat and laugh about that strange day high in the Himalayas.

In March of 1983, my Tibetan helper finally came to visit and brought new supplies. It was good to see him again. He had been worried about my safety. Shortly after that, the local Indian farmers also started traveling on the path above my rock. Although I cannot say that I had a lot of visitors, I did get one or two brief visits a week. The remaining six months were spent doing the final small retreats that were included within the great retreat. I completed all the requirements except the final fire rituals by October.

A great retreat requires doing an elaborate series of fire rituals. I left the mountain hut and returned to Tushita Retreat Center. They gave me a small room to live in and I started these last rituals. Ling Rinpoche suffered his first stroke at this time. I was shocked by the news. I managed to visit him once after that and he congratulated me on my completion of the retreat. That was important for me, as his words of encouragement meant a great deal. He had become like my father.

His health declined over several months with a series of small strokes until he finally passed away on Christmas Day in 1983. A few hours before his death, four of his closest Western disciples, including me, came to the house. The four of us were talking quietly downstairs. At noon, his manager came and told us that Ling Rinpoche had died. It was curious that we had all come there spontaneously and were able to be close to this man who had meant so much to us. This event also coincided within two days of Uranus transiting my Ascendant. The next year, my first year in Canada, was a year of tremendous change for me.

Ling Rinpoche seldom showed his enlightened capacity. At this time, he did perform one miracle. It is common in Tibet for great masters to show their power of realization at the time of death. One way to show this is to remain in meditation even after they stop breathing. As the lama enters into this meditation state, the body maintains its composure and color. There is no breath—the person is dead—but the appearance of quietude remains for several days. The smell of death is not detectable. This is called *the meditation on the clear light of death*. As long as the lama maintains this meditation, the body will remain pleasant to view and be around.

Swami Yoganada is the only other noted mystic who accomplished this feat in recent times. Swami Yoganada died in California, and people commented that they could smell roses when in the presence of his corpse. Ling Rinpoche stayed in his meditation of the clear light of death for thirteen days. His head turned slightly at the end of this time. His Holiness the Dalai Lama said that Rinpoche's consciousness had departed. His Holiness asked for the body to be embalmed in respect for this profound feat and the exemplary life Ling Rinpoche had lived. It now resides in His Holiness' residence in Dharamsala, India.

I only lived a short time in Dharamsala after Ling Rinpoche's passing. I took a few minor teachings and then received a special audience with His Holiness the Dalai Lama. He had periodically asked about me during the retreat, and in our audience he congratulated me strongly for persevering for so long. I then moved to Delhi and arranged for my flight home.

Return to Canada

Over the next two years after my return in 1984 I went through a long period of cultural readjustment. I returned my Buddhist ordination as a monk in September, 1984. This coincided with the final transit of Uranus to my Ascendant. It is difficult to be an ordained Buddhist monk in Western culture. Asian culture supports this, but in North America there is very little support. One is more an oddity than a valued member of society. I married and adopted two children by the end of 1985. My wife, Maria, was a Buddhist who had lived in India for seven years. We had known each other during my years in Dharamsala. Much of my capacity to readjust successfully was due to her kindness and help during those first difficult years.

Maria and I decided to establish a more stable meditation center in 1988. We looked for some property that would suit our needs. I took a regular job in a local hardware store in order to qualify for a mortgage loan. Prior to that, I hoped that somehow I could find employment to suit my skills. A local college had hired me as a part-time instructor for some of their courses. I also received training as a hospital chaplain, but neither of these pursuits worked out very well. Although I received good evaluations as a teacher, I had no degree and was not acceptable as a college instructor. I enjoyed the training as a chaplain, but again could not find acceptance to work. The hospital saw it as unacceptable to hire a Buddhist chaplain for a mostly Christian society. The local hospital administrator gave me an interview but concluded it by not even shaking my hand. He seemed rather uncomfortable with my being a Buddhist.

I finally decided to take a regular job. I was hired by a local lumber and hardware store in September of 1988. Maria and I qualified for a mortgage, and we purchased one acre of land in Duncan. His Holiness the Dalai Lama named the center *Thubten Choling* and it has functioned ever since.

I found my new employment enjoyable interacting with the public on a daily basis, and I became known as the Buddhist staff member. I also managed to incorporate my Buddhist practice into serving customers by saying, "May I help you?" Although no one understood what I was really asking, it suited my bodhisattva vow to be of assistance to others. It didn't matter if they only bought a screwdriver at the time; maybe later I would help them become enlightened.

His Holiness the Dalai Lama also granted me a spiritual advancement after the purchase of the property. He gave his full blessing for me to bestow both initiations and teachings on all aspects of Tantra. I looked at this as a particularly great step forward for all Western Buddhists. I am only one of many Western practitioners qualified to initiate and teach the Tantras. His Holiness' permission opened the door for all Westerners of the Tibetan tradition to transmit both Mahayana and Vajrayana teachings. It was one of the final steps in the arrival of Buddhism to North America.

My intention in this brief autobiography is to share some stories with you. I have had an interesting life, and by sharing some of these events, maybe some serious practitioners may feel inspired to do similar activities. I spent seven of the fourteen years that I was a monk in retreat. That is not a lot of time on the scale of one's whole life, but it was enough to satisfy me for a little while. Nowadays, with so many exciting things to do, few people devote time and energy to inner transformation. Although much can be done with daily practice, periodic sessions in intensive contemplation are invaluable. I personally recommend an individual stay with a daily practice to support gradual development. That is crucial. If each day is not an enactment of one's beliefs, then even retreats will do little to help. Regular practice and sincere retreat time combined help develop higher conscious awareness. This can translate into an expression of love, compassion, and wisdom.

In 1994, I left the hardware store and started Daka's Buddhist Consulting. I had practiced astrology over the years in Canada. In the fall of 1993, while translating for Geshe Tashi Namgyal, a Tibetan lama from Victoria, I met Kasandra, a professional numerologist. Kasandra was impressed with my ability as a translator and then became aware that I could do astrology. She suggested that I take astrology to a professional level. I initially felt uncertain about whether this was feasible. After some research, I was confident enough to change my profession. I now work as a professional Buddhist consultant and astrologer. This way, I continue to both teach Buddhism and help people understand their astrology charts.

Glossary of Buddhist Terms

Amitayus

Amitayus is the Buddha of long life. He is the Sambhogakaya form of Amitabha Buddha. That refers to Amitayus as a pure astral form that does not manifest on a physical level. He is red in color, sits cross-legged, and holds a vase of long life nectar in his two hands.

Anapanasatti

This is a form of Calm Abiding meditation. (See *Calm Abiding Meditation*.)

Anicha

Anicha is the Pali word for *impermanence*.

Anutara Yoga Tantras

Tantra is divided into four classes of practice: Kriya, Carya, Yoga, and Anutara Yoga. The highest class of Tantric practice is the Anutara Yoga Tantra. Each level has a particular manner in which the visualization is done. For example, Kriya and Carya Tantras normally visualize the deity in front of or above the practitioner.

Attitude Transformation Techniques

Intention and attitude are primary factors in Buddhist practice. These establish the goal that a spiritual aspirant can attain. Mahayana Buddhism considers working for the benefit of all sentient beings to be the highest goal to strive toward. It is a natural outcome of true compassion and altruism. The desire to develop a stable, compassionate attitude is the basis of attitude transformation teachings. There are two lineages of this practice. One focuses on the idea of beginningless rebirths and the second on the interconnectedness of all sentient beings. His Holiness the Dalai Lama has said that the second technique is easier to grasp, as it does not require belief in past and future lives. Both strive to develop a noble and altruistic heart of love and compassion.

Avalokiteshvara

The Buddha of love and compassion. He is part of the Amitabha family of Buddhas and relates to loving compassion. His normal aspect is a white body with one face and four arms. His mantra is famous throughout the world: OM MANI PADME HUM. His Holiness the Dalai Lama is felt to be a manifestation of this Buddha.

Bhumi

A Bhumi is a designated spiritual level attained by bodhisattvas. There are ten Bhumi through which a bodhisattva will transit on the way to enlightenment. *Bhumi* literally means "earth" or "ground," so there are ten grounds of spiritual evolution. The term is Sanskrit.

Bimbisara

King Bimbisara lived during the time of Lord Buddha. He was the king of Vanarasi, or Banaras, the holy city of Shiva on the river Ganges. He is famous for his devotion to Buddhism and his support of religious inquiry.

Bodhicitta

Bodhicitta is the altruistic wish to attain full enlightenment in order to liberate all living beings from suffering and guide them to enlightenment.

Bodhisattva

A bodhisattva is one striving for enlightenment to benefit all sentient beings. Many of the greatest disciples of Buddha were bodhisattvas. This includes Avalokiteshvara, Manjushri, Vajrapani, Tara, and others. These beings work endlessly for the benefit of others, unconcerned about their own enlightenment as they wish to ensure that everyone else becomes free of suffering first. These enlightened beings are seen externally as both bodhisattvas and Buddhas. They are enlightened but they manifest in less exulted aspects, as bodhisattvas, to attract even more sentient beings to the spiritual path. They encompass unique qualities such as compassion, wisdom, ability, and grace.

Calm Abiding Meditation

Meditation can be contemplative or calming. Calm Abiding meditation strives to develop a deep focus that avoids all distraction. Distraction to meditation is either scattered thoughts or sluggish feelings. Avoidance of these obstacles allows the mind to attain a deep focus and various special abilities to enhance inner transformation.

Chi Gong

Chi gong is a Chinese set of exercises to generate energy and move it through the body. It is very famous in mainland China, and exhibitions of renowned Chi gong masters can fill a huge stadium with people devoted to these practices. The general focus of the exercises is on health and well-being.

Cittamantrin

This school of Buddhist thought presents the idea that the world is a reflection of the mind. No phenomena exist apart from the conscious mind and these mental phenomena are truly existent.

Contemplative Meditation

Contemplative meditation uses the peaceful environment established by Calm Abiding meditation and investigates a particular subject. Contemplation can focus on impermanence, karma, interdependence, or love and compassion. When a solid intellectual conclusion is arrived at, the meditator stops the contemplation and uses Calm Abiding to deeply integrate the subject. Contemplative and Calm Abiding meditations complement each other.

Dakas and Dakinis

Buddhist male and female angels are called Dakas and Dakinis, respectively. They are seen as messengers of the ultimate nature of reality. The Tibetan translation for Daka or Dakini is "Sky Mover." This means that they move through the sphere of the sky with ease, similar to the way Buddhas move through the sphere of reality flawlessly.

Devadatta

Devadatta was the first cousin of Siddhartha. He became famous for his attacks on the Buddha. He was jealous of Buddha's fame and knowledge. This incited him to constantly stir up both the spiritual community and the laity. At one point, he even tried to have the Buddha murdered. All his attempts failed and in the end he died a sad and lonely death.

Dharma
The Dharma is the teachings of the Buddha that lead one out of suffering to liberation and full enlightenment.

Dharma Protectors
Dharma Protectors are enlightened beings that offer Buddhists assistance.

Dialectic School
This is a Buddhist school for monks, nuns, and laypeople that cultivates precise thinking and analysis. Buddhist dialectics focus on the nature of both mundane and ultimate reality and the implications of this analysis.

Dukha
Dukha is the Pali word for *suffering*.

Fire Sutra
The Fire Sutra is the first sermon Buddha gave on the nature of cyclic existence (samsara). It describes the suffering nature of reality in terms of the senses being burned by the fire of attachment.

Four Immeasurable Thoughts
These are four thoughts that focus on all sentient beings in the universe, of which there is an immeasurable and inconceivable number. The four thoughts are love, compassion, joy, and equanimity: "May all sentient beings have happiness and its causes. May all sentient beings be separated from suffering and its causes. May all sentient beings never be separated from happiness and its causes. May all sentient beings abide in equanimity, free from the bias of those near or far."

Geshe
Geshe is an honorific title indicating great knowledge. The normal course of Buddhist studies takes twenty years to complete. This includes not only knowledge of Buddhist scriptures but also debating and recitation skills. A Geshe must be able to memorize and recite

perfectly the main texts of Buddhist philosophy. The Western equivalent would be a Doctorate of Divinity.

Giving and Taking Meditation

This is a meditation that utilizes inhalation and exhalation with love and compassion. The inhalation is linked to compassion and the wish to take suffering away from all sentient beings. The exhalation is linked to love and the wish to give happiness to all sentient beings.

God Realms

The god realms include the realms of desire, form, and formlessness. The desire-realm gods are similar to the human-realm gods but with more glory and enjoyment. The form-realm gods have enjoyments that are more refined than those of the desire-realm gods, including divine music and thought. The form-realm gods do not rely on physical contact for pleasure. The formless-realm gods are without form and abide in various states of consciousness. They are supported by deep concentration. All of these realms are still part of cyclic existence. These beings have not realized the ultimate nature of reality and so are not free from taking rebirth due to the power of delusion and karma.

Green Tara

Tara is a female Buddha. She is part of the Amitabha family of Buddhas and is known as the Swift Heroine. Among all the Buddhas, it is said that she responds the quickest to requests for help. Her activity is to free sentient beings from fear and suffering.

Guhyasamaja

Guhyasamaja is a deity in the highest class of Tantra. There are thirty-two deities in his mandala. This Tantra was taught by the Buddha directly to King Indrabodhi. This king desired to become a Buddha without leaving his palace. Buddha gave him the initiation and teachings that allowed him to transform his court into the mandala of Guhyasamaja. All the court officials were required to dress and act as divinities. This Tantra is known as the King of Tantras and has the most detailed presentation on the creation of illusory astral bodies. It transforms arrogance and pride into the energy of enlightenment.

Guru Offerings

This prayer of Guru devotion includes a special set of verses of offering. These offerings are traditionally done on the tenth and twenty-fifth day of the lunar month. The Buddhist calendar and holy days are based on the cycle of the Moon. The Tantric commentaries say that the Dakas and Dakinis, Buddhist angels, are more active on these two days. Offering prayers on these days attracts the blessings of divine messengers.

Hara

Hara is the Japanese term referring to the central fulcrum point of the human body. It is considered the emotional center from which people should move in any martial sport. Physiologists have been able to document that the hara is an actual balance point for the body.

Heruka Chakrasambhara

Similar to Guhyasamaja, Heruka Chakrasambhara is an Anutara Yoga deity. This deity stands upon the crest of Mount Meru and blesses sentient beings. There are several lineages of the Heruka. The simplest version has only five deities, and the most complex tradition has a mandala of sixty-four deities. This deity practice transforms lust and passion into the energy of enlightenment.

Hinayana

Hinayana is the small vehicle of Buddhist practice. This spiritual vehicle only takes one individual to liberation and therefore is called small. An individual who strives for personal spiritual realization is a Hinayana practitioner. It is an attitude of spiritual practice and not related to a country or meditation tradition.

Jungpo Trulkor

This is the Tibetan name for Vajrapani, the destroyer of delusion. *Jungpo* translates as either "demon" or "planet," and *Trulkor* as "controlling circle." The circle is three deities and refers to Vajrapani, Hyagriva, and Gauda.

Kalachakra Tantra

The Kalachakra Tantra is a special Tantric lineage dealing with wheels of time. It teaches the primary way to calculate astrological movement and forecast lunar and solar events. The Tantra itself is quite complicated as a meditation practice. His Holiness the Dalai Lama and the Namgyal Monastery are the primary holders of this practice lineage. His Holiness gives this initiation regularly as a blessing for devout Buddhists.

Kar tse

Kar tse is the Tibetan word for the Indian, or Vedic, astrological tradition.

Koti

Koti is the Hindi word for a large house or mansion.

Ketu

Ketu is the tail of the god Rahu. When Ketu meets the Moon, there is a lunar eclipse.

Lankavatara Sutra

This sutra is a Mahayana text explaining the nature of reality according to the Cittamantrin Buddhist philosophy. This school of thought propounds that reality is nothing but a reflection of the mind and external objects hold no objective reality. It is not considered the most profound presentation, although it offers deep insights into the structure of reality.

Madhyamika

This middle-path Buddhist school of thought, founded by Nagarjuna, says that all phenomena, both external and internal, are merely labeled and dependently arising. No phenomena have true existence because everything is interdependently produced. True existence, inherent existence, and self-existence are all synonyms for this philosophy.

Maha Kali

Maha Kali is a wrathful female protector of the Buddhist teachings. She can be seen as a wrathful manifestation of Tara, the female Buddha of virtuous action. When a deity is wrathful, it means their anger is directed at the ignorant mind and not a person. Wrath is an energetic way of creating change for the good.

Mahayana

Mahayana is the large vehicle of spiritual practice. It is a large vehicle that can transport many people to the far shore of spiritual realization. This vehicle represents an attitude of spiritual practice that works for the benefit of all sentient beings. The basis of this concept is that all beings wish to be happy and no one desires any suffering. If one is sensitive to this awareness, then the Mahayana attitude of bodhicitta is born. Bodhicitta is the wish to attain enlightenment for the benefit of all, to bring all beings into enlightenment.

Maitreya

Maitreya is the next Buddha prophesied to manifest in our world system. His arrival is predicted to be many centuries in the future. According to Buddhist tenets, the present teachings of Buddha Shakyamuni have to completely disappear before the next Buddha can manifest and teach the Dharma.

Mandala

A mandala is a three-dimensional image used in Tantra to represent the residence of conscious enlightened experience. The other use of a mandala represents the entire purified solar system, which is offered to the Buddhas when requesting an inspiration.

Manjushri

Manjushri is the Buddha of wisdom. He is golden-colored and holds a sword in his right hand and a Dharma text in his left hand. These represent the ability to cut through delusion and expound on the true meaning of reality. The gold color represents the expanding nature of wisdom.

Mara

A mara is a demon in the Sanskrit language, but actually means "a state of delusion." Mara normally refers to the Lord of Cyclical Existence, who holds all beings in the grip of delusion.

Medicine Buddha

The Medicine Buddha is aquamarine in color and holds a begging bowl full of medicinal nectar on his lap. The meditation involves the absorption of both light and nectars to stimulate a healing process. All Tibetan doctors must do a retreat of this deity before they can practice medical treatment.

Metta

Metta is a Pali term for loving-kindness. The teachings of the Buddha were recorded in two languages, Sanskrit and Pali. The Pali language is used by Theravadin Buddhist countries and principally presents the Vipassana meditation tradition. Sanskrit is the language of Northern Mahayana Buddhism.

Mudra

A mudra is a symbolic spiritual gesture or symbol. All Buddha images have their hands in some form of mudra. For example, the mudra of meditation is the hands placed on the lap.

Nag tse

Nag tse is the Tibetan word for Chinese astrology. Chinese astrology uses a sixty-year cycle divided into twelve animals and five elements. It has no reference to planets or constellations.

Nirvana

Nirvana is the attainment of liberation from suffering. The nirvana of a Buddha differs from that of a Buddhist saint. A Buddha has complete nirvana and a Buddhist saint has personal liberation. The difference is that Buddhas have liberation from both course and subtle obstacles to enlightenment, whereas Buddhist saints have only liberation from course obstacles to liberation.

Perfection of Generosity

The Perfection of Generosity is freedom from miserliness. To attain this perfection, one is not restricted by miserly feelings about possessions, time, or the body. This perfection is identified in three ways: the ability to share materially, the capacity to give protection to those afflicted with suffering, and the wisdom that shares spiritual advice.

Perfection of Morality

The Perfection of Morality or ethics is the abandonment of causing harm to oneself or others. This includes actions of body, speech, and mind. The attainment of the perfection is embodied in this statement: "To the best of one's ability to not cause harm to others."

Perfection of Patience

This perfection can also be translated as bringing resolution to harmful situations. There are three types of patience: to not retaliate against harm, to bear hardship in spiritual practice, and to not lose heart pursuing the ultimate realization of the nature of reality. The last patience refers to the fact that understanding reality in a nondualistic manner is extremely difficult.

Perfection of Enthusiasm

The Perfection of Enthusiasm is experienced as joy moving in a positive direction. Enthusiasm to be busy and attain worldly success is not considered a perfection, but rather is a distraction. An individual who exhibits no fatigue doing positive activities has this perfection. The ability to not become fatigued means that one is joyful about what one does.

Perfection of Meditation

Meditation means to have a calm mind. There are active meditations such as walking meditations, and there are inactive meditations like sitting practices. The definition of *meditation* is "an undistracted ability to focus on whatever one desires to accomplish." It is a product of mental training.

Perfection of Wisdom

Wisdom has two levels. Understanding the relative nature of the world is considered mundane wisdom. This is not just the ability to know how to accomplish tasks. It refers specifically to understanding the nature of actions and their results. Positive actions bring happiness and fulfillment, whereas negative actions bring suffering. This is true relative wisdom. The ultimate wisdom is realizing the nature of reality. This is developmental and arises from understanding the impermanence and voidness of reality. Voidness means all phenomena are empty or void of independent self-existence.

Parinirvana

Parinirvana means the death of a Buddha. It translates as "the final cessation." The attainment of nirvana is everlasting peace. While the body of a person who has attained this state is alive, he or she has nirvana. When the person dies, he or she attains Parinirvana—complete cessation, no further rebirths.

Quietude Meditation

Meditation that focuses on single-pointed concentration is a quietude technique. It means that the consciousness of the individual does not become distracted by extraneous thoughts. There is an unbroken flow of conscious awareness that can delve deeply into its focal point.

Rahu

Rahu is a deity that constantly chases the Sun. When Rahu catches and swallows the Sun, there is an eclipse. The end of the eclipse is when the Sun emerges from Ketu, the tail of Rahu.

Rinpoche

A rinpoche is a precious one. This refers to a bodhisattva who has taken rebirth for the benefit of others. The tradition of finding a reincarnated bodhisattva was perfected in Tibet. The Tibetans use a variety of techniques to find these individuals. The main factor is the death of an individual who demonstrated great spiritual growth. Approximately four years after his or her death, a group of interested individuals would search for this person's rebirth. Suitable children are picked as candidates and are tested until one child proves to be the reincarnation. They are then trained in the meditation practices of the previous saint to stimulate the spiritual memories and abilities in the child.

Rinzi Sect

This is a Zen sect that uses meditation and the koan. A koan is a statement that causes the intellect to stop analysis and seek direct experience. (See also *Soto Sect*.)

Sakyapa Lineage

This Tibetan lineage of Buddhism started in the Sakya area of southern Tibet, close to the Nepalese border. The Sakyapa lineage was founded by Kon Konchok Gyalpo, and the lineage gained its name because of the color of the soil in that area of Tibet.

Samsara

Samsara is translated from Sanskrit as "cyclic existence." It means the wheel of death and rebirth that all sentient beings cycle through repeatedly. The causes of cyclic existence are ignorance and delusion.

Saraswati

Saraswati is the female Buddha of the arts. Manjushri, the Buddha of wisdom, is her consort. She is the equal of Manjushri and she fosters artistic, spiritual growth. People who wish to be excellent poets, singers, artists, writers, or composers rely on her blessings.

Satori

Satori is a Japanese term for a spiritual epiphany. It arises suddenly and breaks through the boundaries of normal perception. Satori refers specifically to sudden enlightening experiences. One has many satori experiences before becoming enlightened.

Seven Point Mind Transformation Texts

These texts emphasize transforming the attitude of being egocentric to one of kindheartedness and empathy toward others. These teachings offer a solid psychological framework to explain the reasons to move from an attitude of self-centeredness to one of openhearted kindness.

Shakya Clan
Siddhartha was born into the Shakya clan in India. A rival clan destroyed the Shakya clan during the time of the Buddha himself. Historians say that the Buddha commented that this came about due to a lack of environmental sensitivity by the Shakyas. The negative karma they accrued by destroying the wildlife in a lake was the primary cause.

Shambhala Centers
These are meditation centers that exist principally in North America and were founded by Chogyal Trungpa Rinpoche. These centers used to be called Dharmadhatu Centers.

Siddhartha
Siddhartha was the crown prince of King Suddhodana of the Shakya clan. He is often referred to as the bodhisattva who attained enlightenment after renouncing the luxuries of palace life.

Soto Sect
This is a Zen sect that uses meditation and private interviews with the instructor. This sect does not use the koan. (See also *Rinzi Sect.*)

Stupa
A stupa is a symbolic religious monument representing the body, speech, and mind of a Buddha.

Tantra
The Tibetan language translates the Sanskrit word *Tantra* as "continuum." Buddhist tantra is the practice of the Vajrayana, the Vajra vehicle. This refers to bodhisattvas who wish to attain enlightenment as quickly as possible in order to benefit other sentient beings. The practices require guidance from a spiritual teacher and initiations. The commitment between the Vajra mentor and the student is an important facet of this practice.

Tushita Pure Land
Tushita is a heavenly realm where bodhisattvas receive teachings from Maitreya Buddha. Beings in this realm live for a long time. It is

said that one day there is equal to 200 years in our realm. This place is very conducive to spiritual practice.

Vajrapani

Vajrapani is the Buddha of power and ability. He is dark blue in body color with a wrathful expression. The color dark blue represents being immutable, and the wrathful expression symbolizes the fact that he is fierce when dealing with obstacles.

Vajravahari

Vajravahari and Vajrayogini are synonymous.

Vajrayogini

Vajrayogini is the enlightened principle of wisdom. Female Buddhas are identified as the bears of intuitive insight. Vajrayogini cuts through delusion with her cleaver and consumes reality in her skull cup of nectar. Her color is red and her aspect is wrathful. Many of the greatest male saints are blessed by her direct and powerful inspiration.

Vajrayana

Yana means "vehicle" in the Sanskrit language. The Vajra vehicle is an indestructible vehicle that takes one quickly to enlightenment. Vajrayana is part of the Mahayana tradition as it relies on great compassion as the motive for practice. One must enter the bodhisattva vehicle to practice Tantra, the Vajra vehicle.

Vipassana

Vipassana is a meditation technique called *penetrative insight*. It refers to gaining insight into the nature of reality. Nowadays, it refers to a tradition of meditation that is practiced in Burma and Thailand.

Wheel of the Dharma

This is a set of instructional teachings Buddha gave during a particular period of time that expounds the Buddhist path to enlightenment. There are three recognized Turning of the Wheel of Dharma periods during Buddha's life.

White Tara

White Tara is the female Buddha of long life and prosperity. She is white in color with one face and two arms. She is similar to Green

Tara except her main activity is to grant longevity to those who rely on her. People who are fearful of a short life, poverty, or illness can change their karmic potential in a positive manner by doing daily meditations with her. She is part of the Amitabha family of Buddhas and is crowned by Amitayus, the Buddha of long life.

Wrathful Buddhas

Wrathful Buddhas are used in meditative processes to help transform personal or external problems.

Bibliography

Berzin, Alexander. *Relating to a Spiritual Teacher*. Ithaca, N.Y.: Snow Lion Publications, 2000.

Blofeld, John. *The Book of Change: A New Translation of the Ancient Chinese I Ching*. New York: Dutton, 1965.

Chodron, Thubten. *Buddhism for Beginners*. Ithaca, N.Y.: Snow Lion Publications, 2001.

———. *Open Heart, Clear Mind*. Ithaca, N.Y.: Snow Lion Publications, 1990.

———. *Working with Anger*. Ithaca, N.Y.: Snow Lion Publications, 2001.

Clement, Stephanie Jean, Ph.D. *Charting Your Spiritual Path with Astrology*. St. Paul, Minn.: Llewellyn Publications, 2001.

Dalai Lama, His Holiness the XIV. *The Dalai Lama, A Policy of Kindness: An Anthology of Writings by and about the Dalai Lama*. Compiled and edited by Sidney Piburn. Ithaca, N.Y.: Snow Lion Publications, 1990.

———. *Kindness, Clarity, and Insight*. Translated and edited by Jeffrey Hopkins. Coedited by Elizabeth Napper. Ithaca, N.Y.: Snow Lion Publications, 1984.

———. *The Path to Enlightenment*. Edited and translated by Glenn H. Mullin. Ithaca, N.Y.: Snow Lion Publications, 1995.

Forrest, Jodie, and Steven Forrest. *Skymates.* Chapel Hill, N.C.: Seven Paws Press, 2002.

Forrest, Steven. *The Book of Pluto.* San Diego, Calif.: ACS Publications, 1995.

———. *The Changing Sky.* San Diego, Calif.: ACS Publications, 1999.

———. *The Inner Sky.* San Diego, Calif.: ACS Publications, 1989.

Gleadow, Rupert. *The Origin of the Zodiac.* Dover edition. Mineola, N.Y.: Dover Publications, 2001.

Humphreys, Christmas. *Concentration and Meditation: A Manual of Mind Development.* Third edition. London: Stuart & Watkins, 1968.

Mackenzie, Vicki. *Reincarnation: The Boy Lama.* Boston: Wisdom Publications, 1996.

Negus, Ken, trans. and ed. *Introduction to Tibetan Buddhism.* Ithaca, N.Y.: Snow Lion Publications, 1995.

———. *Kepler's Astrology Excerpts.* Princeton, N.J.: Eucopia, 1987.

Nhat Hanh, Thich. *Old Path, White Cloud.* Berkeley, Calif.: Parallax Press, 1991.

Powers, John. *Introduction to Tibetan Buddhism.* Ithaca, N.Y.: Snow Lion Publications, 1995.

Ribush, Dr. Nicholas. *The Lama Yeshe Wisdom Archive.* P. O. Box 356, Weston, Mass., 02493, Dr. Nicholas Ribush, Director, www.LamaYeshe.com.

Rinpoche, Khempo Karthar. *Dharma Paths.* Translated by Ngödup Burkhar and Chöjor Radha. Edited by Laura M. Roth. Ithaca, N.Y.: Snow Lion Publications, 1992.

Salzberg, Sharon. *Lovingkindness: The Revolutionary Art of Happiness.* Foreword by Jon Kabat-Zinn. Boston, Mass.: Shambhala Publications, 1995.

Schumann, H. W. *The Historical Buddha.* London: Arkana, 1989.

Scofield, Bruce. "The Great Zodiac Debate." *The Mountain Astrologer,* April/May 2002.

Segal, Zindel V., J. Mark G. Williams, and John D. Teasdale. *Mindfulness-Based Cognitive Therapy for Depression: A New Approach to Preventing Relapse.* Foreword by Jon Kabat-Zinn. New York: Guilford Press, 2002.

Tyl, Noel. *The Creative Astrologer.* St. Paul, Minn.: Llewellyn Publications, 2000.

———. *Synthesis & Counseling in Astrology.* St. Paul, Minn.: Llewellyn Publications, 1994.

Wallace, Alan. *Buddhism with an Attitude.* Ithaca, N.Y.: Snow Lion Publications, 2001.

Yeshe, Lama Thubten. *Becoming Your Own Therapist.* Edited by Dr. Nicholas Ribush. Weston, Mass.: Lama Yeshe Wisdom Archive, 1998.

———. *Essence of Tibetan Buddhism.* Edited by Dr. Nicholas Ribush. Weston, Mass.: Lama Yeshe Wisdom Archive, 2001.

———. *Introduction to Tantra.* Compiled and edited by Jonathan Landaw. Boston: Wisdom Publications, 1987.

———. *Make Your Mind an Ocean.* Edited by Dr. Nicholas Ribush. Weston, Mass.: Lama Yeshe Wisdom Archive, 1999.

———. *The Tantric Path of Purification.* Edited by Dr. Nicholas Ribush. Boston: Wisdom Publications, 1995.

Yeshe, Lama Thubten, and Lama Thubten Zopa Rinpoche. *Wisdom Energy: Basic Buddhist Teachings.* Boston: Wisdom Publications, 1985.

———. *Wisdom Energy: Two Tibetan Lamas on a Lecture Tour in the West.* Boston: Wisdom Publications, 1985.

Zopa, Lama Thubten Rinpoche. *Ultimate Healing: The Power of Compassion.* Edited by Ailsa Cameron. Boston: Wisdom Publications, 2001.

Index

Amitabha, 210, 339–340, 343, 352
Amitayus, 251, 265, 298–299, 339, 352
Anapanasatti, 280, 339
Anicha, 281, 339
Anutara Yoga, 247, 339, 344
Ascendant, 41, 285, 326, 335–336
Attitude Transformation, 24, 119, 134, 339–340
Avalokiteshvara, 136, 206, 209–210, 298, 340

Bhumi, 94, 340
Bodhicitta, 43, 106, 113, 135, 213, 340, 345
Bodhisattva, 1, 12, 14, 90, 98–99, 101–102, 108, 115–116, 121, 123, 143, 165, 211–212, 279, 337, 340, 348, 350–351
Buddha, 1–5, 8, 11–47, 52–53, 56, 65, 67–68, 71, 73, 78, 81–82, 88–89, 94, 96, 101–103, 108, 121–123, 131, 136, 146, 148–150, 200–201, 206–207, 218, 220, 232, 239, 244, 251, 265, 276–277, 279–280, 283, 286–288, 290–291, 298–299, 312, 316–317, 320, 326, 329, 339–343, 345–352

Castenada, Carlos, 70
Chi, 41, 161, 166, 222, 233, 255–257, 263, 265, 275, 341
Chiron, 44–45
Cittamantrin, 83, 341, 345

Daka, 329, 338, 341
Dakini, 341
Dalai Lama, His Holiness the Fourteenth, 103, 173, 280, 316
Dalai Lama, His Holiness the Sixth, 57, 67, 110, 113, 134, 140, 148, 155, 162, 169, 176, 179, 185, 193, 200, 332
Deities, 9, 33, 136, 209–210, 215–216, 221, 223, 225, 232, 235, 247, 256, 266, 297–299, 333, 343–344

Depression, 54, 197–198, 200,
    202–203, 215, 219, 229, 240, 251,
    265, 270, 295–296, 302
Descendant, 285, 318
Dhargaye, Geshe Ngawang,
    317–318, 324–325, 329
Dharma, 14, 56, 81, 91, 108, 252,
    288, 291, 317, 328, 342, 346, 351
Dukha, 281, 342

Forrest, Steven, 16

Geshe Rabten, 99–100, 315–316,
    326
Giving and Taking Meditation, 343
Goenka, 280–282
Great Retreat, 328–330, 333, 335
Green Tara Meditation, 8, 298, 343

Hinayana Buddhism, 39, 167, 171,
    289, 344

I Ching, 310
Impermanence, 49, 56–71, 84, 87,
    89, 131, 138, 151–153, 201,
    251–252, 281, 297, 339, 341, 348
Interdependence, 2–4, 11, 24, 49, 56,
    73, 82–83, 87–89, 96–97, 119,
    125, 153, 291, 297, 300, 341

Jataka Tales, 78

Kadampa, 56–57
Kalachakra Initiation, 311
Kalachakra Tantra, 6–7, 344
Kar tse, 7, 345
Karma yoga, 111, 160, 163, 169
Karmic Potential, 9, 12–13, 352
Kornfield, Jack, 283

Lauduo Gompa, 318, 321

Madhyamika, 84, 345
Mahamudra, 224
Mahayana, 3, 24, 39, 43–44, 98–99,
    116, 119–121, 130, 133–134, 146,
    149, 165, 167, 169, 212–213, 253,
    277, 279, 283, 289, 296, 301, 317,
    321, 337, 339, 345–346, 351
Maitreya, 3, 346, 350
Mandala, 138, 324, 329, 333,
    343–344, 346
Manjushri, 37, 146–150, 210, 218,
    220, 223, 225, 231–232, 234–235,
    239, 340, 346, 349
Mara, 92–94, 346
Medicine Buddha, 200–201, 251,
    265, 276–277, 298–299, 346
Metta Meditation, 282, 289, 346
Midheaven, 4, 50, 285, 310, 326,
    330
Mindful Awareness, 5, 229,
    282–284, 286–287
Mindfulness, 32, 36, 59, 71, 139,
    160, 170, 182–183, 193, 263–264,
    276, 284, 290
Mudra, 290, 346

Nag tse, 7, 347
Nagarjuna, 97, 312, 345
Newtonian Physics, 82
Nirvana, 17, 82, 91, 285, 347–348

Optimism, 44, 123, 167, 212, 223,
    243–244, 252–253, 261–265, 287

Palmo, Tenzin, 326
Parinirvana, 14, 23, 35, 348
Perfections, the Six
    Perfection of Enthusiasm, 114,
        160, 347
    Perfection of Generosity, 107,
        347

Perfection of Meditation, 116, 348

Perfection of Morality, 112, 347

Perfection of Patience, 112, 159, 347

Perfection of Wisdom, 35, 113, 348

Planets, 2, 6-7, 11, 16, 18-19, 23, 28, 35-36, 41, 43, 45, 47, 50, 59, 73-75, 77, 89, 92, 96, 105-127, 129, 145-203, 205, 207, 209-210, 212, 218-219, 221-222, 230-271, 273-278, 284-286, 293, 298-299, 347

Posture, 92, 207, 289-290, 294-295, 304

Quantum Mechanics, 74, 82, 302

Quietude Meditation, 26, 116, 120, 131, 143, 180, 211, 214, 216-217, 221-222, 231, 233, 237, 239, 256, 258, 265, 267, 270, 275-276, 335, 348

Rinpoche, Kyabje Ling, 323

Rinpoche, Lama Zopa, 313, 318

Rinpoche, Trungpa, 101, 350

Samsara, 82, 92, 100, 110, 153, 237, 342, 349

Satori, 268, 274, 291, 294, 314, 349

Saturn Return, 50-51, 53-54

Shaneman, Jhampa, 103, 280, 309-338

Shantideva, 57, 99, 284

Siddhartha, 1-4, 11-13, 15, 17, 19-31, 33-34, 36, 39, 42, 44-47, 49-71, 78-82, 90-94, 98-99, 102-103, 133, 286, 341, 350

Skillful Attitude, 70, 130, 162, 164, 176-178, 192, 202

Soto Buddhism, 288, 290, 349-350

Suchness, 89

Tai Chi, 161, 255, 257, 263

Tantra, 6-7, 35, 38-39, 152-153, 155, 157, 196, 200, 242, 247-248, 296-297, 300-301, 337, 339, 343-344, 346, 350-351

Tantras of Heruka Chakrasamb-hara, 247, 344

True Nature, 138

Vajra Daka, 329

Vajradhara, 320

Vajrapani, 42, 123, 211, 235, 298-300, 340, 344, 351

Vajrayana, 149, 221-222, 337, 350-351

Vipassana, 166-167, 182, 189, 208-210, 214, 217-218, 277, 280-289, 291, 293, 296, 301, 346, 351

Voidness, 49, 88, 97, 152-153, 297, 348

White Tara, 200-201, 251, 265, 298-299, 351

Wrathful Deities, 215-216, 221, 256, 332, 345, 351-352

Yeshe, Lama Thubten, 54, 59, 68-69, 99, 312-318, 320, 322-324, 327, 329

Yodishvara, 13

Yoga, 111, 160, 163, 169, 235, 247, 255, 263, 297, 315, 339, 344

Yoganada, Swami, 336

Zen Buddhism, 38, 273-274, 288, 312

Zen Meditation, 166, 233, 270, 288, 292-294, 301

Zengi, Dogen, 288

Zodiac, 11, 15, 52, 80

For readers of

Buddhist Astrology

only

FREE Birth Chart Offer

Thank you for purchasing *Buddhist Astrology*. There are a number of ways to construct a chart wheel. The easiest way, of course, is by computer, and that's why we are giving you this one-time offer of a free birth chart. This extremely accurate chart will provide you with a great deal of information about yourself. Once you receive a chart from us, *Buddhist Astrology* will provide everything you need to know to interpret your chart from a Buddhist perspective.

Also, by ordering your free chart, you will be enrolled in Llewellyn's Birthday Club! From now on, you can get any of Llewellyn's astrology reports for 25% off when you order within one month of your birthday! Just write "Birthday Club" on your order form or mention it when ordering by phone. As if that wasn't enough, we will mail you a FREE copy of our fresh new book *What Astrology Can Do for You!* Go for it!

Complete this form with your accurate birth data and mail it to us today. Enjoy your adventure in self-discovery through astrology!

Do not photocopy this form. Only this original will be accepted.

Please Print

Full Name:_____

Mailing Address:_____

City, State, Zip:_____

Birth time:_____ A.M. P.M. (please circle)

Month:_____ Day:_____ Year:_____

Birthplace (city, county, state, country):

_____

_____

Check your birth certificate for the most accurate information.

Complete and mail this form to: Llewellyn Publications, Special Chart Offer,   P.O. Box 64383, 0-7387-0315-X, St. Paul, MN 55164.

Allow 4–6 weeks for delivery.